The Taylor Effect

The Taylor Effect:
Responding to a Secular Age

Edited by

Ian Leask with Eoin Cassidy, Alan Kearns,
Fainche Ryan and Mary Shanahan

CAMBRIDGE SCHOLARS
PUBLISHING

The Taylor Effect: Responding to a Secular Age,
Edited by Ian Leask with Eoin Cassidy, Alan Kearns, Fainche Ryan and Mary Shanahan

This book first published 2010

Cambridge Scholars Publishing

12 Back Chapman Street, Newcastle upon Tyne, NE6 2XX, UK

British Library Cataloguing in Publication Data
A catalogue record for this book is available from the British Library

Copyright © 2010 by Ian Leask with Eoin Cassidy, Alan Kearns, Fainche Ryan and Mary Shanahan
and contributors

All rights for this book reserved. No part of this book may be reproduced, stored in a retrieval system, or transmitted, in any form or by any means, electronic, mechanical, photocopying, recording or otherwise, without the prior permission of the copyright owner.

ISBN (10): 1-4438-2263-9, ISBN (13): 978-1-4438-2263-3

Contents

Preface vii
Dermot A. Lane

Introduction 1

Part One: Analyses and Dialogues

A Secular Age: The Missing Question Mark 8
Ruth Abbey

"Transcending Human Flourishing": Is There a Need for Subtler Language? 26
Eoin G. Cassidy

Beyond Flourishing: "Fullness" and "Conversion" in Taylor and Lonergan 39
Stephen J. Costello

Our "Ethical Predicament": Getting to the Heart of *A Secular Age* 53
Joseph Dunne

Deism, Spinozism, Anti-Humanism 69
Ian Leask

Establishing an Ethical Community: Taylor and the Christian Self 84
Mary Shanahan

Part Two: Applications and Explorations

The Chaste Morning of the Infinite: Secularization between the Social Sciences and Theology 96
Michael Conway

Translating Taylor: Pastoral and Theological Horizons 113
Michael Paul Gallagher

Ireland: A Secular Age? 124
Patrick Hannon

Religious Inheritances of Learning and the "Unquiet Frontiers
of Modernity" 134
Pádraig Hogan

Codes of Ethics in a Secular Age: Loss or Empowerment of Moral
Agency? 146
Alan Kearns

Sources of the Sacred: Strong Pedagogy and the Making
of a Secular Age 160
Andrew O'Shea

"Code Fixation", Dilemmas and the Missing Virtue: Practical Wisdom
in a Secular Age 175
Fainche Ryan

Contributors 191

Notes 193

Index 215

PREFACE

It is a pleasure for me, as President of the Mater Dei Institute of Education, to write the preface to this collection of papers on the work of Charles Taylor, distinguished Professor Emeritus of Political Science and Philosophy of McGill University in Montreal, respected practitioner of civic engagement, recipient of the Templeton Prize for his contribution to religious thought in 2007 and the Kyoto Prize, known as the "Japanese Nobel", in 2008.

In June 2009, Mater Dei Institute hosted an international conference on the work of Charles Taylor, with particular reference to his book *A Secular Age*. Fourteen scholars offered plenary papers over four days, most of which are now published in this collection. In addition, fifty other scholars presented papers in parallel sessions, many of which will become available through the online electronic journal of the Institute, *REA: A Journal of Religion, Education and the Arts*. The Institute also offered a Summer School for students on Taylor's book, at the time of the conference.

Mater Dei Institute is a College of Education in Dublin City University, specialising in the formation of teachers for second-level schools in Ireland in the areas of Religious Education and the Humanities. The Institute is made up of three schools: Theology, Education and the Humanities. Given the inter-disciplinary character of the curriculum in Mater Dei Institute, *A Secular Age* was an ideal text around which to gather students, staff and visiting scholars in conversation.

It is a rare enough phenomenon that an academic text, especially a text on philosophy and religion, should generate such widespread interest, public debate on the internet, and international discussion in both academia and *ecclesia*. It is even more rare when the text in question is over 875 pages long. Such is Taylor's *A Secular Age*, which is analysed and discussed in depth in the following pages.

It can be said that this book is a comprehensive account of the process and meaning of secularisation. It has been described by one reviewer in the following way: "Rather than clever and dramatic, the book is fine-grained, subtle, exhaustive and exhausting" (Peter Steinfels, *Commonweal*, 9th May 2009).

Taylor tells the story of secularisation by answering the question: How is it that in the year 1500 most people believed in God and that in the year

2000 most people find it difficult to believe in God? In his answer, Taylor maps out the changing conditions and circumstances surrounding the rise of widespread un-belief. He is quick to reject early on in the narrative that secularism is the result of public spaces being emptied of God, what he calls Secularism 1, or the result of the falling off of religious belief and practice, which he calls Secularism 2. Instead, the story of secularism is far more subtle and complicated.

The problem with subtraction theories is that they short-change the integrity of secularism and religion as well as the possibility of critical engagement between secularism and religion. Secularism, rather, is a process in which a number of significant shifts have take place over centuries: shifts from an enchanted universe to a disenchanted world; from *kairos* to *chronos;* from theism to a providential deism to an impersonal order; from transcendence to an immanent frame; from a hierarchical social order to a self-sufficient society; from a moral order with transcendent roots to an order of exclusive humanism.

Anthropology plays a key role in this unfolding narrative. As the author of a major volume on anthropology entitled *Sources of the Self* (1989), Taylor appreciates better than most the centrality of anthropology to the modern project. In *A Secular Age*, Taylor traces what he calls the move from a pre-modern "porous self" to a modern "buffered self" as a one of the major sources of unbelief. Towards the end of the book he returns to the theme of anthropology, noting that it was the Catholic view of the human as "part angel and part beast" that led to Walker Percy's conversion, a perspective that stands out in contrast to the scientific view which sees the human as a "mere organism in an environment" (SA 731). And yet he notes that "our modern culture is restless at the barriers of the human sphere" (SA 726): through the search for meaning, the presence of empty-time, the denial of death, and the lack of human contact with nature.

A second significant theme is the debate about the difference between Europe and America in the context of secularism. Is America the exception to Taylor's phenomenology of the rise of secularism and its promotion of an exclusive humanism? Most Americans would describe themselves as religious humanists in contrast to the secular humanist of Europe. Taylor explains this difference between Americans and Europeans by noting that America did not have to overcome established ecclesiastical institutions in the way that Europe had. In the context of this debate it is opportune to have had a conference on Taylor in Ireland, since Ireland exists somewhere in-between the religiosity of America and the secularity of Europe. Ireland has much to learn from Taylor in understanding the social transformations of the last twenty five-years, and especially in relation to the religious turmoil in Ireland in the light of the Ferns Report (2005), the Ryan Report (2008) and the Murphy Report (2009).

A third theme running through the book is the role that imagination plays in shaping the conditions of belief and unbelief. Taylor had previously written an important book on *Modern Social Imaginaries* (2004). In that text, he described the social imaginary as "something much broader and deeper than the intellectual schemes people may entertain when they think about social reality in a disengaged mode". Instead, the social imaginary is about "the ways people imagine their social existence, how they fit together with others, how things go on between them and their fellows". The social imaginary is a set of background understandings operative in the way society functions. Taylor singled out three particular areas of the social imaginary that are central to the emergence of secularity, namely the modern economy, the public square and the sovereignty of the people, each of which has no need of transcendence and as such is self-sufficient. In *A Secular Age* he takes up these themes again and articulates what has happened to the imagination in the modern era.

Taylor's *magnum opus* renders a singular service to the academy and religion by outlining in a very coherent and compelling manner the transitions that have taken place since the Enlightenment. His book raises as many questions as it answers. Allow me to ask three questions:

First, is Taylor's narrative a point of arrival or a point of departure? It is of course both. As a point of arrival it illuminates what has happened to religion over the course of centuries, and this is a real service and something of a wake-up call for theology, the churches, and religion. As a point of departure, it paves the way for further engagement between faith and late modernity, challenges the reader to explore the possibility of a re-enchanted immanence, and opens up a new space for dialogue about the role of religion in a post-secular society. Taylor is hopeful about the future of religion, partly because he believes the sources of secularisation are Christian in inspiration. However, it must be asked: what are we to make of secularism in non-Western societies untouched by Christianity?

Secondly, why is it that within such a comprehensive account about the conditions of belief and unbelief, Taylor has little to say about the biblical narrative? More particularly, what has become of the prophetic role of biblical religion in Taylor's discussion of belief and unbelief?

Thirdly, why is it that Taylor gives so little attention to the story of the Second Vatican Council? I believe that Taylor's narrative would have been enriched if he had paid more attention to the events of Vatican ll. This is especially true of the document from the council entitled *Gaudium et Spes* (1965). That document outlines how the Catholic Church at Vatican ll embraced modernity, albeit in a qualified manner. There are interesting echoes of Taylor's account of the modern social imaginary within *Gaudium et Spes* and these have been brought out in a noteworthy way in the work of Australian theologian James Gerard Mc Evoy. Further, the Council had significant things to say about secularisation, atheism, unbelief, freedom and faith, as well as pointing the Church towards the importance of interreligious dialogue.

In spite of these questions and the many others that arise in this collection of papers, Taylor's book stands out as a landmark study of the conditions of belief and unbelief. Taylor provokes all to reflect on what he calls the "unthought" aspects of secularism and religion.

It is hoped that the publication of these proceedings will contribute to the many conversations already initiated by Taylor's work—in Yale University in 2008, Fordham University in 2009, the Catholic University of America, Washington DC, in 2009, in University College Dublin in 2010, and elsewhere.

In conclusion, I want to thank: the organising committee of the conference, chaired by Dr Eoin Cassidy; Ms Mary Shanahan who co-ordinated the preparations for, and activities of, the conference; Dr Ian Leask, who acted as the editor-in-chief of the proceedings; Dr Andrew Mc Grady, Director of the Institute, who supported the conference; and finally the Research and Finance Committees of the Institute for sponsoring the conference.

Dermot A. Lane
Dublin
May 2010

Introduction

This volume presents an original and diverse collection of essays addressing various aspects of Charles Taylor's magisterial *A Secular Age*. Ranging from close and critical readings of Taylor's formulations and suppositions, to comparative studies of Taylor and various "interlocutors", to applied approaches utilizing Taylor's concepts, to explorations launched from a Taylorian foundation, the thirteen chapters comprise a multifaceted exploration of Taylor's multifaceted achievement.

The volume has emerged from a highly successful international conference on *A Secular Age*, held at the Mater Dei Institute, Dublin, in June 2009, and its various chapters have been further honed and crafted as a result of the vigorous engagement that characterized those four days of debate and dialogue. Given the vast, synoptic sweep of Taylor's *magnum opus*, the contributors represent a suitably diverse range of interests, backgrounds and expertise—members of departments of philosophy, literature, philosophical theology, systematic theology, moral theology, education, and political science, whose interests stretch from Plato to Girard, *phronesis* to pedagogy, Deism to dogmatics, medical ethics to aesthetics...

To help orientate readers within this diverse spread, the collection has been divided into two, broad-ranging sections: "Analyses and Dialogues", in which particular areas of *A Secular Age* are examined and, in some cases, placed in "conversation" with other aspects of the philosophical and theological traditions; and "Applications and Explorations", in which Taylor's work becomes both the inspiration and foundation for further (and often critical) investigations across a swathe of different concerns.

In the first chapter of the first section, Ruth Abbey examines Taylor's attempts to articulate the contemporary conditions of religious belief and experience in westernized societies. These include: the quest for Religious Authenticity; the phenomenon of Cross Pressures and Fragilization; the Three Cornered Contest between Exclusive Humanism, the Immanent Counter-Enlightenment and Religion; the Ideal of Fullness; and the Immanent Frame. Scrutinizing each in turn, and posing some unanswered questions about both the meaning of each and the relationship of the questions to one another, Abbey concludes that Taylor's own framework can be used to show that religious belief is not as marginal as many of his own remarks suggest.

Complementing Abbey's approach, Eoin Cassidy argues against a strict demarcation between "transcendence" and "immanence", in terms of the fate of religion in a secular age: for Cassidy, the distinction risks fuelling the suspicion that religion is an escapist or cowardly flight from the world. Moreover, Cassidy suggests, the distinction can too easily become a supposed "explanation" for the decline of religion, and can thus occlude the possibility of the "immanent frame" acting as a catalyst for religious renewal.

Stephen J. Costello provides a wide-ranging exploration of the notion of "fullness" and its relationship with fulfilment and flourishing. Making the issue of "conversion" the culmination of his piece, Costello suggests that Bernard Lonergan provides a more nuanced account, and is thus able to fill in certain gaps in Taylor's narrative; the result, he suggests, is a suitably "fuller" appreciation of the dynamics involved in moral, intellectual and religious conversions.

In a powerful example of Taylorian "self-interpretation", Joseph Dunne provides an exegesis that begins—appropriately—with his own life and times (viewed in terms of Taylor's philosophical anthropology), before going on to consider the links between Taylor's particular conception of "the ethical" and his valorisation of "lived experience". Finally, Dunne also explores more fully the tensions entailed in what Taylor calls our "ethical predicament", and the three cornered contest it produces between humanists, believers and defenders of the "immanent counter-Enlightenment".

Meanwhile, as regards the historical "ballast" beneath Taylor's understanding of contemporary society, Ian Leask takes issue with Taylor's depiction of Deism as the effective foundation of the "exclusive humanism" that (supposedly) characterizes modernity. By showing the importance of the influence of Spinoza's thought on Deism—an influence unacknowledged by Taylor himself—Leask seeks to challenge the correlation operative within *A Secular Age* and suggests that, once it is located in a more Spinozistic context, Deism is better understood as a kind of *anti*-humanism.

Finally, and exemplifying the "dialogical" approach of Taylor's own work, Mary Shanahan considers Taylor's analysis of the fragmentation of society and its lack of shared projects in the light of Plato's analysis of friendship. Drawing upon the *Phaedrus*, *The Ethics of Authenticity* and *A Catholic Modernity*, as well as *A Secular Age*, she argues that it is ethics, or, more specifically, "ethical intersubjectivity", that provides the ultimate shared project.

Part Two, "Applications and Explorations", begins with Michael Conway's resolutely theological take on the theory and process of secularization, as expounded in the social and historical sciences. In the light of Taylor's specific contributions, Conway considers a variety of key issues—like autonomy of discipline, dependency of discourse, and legitimacy of statement—before outlining a critical and deep-seated inadequacy in so much current discussion of secularization. This inadequacy, in turn, is taken as an invitation to dialogue with the *logos* of theology.

Following Conway's theological exploration, Michael Paul Gallagher offers a non-specialist introduction to Taylor for those engaged in religious education. He explores five major dimensions of Taylor's thought, all of them touching on the culture that conditions faith today, examining in turn his key positions on modernity, secularisation, religion in general, Christianity in particular, and emerging languages of faith. A closing section of the paper imagines Taylor speaking directly to teachers of religion today.

Moving to issues of moral theology, Patrick Hannon offers reflections on some implications of Taylor's account of secularity for evolving relationships between religion (especially Catholicism) and society in Ireland. He argues that if the Christian churches are to play a constructive role in the shaping of modern Ireland, their efforts must be ecumenical, and responsive to a new pluralism of religious belief and practice, as well as to secularism itself. He suggests that a way ahead may be found in a joint exploration and pursuit of the common good of Irish society today.

Pádraig Hogan examines the possibilities for religious education as an "unforced pursuit", in the light of some key arguments in *A Secular Age*. Taking stock of the challenges posed by the complex relationship between the "massive unlearning" of modern society and more militant religious conviction that the same society engenders, Hogan explores the kinds of engagement that religious inheritances of learning might fruitfully be afforded in today's education.

Shifting the focus, Alan Kearns presents an examination of the way in which Taylor's work questions the use of codes and indirectly raises questions about the impact of codes on moral agency in contemporary professional practices. For Taylor, it seems, the ever-expanding plethora of professional codes of ethics implies a reduction in individual moral agency. For Kearns, however, a code of ethics does not necessarily diminish professional agency, but, instead, can provide a structure of support and guidance for dealing with increasingly complex ethical issues.

Andrew O'Shea explores what Taylor calls the conflicts of modernity within the context of the new modern imaginary, and shows how the dilemmas that Taylor addresses in *A Secular Age* have their roots in an account of the pre-Axial sacred and the seemingly progressive stages that mark an internal critique of archaic violence. By explicating Taylor's analysis of the pre-Axial in the context of the two divergent accounts of religion that he deals with (in the works of Bataille and Girard), O'Shea highlights what he sees as the significance of the still resonant impulses toward violence, and shows how the theme of "dark origins" emerges as a defining motif in the debate concerning transcendence. O'Shea argues that a Christian hermeneutics can meet the challenge posed by violence and excess, a challenge that understands "sacrifice" as a central feature of human experience.

Finally, Fainche Ryan considers the implications of Taylor's observation that, today, "we need *phronesis* even more". Writing from an explicitly Thomistic perspective, Ryan addresses the need, not so much for *phronesis*, but for a recovery of the virtue of *prudentia*, or practical wisdom. She considers in detail, not just the virtue *in se*, but also how one can learn to "play the game of life well", how one can become good at the project of becoming a human being, and how a human might flourish, if the criteria of being human rests in creation after the image and likeness of God.

The sheer range of voices and issues gathered in the volume is obvious enough, from the above summary. Accordingly—and even if the extent of Taylor's provocation makes it inconceivable that further studies of his monumental text will not follow—the editors of this volume are confident that *The Taylor Effect* will not just represent one of the first major responses: its breadth and quality should ensure that it remains a central reference point in any future discussion of Taylor's work.

Acknowledgements

As already indicated, this volume emerged from a conference and summer school on *A Secular Age*, held at the Mater Dei Institute, Dublin, in June 2009. The editors should like to thank the various speakers and delegates at those events, as well as the academic and support staff involved, the Institute's Director, Dr Andrew Mc Grady, and its President, Dr Dermot Lane.

Bibliographical Note

Given its centrality and ubiquity in this volume, Taylor's *A Secular Age* has been rendered throughout as SA, with appropriate references following immediately. Its full details are:

Taylor, Charles, 2007. *A Secular Age*. Cambridge, Ma.: Harvard University Press.

Part One:

Analyses and Dialogues

A SECULAR AGE:
THE MISSING QUESTION MARK

RUTH ABBEY

Introduction

A *Secular Age* represents the culmination of a decade or more of Charles Taylor's thinking about religion and its place in modernity in particular and in human life more generally. Earlier formulations of some of the ideas that make up this vast work appear in the Gifford Lectures which Taylor delivered in Edinburgh in April and May, 1999. Versions of some of its arguments have also been expressed in his short work from 1999, *A Catholic Modernity?*, in another short work, this time from 2002, *Varieties of Religion Today*, and in *Modern Social Imaginaries* published in 2004. There are also links with Taylor's 1989 book *Sources of the Self*. Indeed, as I understand Taylor's trajectory, the explicit manifestation of his religious views began tentatively in the closing pages of *Sources of the Self* where he talked about high standards needing strong sources and raised doubts about the capacity of a purely humanist outlook to go on powering the ethically demanding commitment to practical benevolence (Taylor 1989, 516-517). When posing these questions Taylor reveals his own hunch that "great as the power of naturalist sources might be, the potential of a certain theistic perspective is incomparably greater" (Taylor 1989, 518). And of course, having been a practicing Catholic all his life, we can assume with some confidence that Taylor must have been thinking about issues like these even before they began to surface in his writings.[1]

Yet although Taylor has clearly given a great deal of thought to these matters, I want to raise some questions about his depiction of what he calls Secularity 3. In particular I want to ask how secular the age we are said by Taylor to live in really is. This is what the missing question mark in this chapter's title refers to: just how secular is the age in which we are living? Posing this question is, however, designed, not to undermine, but to complement Taylor's overall analysis. Given that one of Taylor's larger aims in this work is to demonstrate the tenacity of religion in modern western societies,[2] I advance a line of argument that he could have followed in adducing the conditions of contemporary religious belief and non-belief in such societies, but did not. In short, I propose that Taylor's own framework can be used to show that religious belief is not as marginal to the lives of most contemporary Westerners as many of his remarks suggest. From this point of view, an alternative title for his book could have been *What Secular Age?*[3]

A chapter of this length can, of course, deal only with a sliver of a work as formidable as *A Secular Age*. This chapter draws from those sections dealing with the conditions of contemporary religious belief and practice without engaging the historical material that constitutes such a large section of the book. My comments pertain, therefore, to material from the Introduction and from Chapter 13, "The Age of Authenticity", to the end.[4] I begin by discussing what Taylor means by Secularity 3, and consider the conceptual tools he employs to examine religious belief and non-belief in contemporary western societies. As part of this process, I underline the inclusive way in which Taylor defines religion. The chapter goes on to question how embattled an option religious belief really is in modern western societies, and draws from opinion poll data to show that most members of most western societies claim to adhere to some form of religion, at least in the way Taylor defines it. I conclude by arguing for the value of such data in rounding out Taylor's picture of life in a supposedly secular age. This sort of data supports Taylor's signature story about religion's endurance in the modern western world while at the same time checking his tendency to exaggerate the reach of what he calls exclusive humanism or closed immanence.

What is Secularity 3?

One of Taylor's central ambitions—and perhaps even his central ambition—in *A Secular Age* is to shed light on Secularity 3 as he calls it, or the current conditions of modern religious belief and experience in western societies. This is what, in Taylor's eyes, sets his approach apart from other analyses of secularity which see it as referring either to the evacuation of religion from the public and other social spheres—which is what he calls Secularity 1—or to the decline in the number of people expressing allegiance to traditional religious views and in particular Christianity—which he dubs Secularity 2. While Taylor's preferred approach to secularity cannot ignore completely either of these developments, what distinguishes it is its focus on experience, on what it is like to be a religious believer or non-believer in contemporary western societies (SA 2-3; cf. 423).⁵ In making his distinctive contribution, Taylor seeks to "shift the focus to the conditions of belief, experience and search ..." (SA 4). At the work's outset he announces his intention to "focus attention on the different kinds of lived experience involved in understanding your life in one way or the other, on what it's like to live as a believer or an unbeliever" (SA 5; cf. 8, 13-14).

As this indicates, he attributes great importance to the issue of how individuals living in a secular age experience religion (or its absence). Being religious or not is for him more than simply adhering to a particular belief system: rather, "there is a way in which our whole experience is inflected if we live in one or another spirituality" (SA 11). Readers familiar with Taylor's thought will recognize that this concern with what it is like to live as a believer or non-believer in contemporary western societies is an extension of his career-long concern with self-interpretations, with how individuals understand themselves. Self-interpretations are, for him, crucial components of human identity and, therefore, of social reality. As he says, "man [sic] is a self-interpreting animal... he is always partly constituted by self-interpretation" (Taylor 1985, 72). In "Interpretation and the Sciences of Man" Taylor insists that we "think of man as a self-interpreting animal. He is necessarily so, for there is no such thing as the structure of meanings for him independently of his interpretation of them" (ibid., 26; cf. 54).⁶

Before exploring in any detail how Taylor wrestles with what he calls Secularity 3, it is necessary to reflect on what he means by religion. Such an appreciation is also essential to my thesis that the secular age is not as secular as Taylor often suggests. This question of what Taylor means by religion is taken up by only a few of the many commentaries I have seen on *A Secular Age*,⁷ yet it is an important and complicating component of his whole argument.

Taking a capacious approach to defining religion, Taylor counts any perspective or worldview that remains open to transcendence of the human, all too human, as religious. Thus he says that "a reading of 'religion' in terms of the distinction transcendent/immanent is going to serve our purposes here" (SA 15; cf. 16, 20, 544). His is not primarily an institutional or doctrinal approach: it is not really about practices or groups or institutions or bodies of belief. What counts for Taylor is whether an outlook has a transcendent axis and whether its sense of the transcendent informs its conception of human flourishing. Taylor thus defines religious faith in what he calls the strong sense "by a double criterion: the belief in transcendent reality, on one hand, and the connected aspiration to a transformation which goes beyond ordinary human flourishing on the other" (SA 510). As I understand this working definition of religion, all belief in God is likely to qualify as religion—unless someone holds that God exists but that this has no bearing upon that person's conception of human flourishing or ideal of fullness. This is the sort of position Taylor finds in ancient Epicureanism which "admitted Gods, but denied them relevance to human life" (SA 19). But Taylor's capacious approach must allow that religion is more than simply theism—theism is but one form of religion. Any orientation toward the transcendent where the understanding of transcendence feeds back into a conception of human flourishing and fullness, counts as religion for the purposes of Taylor's analysis of the secular age. He offers Buddhism as an example of this—it has a transcendent axis that informs its conception of human flourishing, but it is not a traditional form of theism (SA 17).[8]

His inclusive and generous approach allows Taylor to avoid invidious distinctions and decisions about what does and does not qualify as religion. This is especially advantageous given the repeated emphasis in *A Secular Age* on the dazzling diversity of approaches and attitudes toward religion evident in the contemporary western world. He calls this the "nova effect"[9] and it is, in turn, connected to the quest for religious authenticity which is one of the hallmarks of a secular age. Casting a wide net in defining religion also allows agents to decide for themselves whether they have a religious orientation or not, which is compatible with his wider commitment to attention to self-interpretations. Taylor's generous approach to what counts as religion is also, more generally, a reflection of his flexible, open-minded and characteristically relaxed attitude towards matters of definition.

Taylor's ambition to shed light on what it is like to be a religious believer or non-believer in contemporary western societies is a massive task, and one of the striking things about *A Secular Age* is the way he comes at this complex question from a number of angles. It is as if he is trying out a series of formulations for capturing life in a secular age. As I understand it, Taylor advances five major entrées into this question about what is distinctive about the current conditions of modern religious belief and practice in western societies. These are:

1. the Phenomenon of Religious Authenticity;
2. the Experience of Cross Pressures and Fragilization;
3. the Three Cornered Contest between Exclusive Humanism, the Immanent Counter-Enlightenment and Theism;
4. the Ideal of Fullness; and
5. the Immanent Frame.

Only the latter two—the ideal of fullness and that of the immanent frame—are, to my knowledge, unique to *A Secular Age*. Versions of all of the other ideas have appeared in the earlier works mentioned above.[10] Even the ideal of fullness is best understood as a variation on Taylor's earlier arguments about the inescapability of strong evaluations, so of the ideas listed here, that of the immanent frame is the only conceptual innovation in *A Secular Age*.

When we boil down what Taylor means by living in a secular age, we find that the following things are central. From Item 3—the Three Cornered Contest between Exclusive Humanism, the Immanent Counter-Enlightenment and Theism—what is really crucial is the existence of exclusive humanism and the immanent counter-enlightenment, for both shut the transcendent window. From Item 4—the Ideal of Fullness—what is crucial is the evolution of conceptions of fullness that make no reference to anything beyond the human. From Item 5—the Immanent Frame—what is crucial is the possibility of closed immanence. Items 1 and 2—the rise of religious authenticity and the experience of cross pressures and fragilization—could, in principle, occur in societies where everyone was religious—in Taylor's loose and inclusive sense. The three things that I submit as being central to Taylor's analysis of life in a secular age are, moreover, three ways of depicting the same phenomenon—the possibility of a life led without reference or attention to the transcendent. This plays a constitutive role in what Taylor takes to be the conditions of belief in the secular age. As Taylor puts it, "secularity 3 came to be along with the possibility of exclusive humanism... the crucial transforming move in the process is the coming of exclusive humanism" (SA 19). One of the things that he finds to be unprecedented in the contemporary western world is that humans can now live without any personal connection or aspiration to religion or any form of transcendence. As he announces in the Introduction to *A Secular Age*:

> ... the coming of modern secularity in my sense has been coterminous with the rise of a society in which for the first time in history a purely self-sufficient humanism came to be a widely available option ... a humanism accepting no final goals beyond human flourishing; nor any allegiance to anything else beyond this flourishing. Of no previous society was this true. (SA 18)

Shortly after he expresses the point thus: "a secular age is one in which the eclipse of all goals beyond human flourishing becomes conceivable... This is the crucial link between secularity and a self-sufficing humanism" (SA 19-20).[11]

Religious non-belief and denial or indifference to the transcendent realm in any form has thus become a viable option for people in modern western societies. It is possible and for some desirable to live a life with neither personal participation, nor interest, in religion nor any orientation toward the transcendent. (It is, of course, much harder for such individuals to escape religion altogether—take, for instance, the simple existence of Christian public holidays such as Christmas and Easter in western countries.) Although Taylor initially says that the possibility of living life without any personal connection or aspiration toward religion or any form of transcendence is an unprecedented phenomenon, he later qualifies this by explaining that what is novel is the spread of this doctrine, rather that its mere existence. He casts ancient Epicureanism as a form of exclusive humanism, but one which remained confined to an elite. Contemporary exclusive (or self-sufficient, self-sufficing or atheist—see, for example, SA 569) humanism is, by contrast, available to those at any level in western societies (SA 19).[12] However, as I will argue, just because it is widely available does not mean that it is widely adopted.

As its name suggests, exclusive humanism shows no interest in, and sometimes hostility toward, things or forces that claim to go beyond the human realm. But as Taylor's account of Luc Ferry's work shows, this does not doom its adherents to seeking fulfillment in the dull round of daily life nor to heralding consumerism as the highest human good. Exclusive humanists can be committed to improving human welfare, to ending poverty and violence or to any number of large-scale and ethically demanding projects. What defines exclusive humanism is that all this energy is expended for the good of one's fellow human beings only—no extra-human goal or purpose is sought or served (SA 677). Even moral outlooks that pay attention to questions of intergenerational justice would, as I understand it, fall into the exclusive humanist category, for although their concerns transcend the here and now to embrace imaginatively the welfare of those yet to be born, their purpose remains the promotion of strictly human flourishing. As Taylor's recognition of, and even admiration for these large-scale, and sometimes long-term projects indicates, even those whose life includes no transcendent dimension harbor ideas of fullness. Working for the betterment of one's fellow human beings is one non-transcendent ideal of fullness; the dignity conferred by a life lived in accordance with reason is another (SA 8-9, 694).[13]

Moreover, as the addition of the adjective "exclusive" implies, not all humanism is of this sort. Taylor makes room, albeit briefly, for a non-exclusive form of humanism, taking as his example the idea of deep ecology—the belief that humans can experience a form of transcendence through communing with the natural world. From this perspective, nature's worth is intrinsic rather than instrumental and it represents an eminently valuable good above and beyond human life (SA 19).[14] Non-exclusive humanism thus offers transcendence *sans* traditional religion.[15] This also denies traditional religion any monopoly on transcendence, which is in keeping with Taylor's capacious approach to religion.[16]

I suggested previously that the ideal of fullness is best understood as a variation on Taylor's earlier arguments about the inescapability of strong evaluations. There Taylor held that individuals rank some of their desires, or the goods they desire, as qualitatively higher than others. Some of the goods in our lives are seen to be more worthy, valuable, meaningful or important than others. The fact of strong evaluation means that humans are not only simple weighers of preferences: instead, with some choices, we make qualitative distinctions among the things we value or seek.[17] So Taylor has long held that all humans live with some sense of higher and lower in their lives. In *A Secular Age* this comes to be expressed in terms of an ideal (or intimation) of fullness. In its Introduction, Taylor gives an account of fullness in terms that resonate powerfully with his older conception of strong evaluation. As he says,

> We all see our lives, and/or the space wherein we live our lives, as having a certain moral/spiritual shape. Somewhere, in some activity, or condition, lies a fullness, a richness; that is, in that place (activity or condition), life is fuller, richer, deeper, more worth while, more admirable, more what it should be… Perhaps this sense of fullness is something we just catch glimpses of from afar off; we have the powerful intuition of what fullness would be, were we to be in that condition, e.g., of peace or wholeness; or able to act on that level, of integrity or generosity or abandonment or self-forgetfulness. (SA 5; cf. 16, 677)[18]

The ideals of fullness followed by those who are religious will differ one from another but all will be informed in some way by their religious beliefs (SA 11). And as we have just seen, even those whose life includes no transcendent dimension have ideas about what makes their lives more fulfilling. Indeed, one of the things marking the secular age is that exclusive humanism has advanced a number of ideals of fullness that make no reference to the divine or transcendent. This is one of the achievements of modernity that renders it possible for people to live their whole life in a condition of closed immanence.

As this specification of "closed" immanence intimates, exclusive humanism is not synonymous with what Taylor means when he coins the phrase "the immanent frame". He believes that all denizens of western society live within the immanent frame which offers a way of making sense of one's life without reference to God, the divine or the transcendent (SA 594). This argument relies heavily on Taylor's account in *Modern Social Imaginaries* of how three major arenas of modern life—the market economy, the public sphere and popular sovereignty—have come to be understood as self-constituting and self-regulating, as not relying on any conception of God, religion or transcendence for their legitimacy or smooth functioning. However, Taylor is at pains to point out that exclusive humanism is but one option within the immanent frame. It is possible to live within the immanent frame while remaining open to religion and the transcendent, to live within the immanent frame without closing the transcendent window, as Taylor sometimes puts it. The offer made by the immanent frame—that people can live their lives without reference to anything beyond the human all too human—is not too good to be refused. As Taylor declares in the first part of Chapter 15, entitled "The Immanent Frame", it "permits closure, without demanding it" (SA 544. Cf. 545; 556).[19] Indeed, his target throughout much of *A Secular Age* is those who portray the closing of the transcendent window as inevitable in western modernity (SA 548, 555-6; 579, 595). Modern westerners might have little or no choice but to live within the immanent frame, but this does not necessitate closing the transcendent window nor, by Taylor's definition, excluding religion.[20]

The Embattled Option?

Taylor works hard to point out that the immanent frame can be lived in a closed or open way and in so doing, makes his case for the enduring role of religion—as he loosely defines it—in a secular age. Yet despite this achievement, Taylor sometimes undermines his own goal of demonstrating religion's tenacity by exaggerating the threat to it in the secular age. On a number of occasions he overstates the power and presence of exclusive humanism, writing as if closed immanence were in the ascendancy in western societies. In the book's Introduction, for example, he explains that

> [t]he shift to secularity... consists, among other things, of a move from a society where belief in God is unchallenged and, indeed, unproblematic, to one in which it is understood to be one option among others, and frequently not the easiest to embrace... belief is an option, and in some sense an embattled option in the Christian (or post-Christian) society... (SA 3)

Note here, however, the shift in his concerns, for his interest in this passage seems to be belief in God specifically rather than transcendence more generally. And this is not the only passage where Taylor deviates from his own larger, more capacious definition of religion. Consider the way he formulates the key question regarding Secularity 3: "why is it so hard to believe in God in (many milieux of) the modern West, while in 1500 it was virtually impossible not to?" (SA 539).[21] Yet as we have seen, religion as Taylor defines it is not co-extensive with belief in God. What he officially cares about in *A Secular Age* is religion rather than simply theism, and so the difficulty or decline of belief in God is only relevant if it is not in any way replaced by other transcendent perspectives. Diminishing faith in traditional forms of theism is only relevant if superseded by exclusive humanism or closed immanence. I am not suggesting that declining belief in traditional forms of theism or dwindling church attendance and affiliation are utterly irrelevant to understanding religious experience, nor without significance for churches themselves or social life more generally. But the move Taylor makes in adopting his capacious definition of religion and his focus on Secularity 3 combine to suggest that these things are not decisive in understanding a secular age. What is decisive is the dissemination of exclusive humanism or closed immanence.

Further evidence that Taylor sometimes undermines his own goal of showing religion's endurance in the modern western world by exaggerating the threat to religion appears in the book's Introduction. Early in *A Secular Age*, we read that

> ... in certain milieux, it may be hard to sustain one's faith. There will be people who feel bound to give it up, even though they mourn its loss... There will be many others to whom faith never even seems an eligible possibility. There are certainly millions today of whom this is true. (SA 3)

Taylor later asserts that for "more and more people, unbelieving construals seem at first blush the only plausible ones" (SA 12). A page later he declares that "the presumption of unbelief has become dominant in more and more of these milieux; and has achieved hegemony in certain crucial ones, in the academic and intellectual life, for instance; whence it can more readily extend itself to others" (SA 13). Shortly after he announces that "unbelief has become for many the major default option" (SA 14). A few pages later we find that "the eclipse of all goals beyond human flourishing... falls within the range of an imaginable life for masses of people" (SA 19-20). The frequency and tenor of these remarks is significant, as is their location, for by placing them in the book's

Introduction, Taylor is setting the tone for what is to come. But such observations about the threats to religion in a secular age are not confined to the Introduction. Later in the book Taylor says that people who are confident that "the existence of God can be 'proven'... are perhaps less numerous today than their secularist opposite numbers, and certainly cannot approach the intellectual hegemony their opponents enjoy" (SA 551). In that same chapter we read that "the same kind of supposition is widespread today, now in favour of atheism, or materialism, relegating all forms of religion to an earlier era... so powerful is the sense created in certain milieux, that these old views just *can't* be options for us" (SA 590; emphasis original). Toward the book's end he speaks of "societies where the general equilibrium point is firmly within immanence, where many people even have trouble understanding how a sane person could believe in God ..." (SA 770).[22]

Many of Taylor's claims about the difficulty of sustaining religious belief in a secular age are quasi-empirical ones. Yet what such formulations fail to capture is that "more and more" of those who see unbelieving construals as the only plausible ones are not *most*. Unbelief might have become the major default option for many people, but it has not become this for most. The masses of people who can now imagine a life of closed immanence are not the mass of people. Taylor provides no evidence for his declaration that those who deny the existence of God outnumber those who believe such existence can be proven, and nothing I have ever seen by way of empirical evidence bears this out. Nor does he supply any support for his secondary point about unbelievers exercising intellectual hegemony. In all these cases, he makes quasi-empirical claims without offering anything approaching empirical support for them.

Doing the Numbers

The "we" who are said by Taylor to live in a secular age are denizens of the western world—the populations of Europe, North America and westernized countries like Australia and New Zealand (SA 1, 435, 594). Elsewhere he refers to "our North Atlantic civilization" (SA 473); he also describes these societies as having their roots in "Latin Christendom" (SA 21). Taylor is correct to say that many people in these societies live a life with neither personal participation nor interest in religion. However, such people remain a minority in almost all of those societies. In the overwhelming majority of the countries of the "we" that supposedly live in a secular age, religious believers—if we use Taylor's inclusive definition of religion—are in the majority.

When it comes to the largest single constituent of the "we", the United States, those occupying positions of closed immanence are a tiny minority. The American Religious Identification Survey (ARIS) conducted in 2008 reported that in response to open-ended questions about religious identification, less than 1% of the US population identify themselves as atheist and less than 1% identify themselves as agnostic. Compare this with the fact that just over 5% of the respondents fell into the "Don't Know/Refuse to Answer" category and we see what a tiny proportion of respondents this comprises.[23] The ARIS findings echo those of the 2008 Pew Forum on Religion & Public Life, where those who describe themselves as either atheist or agnostic are 1.6% and 2.4% of the US adult population respectively (Pew 2008a, 2). To complicate matters, just over a fifth of the 1.6 who identify themselves as atheist in the Pew study express a belief in God or a universal spirit while more than half of the 2.4 who identify themselves as agnostic express such a belief (ibid.,8). This casts doubt upon the very meaning of terms like atheism and agnosticism—at least in the US. But for present purposes, what is noteworthy is that many of these respondents who call themselves atheists or agnostics do not seem to have closed the transcendent window. From within Taylor's parameters, they would seem to count as religious.

As Taylor himself acknowledges, the USA is not the whole of the Western world nor even a microcosm of it.[24] This makes it imperative to consider data for other westernized societies. The 2001 UK Census found 15.1% of people saying they had "no religion". The Australian Bureau of Statistics reports that in the 2001 census, 15.5% of the respondents said they had "no religion". In 2004, 19% of Canadians claimed "no religious affiliation" according to Statistics Canada. The New Zealand census of 2006 records that 34.7% of respondents claimed they had no religion, making New Zealand an outlier compared to its commonwealth cousins. However, declaring that one has "no religion" or "no religious affiliation" does not necessarily mean that one has "closed the transcendent window", to invoke Taylor's metaphor. Respondents to these surveys could be signaling their rejection of or distance from orthodox, traditional, institutionalized religion rather than repudiating any and all forms of transcendence in their lives. Yet it is this latter move that is, as we have seen, what is crucial for Taylor in depicting the secular age. So these figures from Australia, Canada, the UK and New Zealand probably inflate the number of people who actually live in a condition of closed immanence.[25] But even if they do not, these numbers still reveal that in all these countries, the majority of the population does not exist in this condition.

When it comes to Europe, José Casanova summarizes the situation thus:

> A majority of the European population in every European country, except the Czech Republic and East Germany, still affirms 'belief in God' and the proportion of those who declare themselves to be "not atheist or agnostic" is consistently even larger. Only in Eastern Germany do "atheists" constitute a majority of the population (51%). In every other European country, "atheists" remain below 20% of the population. (Casanova 2003, 19)[26]

It becomes hard to avoid the conclusion that the number of people adhering to what Taylor calls closed immanence is a minority across Europe. This is compounded by survey findings from 2005. Asked "Which of these statements comes closest to your beliefs?", only 18% of EU citizens chose "I don't believe there is any sort of spirit, God or life force."[27] A statement like this fits Taylor's description of closed immanence. However, what such an aggregating approach to Europe conceals is the considerable variation among its member countries. Ireland is, for example more like the US than it is like some of its European neighbours when it comes to levels of self-reported religious orientation. According to the European Values Survey, in 1999, a mere 3% of Irish respondents reported "no belief in God or any life spirit."[28] A study conducted in 2007-8 claims that 95% of Irish respondents believe in God.[29] But what the aggregating approach *does* capture is that the "millions" for whom Taylor says "faith never even seems an eligible possibility" are vastly outnumbered by the many more millions for whom it is—or at least the millions who keep the transcendent window open which is, as we have seen (and to repeat my refrain) what is crucial for Taylor in depicting the secular age.

Invoking opinion poll data like this cannot, of course, tell us all there is to know on the question of religion, especially in the loose, inclusive and existential sense in which Taylor defines it. However, four things merit consideration here. The first is that while such data can't tell us everything, they tell us something. Their significance is not negligible, especially for a perspective as broad and sweeping as Taylor's. Secondly, in *A Secular Age*, more so than in any of his earlier writings I can think of, Taylor is entering the terrain of sociology, and so appealing to large scale aggregate data is not out of place in this debate.[30] Thirdly, the use of such evidence strengthens Taylor's dominant narrative about the persistence of religious belief—loosely defined—in modern, westernized societies, even as it undercuts some his more alarmist remarks about the reach of exclusive humanism. Finally, given Taylor's claim that what distinguishes his approach to secularity is the insights it affords into the experience of life in a secular age, data like these are a valuable complement to the evidence he does offer. Opinion poll data are not all there is, but nor should they be ignored. This is especially so given that much of the evidence Taylor does supply to support his claims about the nature of contemporary experience in *A Secular Age* is inadequate to this momentous task.

Evidence of Experience

Taylor's tendency to focus on written texts as evidence of experience, and, within that, to draw on fairly traditional and "high brow" literary and philosophical works, is familiar to readers of *Sources of the Self*.[31] It is also powerfully evident in *A Secular Age*. For non-transcendent sources of fullness, we find references to Kant and Nietzsche and allusions to Romanticism.[32] To illustrate his concept of fullness, Taylor cites the autobiography of Bede Griffiths (without explaining who he is) and declares: "let [this] one example... stand for many" (SA 5). He backs this point up with an allusion to the work of novelist Robert Musil. There is a brief reference to the transcendent sense of fullness experienced by Paul Claudel (SA 14). Indeed, literary references abound in *A Secular Age*—Taylor cites the poetry of Thomas Hardy and Matthew Arnold and invokes the novels of Albert Camus.[33] A heavy reliance on literary sources also characterizes the "Roots of Violence" discussion (SA 656-675; cf. 699-700). Taylor is no doubt correct that "literature is one of the prime loci of expression of these newly-discovered insights" (SA 732), and literature is, more generally, a rich source for the articulation and exploration of experiences of transcendence. I am not, therefore, denying the value of these sources as evidence of experience of Secularity 3. But their value is limited. Given Taylor's repeated ambition to explore the lived experience of a secular age, his preoccupation with literary and philosophical works presents a problem, for these are bound to represent the experience of a very limited stratum of society. Leaning heavily on these genres makes sense when your argument is dedicated to identifying the various sources of the self and the good in western culture, and to demonstrating the invigoration that can come from returning to the sources where these goods are articulated. However, when your ambition is to portray the lived experience of those in a secular age, a wider variety of types of evidence is required.

Other sorts of evidence are not entirely absent from *A Secular Age*.

Taylor quotes at length Vaclav Havel's experience of fullness (SA 728-9). He offers Taizé as an illustration of young people's quest for religious authenticity and elsewhere refers to popular centres of pilgrimage in the current day (SA 517).[34] On the theme of religious authenticity, he draws from the work of "an astute observer of the American scene", Wade Clark Roof, and cites one of Roof's interviewees on the difference between religion and spirituality (SA 506, 508). Taylor borrows Grace Davie's idea of "believing without belonging" to describe the position of those in England who are not regular churchgoers but who have not abandoned religion altogether. Davie also calls this vicarious religion (SA 520-22).[35] Taylor mentions Germans who could declare themselves *konfessionslos* but who willingly pay taxes to support religion because they value the church's presence in society (SA 598). Elsewhere, he describes the South African Truth and Reconciliation Commission as providing a vertical axis for thinking about human relations which opens up a space for reconciliation and trust (SA 705-6; cf. 710). Quoting from interviews with ordinary people, pointing to events and sites that attract large crowds, drawing on the findings of sociologists, and discussing actions and practices in the political realm are all welcome counterweights to Taylor's inclination to lean on literary and philosophical sources. But it is a pity there was not more of this in the book, given its aspiration to say something about contemporary experiences of religion.

An additional and valuable source of information about people's experiences and self-understandings of religion is available in the form of surveys and questionnaires about religious life. To those who would object that a hermeneutically-inclined critic of the social sciences such as Taylor could have no truck with such data, two countervailing considerations emerge. The first is that such data can be handled with caution and portrayed for what they are—information that needs further interpretation—as the above rider about atheists who retain a transcendent orientation illustrates. In suggesting the value of this sort of information, I am not assuming that it is self-interpreting: opinion poll data need to be carefully interrogated and interpreted, and in this sense resemble literary evidence. Secondly, Taylor does not himself disavow the use of such data. At one point he buttresses his claim about the widening gamut of religious positions with reference to a 1993 Gallup Poll from Britain (SA 828). In an interview published after *A Secular Age*, he invokes the Pew study cited above, mentioning its findings about the number of American respondents who claim to have changed their religious affiliation in their lifetime. He concludes that this information "does indeed say something about the nature and future of Western societies" (Taylor 2009). The Pew study reveals that "religious affiliation in the U.S. is both very diverse and extremely fluid" (Pew 2008a, 1) just as Taylor contends that "the religious life of Western societies is much more fragmented than ever before, and also much more unstable, as people change their positions during a lifetime, or between generations, to greater degrees than ever before" (SA 594).[36] So Taylor is correct to suggest that the Pew study vindicates his point about the great variety and mobility in contemporary religious experience—at least in the US.

Conclusion

When we consider religion in the loose and flexible way that Taylor recommends, there is very little evidence that we are living in a secular age. The overwhelming majority of people in the western world continue to have some form of religion. Those who live in a condition of what Taylor calls closed immanence are firmly within the minority. While there can be pitfalls and problems in using opinion poll data, and they cannot paint anything approaching a complete picture of contemporary religious experience in westernized societies, they do provide an additional valuable perspective on this issue. Moreover, when making large, cross-national claims as Taylor does, these sorts of data are particularly useful. So one of the things I am recommending in this chapter is that Taylor could have enriched his discussion of Secularity 3 by drawing on such data. I am proposing, further, that the empirical figures about the presence of what Taylor would call closed immanence support his signature story about the persistence of religious belief as he defines it in his capacious way. Were Taylor to engage this sort of data, they would not only broaden his depiction of experience in a secular age but also strengthen his claim about the endurance of religious belief—loosely defined. After all, an important part of Taylor's purpose in writing *A Secular Age* is to show that religion is neither dead nor dying in the modern west and to make room for the recognition of religious faith and orientations toward transcendence in all their variety and motility in these societies. As he states:

> the developments of Western modernity have destabilized and rendered virtually unsustainable earlier forms of religious life, but... new forms have sprung up. Moreover this process of destabilization and recomposition is not a once-for-all change, but is continuing. (SA 594; cf. 437)

Elsewhere, he concludes that

> ... a crucial area of work is to recognize the nature and spread of the new

forms. New kinds of devotion, discipline, congregational life... the decline of old and coming of new forms in the West has created a new over-all place of religion or the spiritual in society. Spiritual/religious life is much more self-consciously pluralistic, with ever new forms arising, and with much more scope for individual affinities and conversions. (Taylor 2007)[37]

Yet in light of his desire to emphasize religion's endurance in the modern western world, Taylor's tendency to exaggerate the effects of closed immanence is counter-productive. Engaging the sort of data marshaled in this chapter would force him to modify or retract some of his more alarmist claims about the difficulty of and threats to religious belief—loosely defined.[38]

References

Abbey, Ruth, 2000. *Philosophy Now: Charles Taylor*, Princeton: Princeton University Press.
Berger, Peter L., 2005. Religion and the West. *The National Interest* (Summer) 112-119.
Casanova, José, 2003. Beyond European and American Exceptionalisms: towards a Global Perspective, in *Predicting Religion: Christian, Secular, and Alternative Futures*, ed. Grace Davie, Linda Woodhead and Paul Heelas, 17-29. Aldershot: Ashgate.
Davie, Grace, 2006. Is Europe an Exceptional Case? *The Hedgehog Review* (Spring and Summer): 23-34.
Gordon, Peter E., 2008. The Place of the Sacred in the Absence of God: Charles Taylor's A Secular Age. *Journal of the History of Ideas* 69.4 (October): 647- 673.
Gourgouris, Stathis, 2008. "A Case of Heteronomous Thinking." http://www.ssrc.org/blogs/immanent_frame/2008/01/19/a-case-of-heteronomous-thinking/
Greeley, Andrew, 2002. *Religion in Europe at the End of the Second Millennium: A Sociological Profile*. New Jersey: Transaction Publishers.
Hervieu-Léger, Daniele, 2008. Religion as Memory. In *Religion: Beyond a Concept*, edited by Hent de Vries, 245-58. New York: Fordham University Press.
Jay, Martin, 2009. Faith-Based History. *History & Theory* 48.1 (February): 76-84.
Miller, James, 2008. What Secular Age? *International Journal of Politics, Culture and Society* 21.1-4: 5-10.
Pew Forum on Religion & Public Life, 2008a. The U.S. Religious

Landscape Survey Reveals a Fluid and Diverse Pattern of Faith. February 25: 1-4. http://pewresearch.org/pubs/743/united-states-religion
—. 2008b. US Religious Landscape Survey: Summary of Key Findings 1-20. http://religions.pewforum.org/
Polebaum, Jessica and Charles Gelman, 2009. Religious "nones" and the future of American religion. *The Immanent Frame: Secularism, Religion and the Public Sphere*, http://blogs.ssrc.org/tif/2009/09/28/religious-nones-and-the-future-of-american-religion/
Rosa, Hartmut, 2004. Four levels of self-interpretation. *Philosophy & Social Criticism* 30.5-6: 691-720.
Redhead, Mark, 2002. *Charles Taylor: Living and Thinking Deep Diversity*. Lanham, Md.: Rowman and Littlefield.
Smith, Nicholas H., 2002. *Charles Taylor: Meaning, Morals and Modernity*. Cambridge: Polity.
Taylor, Charles, 1985a. What is Human Agency? *Human Agency and Language: Philosophical Papers 1*, 15-44. Cambridge: Cambridge University Press.
—. 1985b. Self-Interpreting Animals. In *Human Agency and Language: Philosophical Papers 1*, 45-76. Cambridge: Cambridge University Press.
—. 1985c. Interpretation and the Sciences of Man. *Philosophy and the Human Sciences: Philosophical Papers 2*, 15-57. Cambridge: Cambridge University Press.
—. 1989. *Sources of the Self: The Making of the Modern Identity*. Cambridge, Mass.: Harvard University Press.
—. 1995. Heidegger, Language and Ecology. In *Philosophical Arguments*, 100-126. Cambridge, Mass.: Harvard University Press.
—. 1999. *A Catholic Modernity? Charles Taylor's Marianist Award Lecture, with responses by William M. Shea, Rosemary Luling Haughton, George Marsden, and Jean Bethke Elshtain*. Edited by James L. Heft, Oxford University Press, 1999.
—. 2002. *Varieties of Religion Today: William James Revisited*. Cambridge, Mass.: Harvard University Press.
—. 2004. *Modern Social Imaginaries*. Edited by Dilip Gaonkar, Jane Kramer, Benjamin Lee and Michael Warner, Durham, NC: Duke University Press.
—. 2007. Problems around the secular. http://www.ssrc.org/blogs/immanent_frame/2007/11/02/problems-around-the-secular/

—. 2009. The New Atheism and the Spiritual Landscape of the West: A Conversation with Charles Taylor. Part One of Three Interviews with Ronald A. Kuipers, in *The Other Journal.com An Intersection of Theology and Culture,* 11, "Atheism", June 12. http://theotherjournal.com/print.php?id=375

Woodhead, Linda, Paul Heelas and Grace Davie (2003). Introduction. In *Predicting Religion: Christian, Secular, and Alternative Futures,* edited by Grace Davie, Linda Woodhead and Paul Heelas, 2-14. Aldershot: Ashgate.

"Transcending Human Flourishing": Is There a Need for a Subtler Language?

Eoin G. Cassidy

> The change which mattered to people in our (North Atlantic, or "Western") civilization and still matters today… [is that we] have moved from a world in which the place of fullness was understood as unproblematically outside of or "beyond" human life, to a conflicted age in which this construal is challenged by others which place it "within" human life. (SA 15)[1]

Introduction

The attention that Charles Taylor's *A Secular Age* continues to generate is not only a reflection on the significance of the theme—the emergence in our life-time of what is aptly described as the secularisation of culture.[2] It is also a powerful testimony to the quality of a book which is rightly acclaimed for its insightful exploration of the key themes associated with secularisation—themes which include: a "this–worldly" image of human flourishing; an individualist anthropology and a moral framework that is increasingly shaped by emotivism; the cultural embrace of instrumental reasoning; and the emergence of a pluralist ethos.[3] What sets this book apart from others in its genre, however, is the quality of the research and the sharpness of its analysis, particularly the analysis of the impact of the secularisation of culture on foundational beliefs and practices—especially those associated with religion. By any standards, it is a remarkable achievement.[4]

Although the rise of modernity is traced with great attention to detail, it would be wrong to regard *A Secular Age* as if it were an historical treatise. Rather, the whole purpose of the book is to re-invigorate public discourse on foundational beliefs and values for twenty-first century Western society. In pursuit of this goal, Taylor seeks every opportunity afforded to argue for a vision of human flourishing that transcends the exclusively immanent and restrictive boundaries of a materialist ethos. He also devotes space to promoting an ideal or ethic of authenticity as a counter-balance to the excesses of expressive individualism. And, finally, he seeks to restore credibility to the idea of an objective moral framework which alone can counter the excessive pragmatism of an instrumental culture. If for nothing else, he deserves credit for this challenging endeavour.

Prompted solely by a desire to contribute to this debate generated by Taylor, and without taking away from my appreciation of the achievement of *A Secular Age*, this paper takes a rather critical stance regarding the merits of the book. It asks the following question: to what extent, if any, will Taylor succeed in making a lasting contribution to invigorating discourse on foundational beliefs and values for contemporary Western society?

Within the specific parameters of this question, I remain to be convinced that Taylor's thesis will withstand the test of time—and that because of a failure fully to appreciate the significance of the overlapping contours and radical interdependence of the concepts of immanence and transcendence. Not only is this issue something which is clearly of the first importance in understanding an incarnational religion such as Christianity, but it is also of no small significance in comparing and contrasting core beliefs of the other major world religions.

Whilst acknowledging the validity of Taylor's critique of an exclusively immanent horizon of meaning, I shall nevertheless question the appropriateness of Taylor's use of the transcendent/immanent distinction as a template upon which to discuss the fate of religion in a secular age. I shall also contend that it impacts adversely on the accuracy of Taylor's analysis of both the manner and the significance of modernity's influence on religion today.

In pursuing this topic, I am influenced by a profound unease with the thesis which states that the turn towards the subject, which gave birth to modernity, leads inexorably to a cultural embrace of atheism or at least the "practical" atheism that is religious indifference. Does the emergence of an increasingly immanent horizon of meaning lead inexorably to atheism in the guise of positivism, materialism and even relativism?[5] I do not accept that this is an inaccurate reading of the legacy of the Enlightenment and the larger canvas of modernity. From a theistic perspective, I also contend that offers an unduly pessimistic assessment of the current state of religion, other than the questionable belief that the only alternative to theism is the less than attractive prospect of the nihilism of Nietzsche.

In the course of this study, the question will be asked as to whether or to what extent Taylor shares this "pessimistic" reading of the legacy of the culture that is modernity. In *A Secular Age,* he traces in some detail the inexorable rise of an immanent frame of reference that documents the cultural shift that is modernity. Now, if Taylor is to be believed, of even more significance than five hundred years of European cultural history, which preceded this present generation, are the cultural changes that have taken place in the "West" over the past fifty years. In a well argued analysis, he contends that for the first time in the history of "western" civilisation, we have witnessed in this short space of time and on a mass scale a cultural loss of connectedness to any objective horizon of meaning and/or values. At the vertical level, this connectedness would have been in the past shaped by a belief in the presence of God or the Good, and at the horizontal level by a relationship to neighbour or neighbourhood, which is expressive of the belief that human beings are shaped by family, friends and community. As Taylor is at pains to point out, this loss of connectedness with a transcendent horizon of meaning is not without its consequences for individual fulfilment and societal coherence.[6]

The concept of transcendence is of the first importance if one is to make sense of core theological (Christian) belief in a creator God and related truth claims that touch on (1) the relation between creator and creation, (2) the belief in immortality/eternal life, and (3) the belief in the graced character of life. However, for Taylor, the importance of this concept is proposed primarily as a necessary counterpoint to an age of reason which, in proposing exclusively scientific parameters for knowledge, has given rise to the self-confident belief that all questions have observable and measurable answers. Just as importantly, it has given rise to a self-confidence in the power of reason, in the self-sufficiency of the individual, and ultimately, it could be argued, to a belief in absolute freedom—a freedom which has little or no contact with transcendent sources of meaning as outlined above. In Taylor's considered opinion, it is only by acknowledging the validity of a concept such as transcendence, that one will be able to grasp one's connectedness to a horizon of meaning, whose centre of gravity lies outside the limited, restricted and self-defeating boundaries of the self.

Given the appropriateness of the transcendence/immanence distinction to underscore core themes in the cultural shift occasioned by the rise of modernity and the emergence of a secular age, and given the importance of the concept of transcendence to ensure the continued cultural comprehension of core philosophical and theological truths, and, finally, given that Taylor is not claiming that this distinction fully or even adequately captures the phenomenon that is religion, wherein lies my difficulty with his use of this distinction as a template to discuss the fate of religion in a secular age?

Fullness Beyond Human Flourishing?

> I believe that there is no escaping some version of what I called in an earlier discussion "fullness"; for any liveable understanding of human life... The swirling debate between belief and unbelief, as well as various forms of both... [is] a debate about what real fullness consists in. (SA 600)

For anyone seeking to critique Taylor's treatment of the appropriateness of the transcendent/immanent distinction, there is no avoiding the necessity to tackle the subject of the "end of life" issues, and, in this context, what he regards as the correct understanding (from a Christian theist point of view) of the related ideas of fullness and human flourishing. We are fortunate that in the introductory chapter of *A Secular Age* there is to be found quite a detailed analysis of the experiences that draw us beyond "ordinary" reality and point us in the direction of fullness. For example:

> we have to be aware of how believers and unbelievers can experience their world very differently. The sense that fullness is to be found in something beyond us can break in on us as a fact of experience... (SA 14)[7]

What is striking about this passage (and others listed below) is not only Taylor's sensitivity to the epiphanic and/or graced nature of those experiences, but also the stress that he places on their transcendent character, as reflected in his frequent use of the image of something that is "beyond". How should we conceive of this concept of a belief in a beyond? Two obvious answers come to mind, both suggested by Taylor: (1) beyond the boundaries of a self-enclosed material world, and (2) beyond the boundaries of a self-sufficient humanism. However, as the following passage suggests, Taylor has in mind something quite different:

> [D]oes the highest, the best life involve our seeking, or acknowledging, or serving a good which is beyond, in the sense of independent of human flourishing?... The injunction "Thy will be done" isn't equivalent to "Let humans flourish", even though we know that God wills human flourishing. (SA 16-17)[8]

What Taylor is highlighting is that, for the Christian, loving and worshipping God is the ultimate *telos* or goal rather than human flourishing. It is a radical ethic—a *kenotic* ethic, one that demands the renunciation even of the very desire itself for human flourishing itself.[9] It is a reflective piece of writing which challenges any easy assumption that self-sufficing humanism is invulnerable to criticism. But it could legitimately be argued that, in proposing a place of fullness that is beyond human flourishing, not only does Taylor challenge the logic of a self-sufficient humanism, but virtually the whole history of classical thought which was united in its attachment to a eudaemonist ethic—namely, that flourishing/happiness is an appropriate description of our ultimate goal.

There are few Christian apologists who would dispute Taylor's contention that there is a transcendent dimension to human fulfilment—the rejection of an exclusively materialist and/or humanist frame of reference. And, furthermore, there are few who would deny that the path to fulfilment is one paved by acts of self-emptying love. However, neither of those two statements fully captures the meaning intended by Taylor of a belief in a concept of fullness that is beyond human flourishing.

Taylor's contention is that the highest, the best life, involves our seeking, acknowledging and serving a Good/God which is beyond, in the sense of independent of human flourishing. But what does it mean to speak of an ideal of human flourishing/happiness whose significance as a *telos* is so thoroughly compromised by a something beyond human flourishing? It can only be a misplaced or so-called ideal of human flourishing that is so surpassed or supplanted—misplaced because it was perhaps too self-absorbed. If that is indeed the appropriate focus for understanding the issue, then the question for discussion would be: what is the correct way of describing human flourishing that avoids any such misunderstanding? The alternative which discusses whether and how one ought to transcend/go beyond the very ideal of human flourishing is highly problematical, in that it would seem to relativise the significance of human life in a manner that is as difficult to understand as it is to accept.

The importance which Taylor attaches to this distinction between fullness and human flourishing should not be underestimated. As the following passage suggests, it could be argued that, for Taylor, it is the indeed the leitmotif which unpacks core features of the cultural shift engendered by modernity:

> we have moved from a world in which the place of fullness was understood as unproblematically outside of or "beyond" human life, to a conflicted age in which this construal is challenged by others which place it... "within" human life. (SA 15)

If one is to accept the correctness of his insight, the manner in which Taylor lays stress on the word "unproblematically" needs to be carefully nuanced. Did the pre-modern classical culture unproblematically place fullness "outside of" or "beyond" human life'? I am not so sure that it did. A brief examination of this issue from one of the great masters of Greco-

Roman classical civilization, Augustine of Hippo, will help to illustrate my reservations.

Learning from Augustine

It could be argued that Augustine's pre-modern version of the tale of two cities in his celebrated work *The City of God* is proof positive of the correctness of Taylor's description of the Christian tradition. For example, it is quite clear, that for Augustine, fullness—the harmony and peace that is yearned for—transcends the boundaries of all known civilizations, most particularly that civilization represented by the city of Rome. But the crucial question is: why is this the case? Is it because Augustine accepts, as Taylor suggests, that "the place of fullness is understood unproblematically outside of or 'beyond' human life"? (SA 15).

No-one who has read *The City of God* could be under any illusion that there was anything unproblematical about the gulf between the two idealized cities. There is nothing pre-ordained about this gulf—a sort of divinely sanctioned reminder of the transcendent character of human fulfilment. From Augustine's perspective, the reason for the gulf between these two cities is quite simply the baleful reality of sin, which has its roots in human pride. To the mind of Augustine, it was sin, rather than the shortness of human life in this world, which pointed inexorably to the transcendent character of human fulfilment. There is nothing uniquely pre-modern, nor indeed is there anything unproblematical, about that insight.

Staying with this pre-modern Augustine, the question that must be asked is: to what extent is he wedded to the view that the place of fullness is outside of or beyond human life? In the context of the importance that Taylor attaches to the link between the concept of transcendence and a sense of the beyond, it must be acknowledged that the literary structure of Augustine's *Confessions* paints a very different picture. Modelled upon the biblical story of the prodigal son, the *Confessions* remind us that the journey to fullness is not one that draws us beyond human life; rather, it is best described as a return (as in the return of the prodigal son) to the depths of one's own interiority, symbolised by the motif of the restless heart. Interestingly, the core question which Augustine addresses is not where we are on this universal journey of the human heart, but rather where God is to be found. Tellingly, for those who wish to stress the transcendence or otherness of God, Augustine reminds us that God is neither to be found outside of nor beyond us, but is rather to be found in the depths of interiority, even "closer to me than I am to myself" (*Confessions* 10.27).[10]

For the author of the *Confessions* whose opening chapter includes the following: "Thou hast made us for yourself O Lord, and our hearts are restless until they rest in thee" (*Confessions* 1.1). Augustine's acceptance of a transcendent dimension to human fulfilment could not be doubted. But the key question remains, how is this transcendence to be understood? The answer to this question hinges upon how one reads the core Augustinian theological concerns. In this context, it is hard to underestimate the importance to which he attached to the issue of grace in the context of the mystery of sin and redemption. Augustine's deeply held views on this matter are summed up beautifully in the following often quoted passage from the *Confessions,* "The good that I do is done by you in me, the evil is my own" (*Confessions* 7.12).

There is very little if any evidence that Augustine's reflections on the transcendent dimension to human fulfilment are intended to suggest that the appropriate *telos* to life is one that draws us beyond human flourishing. Rather, it has far more to do with the transcendent character of love, reflected in the insight that fulfilment is received rather than grasped—something made very concrete by the painful reality of sin and the need to receive forgiveness. For Augustine, the biblical story of the prodigal son represents the journey made by every person—one that exposes us on a daily basis to the mystery of sin and forgiveness. It is this reality that alone provides an appropriate focus for understanding Augustine's use of the transcendence motif. His own life's experience was a sobering reminder, if one were needed, that this is not a journey which can be successfully negotiated by relying exclusively on one's own resources.

The Appropriateness of the Transcendence/ Immanence Distinction?

In what follows, the debate will be broadened beyond Taylor's discussion of human flourishing/fullness. The intention is to raise, albeit in a very summary fashion, some critical issues which will challenge the suitability of the transcendence/immanence distinction as a template for distinguishing the religious believer from the exclusive/atheistic humanist and, in this context, providing an entry point for the discussion of the fate of religion in a secular age.

My first reason for critiquing the transcendent/immanent template is that, from the point of view of understanding the phenomenon of religion in general, the template is, to say the least, not particularly helpful. I am conscious of the importance of this template to the vast majority of religious believers of whatever religious persuasion. The problem, however, is that the attempt to use it as a template for distinguishing the religious believer from the exclusive/atheistic humanist just won't work because of the wide range of different and indeed widely contrasting positions on the transcendence/immanence scale occupied by the main world religions. For example, the unflinching adherence to the transcendence of God in both the Jewish and the Islamic expressions of monotheism provides a fairly clear-cut contrast with the monist and/or pantheistic tendencies that are to be found in Hinduism. Even the best endeavours of Sikhism failed to reconcile the faith positions of these two great world religions, namely Hinduism and Islam, on this issue. As for Buddhism, is there even internal agreement on this issue? Is there one shared recognisably Buddhist understanding of transcendence? And then there is the rather complex position of a religion such as Christianity. In its espousal of an incarnational theology, it has succeeded, one could justifiably claim, in a most extraordinary endeavour: to have embraced both ends of the transcendence/immanence spectrum.

Learning from Levinas

My second reason for critiquing the transcendent/immanent template is that, unless carefully delineated, the distinction is too undifferentiated to be useful in analysing the impact of modernity on the faith profile of the "western world". Take, for example, the rise of an immanent horizon of meaning, in the form of the emergence over the course of modernity both of an empiricist epistemology and of a more individualist anthropology. Firstly, one could legitimately interpret the impact of both these cultural developments on religion in a positive light, namely as a celebration of the God-given gifts of scientific reasoning and human freedom. And second, even if one was to interpret their impact on religion in a negative light, they would pose very different challenges to the faith profile of religion in general and Christianity in particular. If this is correct, the transcendence/immanence distinction is in and of itself not very helpful in charting the specific character of the challenge posed by either cultural development.

This problem associated with the undifferentiated character of the transcendent/immanent distinction is most evident in Taylor's stress on the concept epiphany/epiphanic, which he uses to describe the experience of transcendence that has engendered religious conversations.[11] I am not denying the epiphanic nature of Christian revelation, but simply to describe something as "epiphanic" tells us nothing about the religious character or otherwise of the experience/revelation. For example, and here I restrict my comments to the Christian religion, unless the epiphany is of the character of a graceful/loving/forgiving/salvific presence, whatever it is, it is not religious in the Christian understanding of that term. In the descriptions of the series of experiences that engendered conversion which Taylor recounts in the concluding chapter of *A Secular Age,* only that attributed to Francis of Assisi would seem to be so differentiated.

For one such as Taylor, for whom the concept of transcendence is so central, it is surprising not to find any systematic treatment of the many and varied ways in which transcendence can be imaged. For example, there is no systematic exploration of transcendence through the prism of the "other"—the transcendence of the neighbour as other which is so provocatively outlined in the philosophy of Emmanuel Levinas. I am referring here to Levinas' penetrating exploration of the manner in which the journey to self-acceptance is commensurate with the character of one's response to the claims of the other—a response which must at all times be conscious of the asymmetrical nature of the relationship with the other, and a response that respects transcendence. In my response to the claims of the other, the other always remains transcendent and can never be subsumed into my orbit.

Deeply influenced by his Jewish faith, Levinas' philosophy thus offers important insights into the manner in which transcendence/otherness can provide an invaluable lens with which to image religious sensibility. Furthermore, it achieves this in a manner which is accessible albeit challenging to those who have been reared in a secular age marked by expressive individualism. Most importantly, it proposes a transcendent frame of reference for human flourishing in a manner that in no way undermines the value of the immanent horizon of meaning that increasingly shapes contemporary culture.

Learning from Marx

My third reason for critiquing the transcendent/immanent template is that, unless carefully nuanced, the distinction could be perceived inaccurately as providing an explanatory hypothesis for the decline of religion—a hypothesis that is enthusiastically embraced by mainstream secularization/subtraction theorists. Not only is there little evidence in favour of this hypothesis, but those proposing it rarely if ever give credence to the possible validity of any alternative hypothesis. One such hypothesis might indeed be the possibility that the emergence of this immanent frame has the potential to be a catalyst for religious renewal of a most profound kind. Even the most cursory glance at an incarnational theology such as is expressive of Christianity could leave one in little doubt about the opportunity afforded by an immanent frame of reference to proclaim "kingdom" values. Freed from the dead weight of the temptation to abandon this world as a vale of tears or a place of temporary and ultimately insignificant abode, this is a unique opportunity to identify with the struggles of the world with a view to proclaiming a civilization of love.

As even a cursory glance at the Marxist critique of religion makes plain, this is an issue which raises the most profound questions that touch on the legitimacy of the Christian religion in the modern world. Although well rehearsed over the best part of two centuries, this critique of religion has lost none of its persuasiveness. There is no doubt but that, once one adopts the transcendence/immanence distinction, either as a point of reference to describe exclusive humanism, or as a synonym for the distinction between theism and atheism, it is hard to break free of the classical criticism of religion, namely that it is both an escapist and cowardly flight from the world.

Learning from Taylor

My fourth and final reason for critiquing the transcendent/immanent template is that it leads inevitably to a belief in the confrontational character of religion's engagement with modernity, which, I would want to argue, is not only unhelpful but also inaccurate—from both theological and philosophical perspectives. From a Christian theological perspective, one could argue that, just as erroneous as an overemphasis on a dialogical (optimistic) interpretation of the relation between faith and culture (for minimising the reality of sin in the world), so likewise, from a Christian theological perspective, it is erroneous to over-emphasise a dialectical (pessimistic) reading of any particular moment in culture, in that it overemphasises the presence of sin in the world and fails to acknowledge Christ's loving presence in each and every culture. From a Christian theological point of view, every culture is composed of light and shadow—and that includes modernity.

In critiquing the conflict model of the relationship between religion and modernity from a philosophical perspective, I wish to draw attention to a little observed ethical ideal that is proposed as worthy counterpoint to those who would seek to categorize the expressive individualism of today's culture in exclusively negative terms, as self-centred, egotistical and selfish. Rather, what is proposed is the ideal or the ethic of authenticity, one which is the product of a self-confident individualism (a true child of modernity)—an ideal which gives recognition to the ethical challenge associated with that eminently contemporary cultural aspiration, namely authenticity, or being authentic or true to oneself. Furthermore, it is a worthy ethical ideal, in that it prioritises the responsible exercise of human freedom over slavish obedience to externally imposed rules. Most importantly it has the potential not only to highlight the rich ethical frame of reference that is a legacy of modernity, but also to challenge the presumption that religion and the culture of expressive individualism are related conflictually rather than as partners in the search to communicate sustainable values in today's world.

Interestingly, it was Charles Taylor himself who first drew my attention to the significance of this insight in a small book which he published exactly twenty years ago under the title *Les Trois Malaises de la Modernité*. Shortly afterwards, it was translated into English and published with the much more positive title of *The Ethics of Authenticity*. Furthermore, as we will have occasion to observe, the juxtaposition of these two titles is no accident, but rather is a powerful reminder that Taylor is conscious of the dangers of a naïve reading of the cultural/ethical legacy bequeathed by modernity.

Again, it is interesting to observe that it is Taylor himself who in this book warns against any over-pessimistic reading of the effects of modernity on the ethical character of contemporary life. As he persuasively argues, one of the most positive aspects of the legacy of modernity was that it facilitated the emergence for the first time of the individual *qua* individual—in other words, a cultural consciousness that life is not inevitably shaped by external forces, but rather by the exercise of human freedom. As Taylor points out, this new consciousness of the dignity of the individual brings with it for the first time a real sense of an ethic of personal responsibility—the importance of being authentic. This is a cultural achievement of no small import.[12]

A Secular Age contains not one but two chapters which host the titles of "The Malaises of Modernity" and "The Age of Authenticity", and which repeat almost word for word the theses of the two 1990 publications. Furthermore, the two chapters in question provide a highly lucid analysis of the salient features of the age of authenticity or the emergence of expressive individualism. However, as we shall observe, these two chapters do not contain the same emphasis on the positive ethical achievement that was proposed twenty years earlier as an integral part of the story of modernity. Rather, Taylor now speaks about what he describes as "the fractured culture of the nova"—the fractured mores of the new cultural reality that is expressive individualism.[13] The chapters also describe in some detail the challenges which these new emerging mores pose to mainstream western theism.

In the chapter entitled "The Age of Authenticity", Taylor offers a phenomenological analysis of the contours of the emerging culture of the Western world. In the course of this chapter he argues that in a culture which is characterized by expressive individualism—an anthropology that gives priority to the conviction that everyone has his/her own way of realising their humanity—it is progressively less feasible to anchor a link to the sacred in any particular broader framework, whether Church or State. Insofar as religious beliefs and/or values are embraced today, this increasingly takes place within what he describes as a post-Durkheimian dispensation.

It is, however, in the earlier chapter entitled "The Malaises of Modernity" that Taylor engages in a detailed analysis of the implications for religion of the emergence of what he describes as "the fractured culture of the nova"—the emergence in Western societies in the last fifty years, of "a generalised culture of 'authenticity', or expressive individualism, in which people are encouraged to find their own way, discover their own fulfilment" (SA 299). In addition, he analyses the manner in which the power or capacity to order the self which underpins this expressive individualism impacts on the emerging shape of an immanent frame of reference.

As always, Taylor's analysis is carefully nuanced. This is particularly evident in the course of this study as Taylor identifies what he describes as "cross pressures"—contrasting positions which emanate from this particular immanent cultural frame of reference. Writing about the impact on religion of the "cross pressures" that emanate from expressive individualism, he describes the combination, within the "buffered identity", of both a "relative invulnerability to anything beyond the human" and "a sense that something may be occluded" (SA 303). What, if anything, could be occluded by a closure to transcendence, a closure to any sense that there may be something beyond the human? From Taylor's perspective, if there is nothing beyond the boundaries of expressive individualism—nothing beyond the boundaries set by the absolute value of freedom—it becomes highly problematic apportioning any sense of worth to one's projects (see SA 308). If free choice is absolute, there is nothing with which to evaluate the quality of one's life; everybody and everything is in consequence trivialized, and we are left with what Taylor describes as "a fragility of meaning" (ibid.). As something which is the unique product of modernity, this fragility of meaning is not something which would have been evident in the earlier pre-Axial or pre-modern culture. As he states:

a crucial feature of the malaise of immanence is the sense that all these answers [to questions in terms of the meaning of life] are fragile, or uncertain; that a moment may come, where we no longer feel that our chosen path is compelling, or cannot justify it to ourselves or to others. (SA 308)

He describes these and other related experiences as the malaises of immanence because, as he says, "everybody recognizes that they come onto our horizon, or onto our agenda, with the eclipse of transcendence" (SA 309). This is the sense of the fragility of meaning, the search for an over-arching significance—the "Is That All There Is?"

Concluding Reflection

In such a manner throughout the book, Taylor clearly and persuasively argues that the advocates of "Closed World Structures" have got it wrong, and here he includes in his critique those who argue for the secularization thesis that the emergence of an immanent horizon of meaning will inevitably lead to the disappearance of religion, or at least the disappearance of the truth claims of religion. I would share his views, which do much to counter the suggestion raised at the outset of this paper that, from a theistic perspective, Taylor may have adopted an unduly pessimistic reading of the legacy of the Enlightenment and the larger canvas of modernity. Nevertheless, I would still wish to argue, in company with the Taylor of the *Ethics of Authenticity*, for a more open acknowledgement of the richness of the immanent frame that is the cultural legacy of modernity, both for religious belief and ethical discourse. With the emergence of a more immanent frame of reference there are new opportunities to appreciate the gift of freedom and to embrace the ideal of a secular age, to accept the challenge to embrace kingdom values in the here and now, freed from the destructive legacy suggested by the imagery of this world as a vale of tears.

References

Bellah, Robert, 2007. *Habits of the Heart: Individualism and Commitment in American Life*. Berkeley: University of California Press.
MacIntyre, Alasdair, 1981. *After Virtue*. London: Duckworth.
Taylor, Charles, 2003. *Ethics of Authenticity*. Toronto: CBC (11th edition).

BEYOND FLOURISHING: "FULLNESS" AND "CONVERSION" IN TAYLOR AND LONERGAN

STEPHEN J. COSTELLO

My aim in this chapter is to unpack and describe the notion of "fullness" as it figures in Charles Taylor's *A Secular Age*. David Walsh's criticism of Taylor, in a footnote in the former's *The Third Millennium: Reflections on Faith and Reason*, makes the point that in *Sources of the Self* Taylor "has drawn our attention to the centrality of ordinary life within the modern worldview, but he fails to exhibit the capacity for transcendence that renders it worthy of celebration" (Walsh 1999, 232). I believe that Taylor's *A Secular Age* answers this criticism. In the last chapter of this work he calls the experiences of fullness "conversions", a notion extensively explored by another Canadian, the Jesuit philosopher and theologian, Bernard Lonergan, in *Method and Theology*, whose reflections on the subject will be adumbrated towards the end of this chapter to fill in the gaps of Taylor's account of the subject.

Taylor on Fullness

For Taylor, "fullness" takes us beyond mere human flourishing and relates us to the realm of the transcendent. Of course, the notion of flourishing was given full voice by Aristotle in his *Nicomachean Ethics*; the word he employs is *eudaimonia*, which is usually translated as "happiness" but which can also be rendered as "flourishing". Taylor is thus critically engaging with this eudaimonistic ethic.

Taylor diagnoses this shift to secularity, where belief in God is no longer axiomatic despite the undoubted search for the spiritual that also abounds. Aristotelian "flourishing" is understood as leading an ethical life, by cultivating the moral and intellectual virtues, in the *polis*. Flourishing in the city-state or society needn't have any reference, though, to ultimate reality. "Flourishing" is a secular symbol. "Secularism" may be defined as the space emptied of God or of any reference to transcendent reality.

"Fullness", by contrast, explicitly relates us to the transcendent, however that is conceived. Before we define what Taylor means by "fullness", and in keeping with Eric Voegelin's injunction that we return to the engendering *experiences* to which subsequent symbols give rise, let me begin with an experiential epiphany enjoyed by Bede Griffiths, the British Benedictine monk, which he reports in his autobiography and which Taylor cites in his introduction to *A Secular Age*:

> One day during my last term at school I walked out alone in the evening and heard the birds singing in that full chorus of song, which can only be heard at that time of the year at dawn or at sunset. I remember now the shock of surprise with which the sound broke on my ears. It seemed to me that I had never heard the birds singing before and I wondered whether they sang like this all year round and I had never noticed it. As I walked I came upon some hawthorn trees in full bloom and again I thought I had never seen such a sight or experienced such sweetness before. If I had been brought suddenly among the trees of the Garden of Paradise and heard a choir of angels singing I could not have been more surprised. I came then to where the sun was setting over the playing fields. A lark rose suddenly from the ground beside the trees where I was standing and poured out its song above my head, and then sank still singing to rest. Everything then grew still as the sunset faded and the veil of dusk began to cover the earth. I remember now the feeling of awe which came over me. I felt inclined to kneel on the ground, as though I had been standing in the presence of an angel; and I hardly dared to look on the face of the sky, because it seemed as though it was but a veil before the face of God. (Griffiths 1979, 9; cited by Taylor SA 5).

Following Taylor, we can describe this conversion experience as one of "fullness"; Lonergan and Viktor Frankl would call it "self-transcendence". The space in which we live has a certain moral and spiritual shape and somewhere, in some condition or activity, there lies a "fullness" or "richness", as Taylor calls it. There "life is fuller, richer, deeper, and more worthwhile, more admirable, more what it should be", as he puts it (SA 5). We often experience it as "deeply moving, as inspiring. Perhaps this sense of fullness is something we just catch glimpses of from afar off; we have the powerful intuition of what fullness would be, were we to be in that condition, e.g., of peace or wholeness… of integrity or generosity or abandonment or self-forgetfulness" (ibid.). Iris Murdoch calls this "unselfing" and Simone Weil labels it *décreation*. These experienced moments bring joy and fulfilment; they are referred to by some as "transpersonal experiences". In such experiences it seems that ordinary reality is abolished or obliterated; they are experiences that unsettle and break through our feelings of familiarity and our tried and tested ways of being in the world. Something other shines through our consciousness and leaves us with a sense of the uncanny, akin to that which Jacques Lacan labels the Real. However, it is important to note, as Taylor does, that the experience of fullness may not always be identified with such limit or "peak experiences", as Maslow calls them, be they uplifting and edifying or frightening and traumatic. They may be moments when "the deep divisions, [Pascalian] distractions, worries, sadnesses that seem to drag us down are somehow dissolved, or brought into alignment, so that we feel united, moving forward, suddenly capable and full of energy" (SA 6). These experiences touch on our highest capabilities and aspirations. They transform us. These experiences situate us morally and spiritually.

> They can orient us because they offer some sense of what they are of: the presence of God, or the voice of nature, or the force which flows through everything, or the alignment in us of desire and the drive to form. But they are also often unsettling and enigmatic. Our sense of where they come from may also be unclear, confused … We are deeply moved, but also puzzled and shaken. We struggle to articulate what we have been through. (SA 6)

We think of Aquinas' reverential silence before the Mystery. Yet so often instead of fullness we experience *ennui* or melancholic *acedia*, when fullness fails. Between these two extremes of fullness and forlornness lies ordinary human happiness which fulfils us in various ways even permitting us to flourish and to contribute to what we conceive of as the good. It is essential, Taylor opines, that we have continuing contact with the place of fullness. For the theist, of course, this place of fullness will be faith, but it need not be so theistically construed. Such faith-filled fullness brings peace and joy, a sense of satisfaction and completeness. The unbeliever may experience satisfaction with his lot or a sense of achievement, but so long as his life is not ordered to God as the divine flow of presence in it, "he still has some way to go" (SA 7); perhaps he hasn't conquered his nostalgia for something really transcendent, Taylor contends.

For the theist, "the account of the place of fullness requires reference to God" (SA 8). For the atheist, fullness may be interpreted naturalistically in terms of human potential and possibility. Experiences of fullness vary but believers often say that it comes to them as a gratuitous gift, as grace; that it is dependent on a relationship of love; that it involves practices of prayer, of charity. Often such people feel very far from such conditions of *caritas* and experience themselves instead as preoccupied with lesser, mortal things. What seems needed or required is a (Christian) conversion (*metanoia*) or opening out, a Heideggerian "clearing" (*Lichtung*), a Platonic *periagoge* or Rilkean "turning", a Murdochian "unselfing" or Weilian *décreation*, whereby the ego is transmogrified. Such experiences of fullness seem to come from a power beyond me. What does this mean? Taylor answers thus:

> the best sense I can make of my conflicting and moral experience is captured by a theological view of this kind. That is, in my own experience, in prayer, in moments of fullness, in experiences of exile overcome, in what I seem to observe around me in other peoples' lives—lives of exceptional spiritual fullness, or lives of maximum self-enclosedness, lives of demonic evil, etc.—this seems to be the picture that emerges. (SA 10)

Let us repeat, such experiences may be construed differently, non-theistically. It seems to me, though, that God is the best explanation of them. Like Lonergan's, Taylor's hermeneutic is avowedly a Christian construal.

Of course, Taylor is aware of the postmodern problems associated with a word such as "fullness". We have just to think of Derrida's critique of the metaphysics of *presence*—Taylor describes Derridean deconstruction as a "non-religious anti-humanism" (SA 19)—or of Levinas' stress on the "trace". Taylor observes:

> "Fullness" has come to be my shorthand term for the condition we aspire to, but I am acutely aware how inadequate all words are here. Every possible designation has something wrong with it. The glaring one in the case of 'fullness' is that according to one very plausible spiritual path, visible clearly in Buddhism, for instance, the highest aspiration is to a kind of emptiness (*sunyata*); or to put it more paradoxically, real fullness only comes through emptiness. But there is no perfect terminological solution here, and so with all these reservations I let the word stand. (SA n8, 780)

These considerations of what constitutes "fullness" contrast with conceptualisations about "flourishing". We all have some conceptions of what human flourishing is, of what constitutes a fulfilled life, of what makes life worth living. These may be codified in moral codes or philosophical or religious practices. The question Taylor poses is: does the highest or best life involve seeking or acknowledging a good that is beyond—in the sense of independent of—human flourishing? The highest human flourishing could include our aiming at something other than human flourishing. Taylor calls these "final goals" (SA 16). Of course, in the Judaeo-Christian tradition the answer to the question just posited is affirmative.

> Loving, worshipping God is the ultimate end. In this tradition, God is seen as willing human flourishing, but devotion to God is not seen as contingent on this. The injunction "Thy will be done" isn't equivalent to "Let humans flourish", even though we know that God wills human flourishing". (SA 17)

Many people on different religious paths detach themselves, or try to do so, from their own flourishing to the point of the extinction of the self. Flourishing is good or a good but seeking it is not our ultimate goal, for Taylor (SA 18). But secular humanism does not accept any final goals beyond human flourishing or ordinary human happiness. By contrast, Taylor defines "religion" in terms of "transcendence", of that something that is higher than or beyond mere human flourishing. Christianity calls this *agape*. Fullness, construed theistically, is "a condition in which our highest spiritual and moral aspirations point us inescapably to God, one might say, make no sense without God" (SA 26); fullness, so, as a gift from God—fullness as the felt presence of God even in our secular society, our disenchanted world. This is what Eric Voegelin, in an equivalent symbol, calls the "flow of presence" (see Costello 2010).

Augustine had held that all times are present to God. "His now contains all time", as Taylor puts it (SA 57)—a *nunc stans*. So God's presence is the intersection of timelessness with time, as T. S. Eliot describes it. Rising to eternity is participating in God's instant. All times are present to Him. This is the beyond of (ordinary) human flourishing which is so crucial to Christianity (see SA 67). But in a world "shorn of the sacred" (SA 80) many people, Taylor contends, are happy living for purely immanent goals; "they live in a way that takes no account of the transcendent" (SA 143). The "secular" age is not only that age that is not tied to religion, but the original sense of the secular was that which pertained to profane rather than sacred time; it posited time as purely profane. Of course Taylor realises that our moral and spiritual resources can be experienced as purely immanent; fullness may be formulated with an exclusively human reference, to human time. The move to immanentisation is a rejection of the Christian aspiration to transcend flourishing. Non-theistic Romantics could interpret Bede Griffiths' experience and description of a moment of fullness pantheistically, as a worship of nature. It will all depend on one's hermeneutic reading. So if flourishing pertains to our human or profane time, fullness belongs to God's "time", or eternity. The secular points or refers to the affairs of the world, to temporality, as distinct from the City of God. (Communism and Fascism, as modes of anti-religion, attempt to capture something of a higher purpose but in purely immanentistic terms (see SA 267).) Modernity is marked by this anthropocentrism in a way the mediaeval period was characterised, in the main, by theocentrism. Our contemporary culture attests to "the eclipse of the transcendent" (SA 307)—Buber had called it the "eclipse of God" in his book of the same title.

The question is: can we find meaning in the malaise of modernity, in the "malaise of immanence" (SA 308)? The sense of emptiness and meaninglessness, of absurdity and nausea, well documented by Sartre and Camus, is ubiquitous. We seem to have lost a sense of the sacred, of truth and goodness and beauty and depth and sense, in our quotidian, dry, flat and banal, mundane modern lives, of the "one thing necessary/needed", in our crass, capitalistic and cardboard culture. Taylor distinguishes *three* modes of these malaises of immanence: 1) the fragility of meaning, the loosening of a sense of or search for an over-arching significance; 2) the felt flatness of attempts to solemnise important moments of our lives; and 3) the emptiness of the ordinary (see SA 309). Transcendence is the answer for some—a return to or deepening relationship with the transcendent; for others who don't share such faith, they will seek their solutions in their own ways, perhaps in working for greater prosperity or peace or justice in a world no longer full of gods/God. For the theist, God's existence is felt and flows through all creation. As Schiller writes in *The Gods of Greece*: "Life's fullness flowed through creation/And there felt what never more will feel/...Everything to the initiate's eye/ Showed the trace of a God" (cited by Taylor, SA 316).

Wordsworth, too, speaks of this presence we are identifying, with Taylor, Lonergan and Voegelin, as God. In *Tintern Abbey*, he writes:

> A presence that disturbs me with the joy
> Of elevated thoughts; a sense sublime
> Of something far more deeply interfused,
> Whose dwelling is the light of setting suns,
> And the round ocean and the living air,
> And the blue sky, and the mind of man;
> A motion and a spirit, that impels
> All thinking things, all objects of all thought,
> And rolls through all things. (cited by Taylor, SA 357-8)

This is an epiphanic experience of the flow, of "the fullness of joy" (SA 358); it is the fulfilment which goes beyond flourishing and even morality and which is the real "point of our existence" (ibid.). This entails, for the

Christian, participating in agapeic love, which calls us to go beyond flourishing and to transform our purely immanentistic perspectives and frameworks, supported as they are by a materialist mentality. Ultimately, it will mean more than pursuing our own happiness. The "pursuit of happiness" in our contemporary commercial culture means the pursuit of private pleasure and self-satisfaction; the modern turn to the self/subject, as in realising my so-called higher or "true self", is a turn to hedonism where the stress is predominantly on personal development and individual self-expression. Self-cultivation represents the higher selfishness involving, not mindless accumulation, but engaging in tasks that are seen to be socially constructive and emotionally enriching or edifying. Taylor calls this the "horizontal" focus and form of the modern worldview; this libertarian *Zeitgeist* lacks the vertical dimension—the irruption of the (W)holy Other.

The question is: can a life encased in a purely immanentistic order provide ultimate purpose or "is this all there is"? Many seekers searching for the self rather than salvation say they are interested in "spirituality" rather than "religion" or institutionalised forms of expression. But this so-called spirituality can be saccharine and subjectivistic, focused, as it is, on the self and its concerns (see Costello 2002). This kind of spiritual quest is often New Age in its immanentistic understandings and frames of reference (see SA 508-9), as "wholeness" is emphasised and cultivated rather than "holiness" and sickness replaces sin in the "triumph of the therapeutic" (see Rieff 1966). This Age of (alleged) Authenticity signifies the retreat of Christendom (see SA 514). It is this hegemony that Taylor is challenging. He calls such a secularist spin a "closed world structure" (SA 551), reminiscent of Bergson's notion of the "closed soul", wherein Capitalism has replaced Christianity and where the entertainment media and advertising encourage egomania, self-satisfaction, the pursuit of pleasure and personal fulfilment. "We feel called to happiness", says Taylor (SA 583); we *demand* to be happy. But alongside this is a longing for clarity or ultimate meaning, for God, if you like, whose call echoes in the human heart. Can we make sense of life without invoking something transcendent? Does the "immanent frame", as Taylor calls it, and which Voegelin calls "the immanentisation of the eschaton", suffice with its relegation of the religious sense of life? Can materialism or Marxism answer our questions about meaning? How do we make sense of our ethical actions or artistic experiences without speaking in terms of a transcendent being which "interpellates us" (SA 597)? The absence of a life of fullness would leave us, according to Taylor, "in abject, unbearable despair" (SA 600). Nietzsche had poured scorn on ordinary happiness describing it as a "pitiable comfort". Camus' Dr. Rieux, in *La Peste*, insisted too on aiming for something higher and engaged in ethical acts despite Sisyphean senselessness and the feeling of futility. There are rival notions of fullness, but for the theist they will probably be mirages, (Baudrillardian) simulacra, merely immanent or naturalistic ontologies. The theist will want, therefore, to include Bede Griffiths' experience or any epiphanic experience we enjoy in our encounter with great music or art within the religious register, what Taylor is calling the fullness beyond flourishing. Commenting on happiness, Taylor has this to say:

> The belief in untroubled happiness is not only a childish illusion, but also involves a truncation of human nature, turning our backs on much of what we are.... Hasn't Christian preaching always repeated that it is impossible to be fully happy as a sinful agent in a sinful world? Certainly this illusion can't be laid at the foot of the Christian faith, however much contemporary Christians may be sucked into this common view of the "pursuit of happiness" today. (SA 635-6)

Humanistic happiness is not what it is ultimately about. Taylor opines: "If the transcendental view is right, then human beings have an ineradicable bent to respond to something beyond life" (SA 638). Conversion. Self-transcendence. Transformation. Attunement or orientation of the soul to God, to the flow of divine Presence. For the Christian consciousness, so, human flourishing, which is the aim of an exclusive humanism, is not the final goal. Christianity needn't and shouldn't crush human flourishing but point beyond it to the fullness of redemption, to the "richness which transcends the ordinary" (SA 677), to the eschatological banquet promised in Paradise. This eschatological emphasis lifts us beyond a teleological tending towards attaining "my happiness" in this historical "here and now". Taylor notes: "Human happiness can only inspire us when we have to fight against the forces which are destroying it; but once realized, it will inspire nothing but ennui, a cosmic yawn" (SA 717).

Taylor speaks of a desire for eternity in human beings, of "a desire to gather the scattered moments of meaning into some kind of whole" (SA 720). Paul Ricoeur similarly speaks of "the narrative unity of a life". Doesn't love call for eternity, as Nietzsche rightly recognised? Doesn't joy strive for it? By contrast, "the collapse of a sense of the eternal brings on a void, a kind of crisis" (SA 722). Mallarmé gives voice to this feeling of *le Rien, le Néant*: "Sprawled in the happiness in which only his appetites/ Feed" (*Mallarmé* 1994, 12; cited by Taylor, SA 724). Taylor observes:

The individual pursuit of happiness as defined by consumer culture still absorbs much of our time and energy, or else the threat of being shut out of this pursuit through poverty, unemployment, incapacity galvanizes all our efforts. All this is true, and yet the sense that there is something more presses in. Great numbers of people feel it: in moments of reflection about their life; in moments of relaxation in nature; in moments of bereavement and loss; and quite wildly and unpredictably. Our age is very far from settling in to a comfortable unbelief. Although many individuals do so, and more still seem to on the outside, the unrest continues to surface. Could it ever be otherwise? (SA 727).

In the concluding chapter of *A Secular Age* entitled "Conversions" Taylor relates another epiphanic experience, that of Vaclav Havel—like Griffiths' one, it is an experience of what Taylor calls *conversion*. Griffiths' and Havel's experiences/conversions broke them out of the immanent frame of focus. In *Letters to Olga*, Havel records:

Again, I call to mind that distant moment in [the prison at] Hermanice when on a hot, cloudless summer day, I sat on a pile of rusty iron and gazed into the crown of an enormous tree that stretched, with dignified repose, up and over all the fences, wires, bars and watchtowers that separated me from it. As I watched the imperceptible trembling of its leaves against an endless sky, I was overcome by a sensation that is difficult to describe: all at once, I seemed to rise above all the coordinates of my momentary existence in the world into a kind of state outside time in which all beautiful things I have ever seen and experienced existed in a total "co-present"; I felt a sense of reconciliation, indeed of an almost gentle assent to the inevitable course of events as revealed to me now, and this combined with a carefree determination to face what had to be faced. A profound amazement at the sovereignty of Being became a dizzy sensation of tumbling endlessly into the abyss of its mystery; an unbounded joy at being alive, at having been given the chance to live through all I have lived through, and at the fact that everything has a deep and obvious meaning—this joy formed a strange alliance in me with a vague horror at the inapprehensibility and unattainability of everything I was so close to in that moment, standing at the very "edge of the infinite"; I was flooded with a sense of ultimate happiness and harmony with the world and myself, with that moment, with all the moments I could call up, and with everything invisible that lies behind it and has meaning. I would even say that I was somehow "struck by love", though I don't know precisely for whom or what. (Havel 1984, 331-2; cited by Taylor SA 728-9).

Men like Griffiths and Havel, as well as sages and saints such as Francis of Assisi and Teresa of Avila, the mystics and the prophets of all time, have all radiated a sense of direct contact with transcendent reality. They have articulated fullness. Taylor writes: "We need to enlarge our palette of such points of contact with fullness, because we are too prone in our age to think of this contact in terms of "experience"; and to think of experience as something subjective distinct from the object experienced; and as something to do with our feelings, distinct from changes in our being: dispositions, orientations" (SA 729-30). But they are experiences as well as events—heart-transforming, life-changing. There are those like Griffiths and Havel and Ignatius who have contemplatively grasped this fullness; they have left us their records and reflections. They have wrought paradigm shifts that signalled a move from an immanent therapeutic perspective and framework to a spiritual one:

> The internal economy of the immanent theory, say a Freudian one, in which the various forces which count are purely intra-psychic, and are rooted in the patient's desires and fears, is now disrupted. The genesis of guilt, alienation, internal division is now found at least in part in the aspiration to something transcendent. (SA 731)

In so doing, they upset the parameters of our time and raise up human life to the divine (*theiosis*). They take us beyond immanent realities and challenge mainstream materialism as well as the nature/supernature distinction. But as Aquinas reminds us, grace builds on nature; it doesn't abolish it. They are responding to transcendent reality which Taylor has called fullness. Others may respond to it too but may misrecognise it such as in the exclusive humanisms. Griffiths initially interpreted his experience in the light of a Wordsworthian Romanticism; only later did he come to see it in the light of Christian Revelation. Rilke, commenting on his poem "Turning", that he penned between the 18th and 20th of June, 1914, to Lou Andreas-Salomé, wrote: "May this gazing out of myself, which consumes me to emptiness, be rid of through a loving preoccupation with interior fullness" (Rilke, 1976; cited by Hederman 2000, 92). For Taylor, our sense of this fullness "is a reflection of transcendent reality (which for me is the God of Abraham)" (SA 769). To find fullness is to find God, ultimately for Taylor. It is to be converted. He writes: "The convert's insights break beyond the limits of the regnant versions of immanent order .... to a larger, more encompassing one, which includes it while disrupting it" (SA 732). While Taylor calls these experiences "conversions", it is Lonergan, who details the dynamics of such conversions in his *Method and Theology* and so it will prove instructive to consider his thoughts on the subject. Taylor defines conversion as "breaking out into the broader field" (SA 769) but it is Lonergan, whom Taylor interestingly doesn't cite, who distinguishes between *three* types of conversion and who offers a more systematic and nuanced account than Taylor, one that can fill in some of the caveats in Taylor's considerations of the subject. We now turn to Lonergan.

Lonergan on Conversion

For Lonergan, by a differentiation of consciousness, we are engaged in a moral pursuit of goodness, a philosophic pursuit of truth, a scientific pursuit of understanding and an artistic pursuit of beauty in our attempt to be attentive, intelligent, reasonable and responsible, as we experience, understand, judge and decide; this is the crux of his transcendental method, as established in *Insight* and *Method in Theology*. It is to this latter work that we will now look for his insights into the nature and dynamic of conversion. Like Taylor, Lonergan holds that being in love with God is "the basic fulfilment of our conscious intentionality" (Lonergan 1957, 105), one which brings a "deep-set joy" (ibid.). In his *Spiritual Exercises*, Ignatius calls such spiritual happiness "consolation" (without a cause).

A conversion ushers in a change in the direction of development, a change for the better as one grows in authenticity. Values are apprehended, scales of preference shift, as Lonergan puts it (see Lonergan 1957, 52). Conversion may issue in a violent change that disrupts psychological continuity, but it may be preceded by transient dispositions. More commonly, conversion is a slow process of maturation as one finds out what it is to be intelligent, reasonable, responsible and loving. Conversion doesn't rest on this once and for all dynamic of change; "conversion is life-long" (Lonergan 1957, 118). The objectification of conversion provides Christianity with its foundations. Lonergan defines conversion thus: "By conversion is understood a transformation of the subject and his world" (Lonergan 1957, 130). Normally it is a prolonged process that results in a change of the course of direction of one's life. "It is as if one's eyes were opened and one's former world faded and fell away... Conversion is existential, intensely personal, utterly intimate. But it is not so private as to be solitary" (ibid.). Conversion affects all of man's conscious and intentional operations. "It directs his gaze, pervades his imagination, releases the symbols that penetrate to the depths of his psyche. It enriches his understanding, guides his judgments, reinforces his decisions" (Lonergan 1957, 131). Conversion is the basic step, after it comes the labour of thinking out everything from the profounder perspective. Conversion heralds in the transition from inauthenticity to authenticity. It is the work of (a good) conscience. The dark decreases and the light increases. Conversion occurs when man discovers what is inauthentic in himself and turns away from it and embraces instead the fullness of authenticity. It is cognate with the Christic edict: "Repent, the kingdom of God is at hand!" Conversion manifests itself in deeds and words; it is radical revision.

According to Lonergan, there are *three* types of conversion. They are three modalities or fundamental forms of self-transcendence. "Conversion may be intellectual or moral or religious. While each of the three is connected with the other two, still each is a different type of event and has to be considered in itself before being related to the others" (Lonergan 1957, 238). He elucidates the three types thus: "Moral conversion changes the criterion of one's decisions and choices from satisfactions to values" (Lonergan 1957, 240). Moral conversion, thus, consists in opting for or choosing the truly good. "Religious conversion is being grasped by ultimate concern. It is other-worldly falling in love. It is total and permanent self-surrender without conditions" (ibid). It is "fated acceptance of a vocation to holiness" (ibid.). For Christians it is God's love flooding our hearts through the Holy Spirit given in the gift of (operative) grace. Operative grace is religious conversion, whereas cooperative grace is the effectiveness of such a conversion; it is "the gradual movement towards a full and complete transformation of the whole of one's living and feeling, one's thoughts, words, deeds, and omissions" (Lonergan 1957, 241). Intellectual conversion "is to truth attained by cognitional self-transcendence" (ibid.). When all three occur within a single consciousness their relations can be conceived in terms of sublation (in Karl Rahner's sense, rather than Hegel's). When religious conversion occurs, desire turns to joy and the subject is held, grasped, arrested, possessed, owned by an other-worldly love; it involves loving with one's whole heart, soul, mind and strength. "Holiness abounds in truth and moral goodness, but it has a distinct dimension of its own. It is other-worldly fulfilment, joy, peace, bliss" (Lonergan 1957, 242). The absence of such fulfilment, in contradistinction, reveals itself as despairing unrest, the absence of joy, depressive disgust with oneself or life, what St. Ignatius calls "desolation".

In relation to the ordering of these three types of conversion, Lonergan delineates their interrelationships thus: "Though religious conversion sublates moral, and moral conversion sublates intellectual, one is not to infer that intellectual comes first and then moral and finally religious" (Lonergan 1957, 243). By contrast, in terms of the causal viewpoint, there is first God's love and the eye of this love reveals values in their luminosity and splendour, while the strength of this love brings about moral conversion. Finally, one discerns in the light of this love the truths taught by the religious tradition; the seeds are thus sown for intellectual conversion. The religious conversion grounds both the moral and intellectual conversion; "it provides the real criterion by which all else is to be judged" (Lonergan 1957, 283). Religious conversion is the experiential event that gives the name "God" its fundamental meaning. The word penetrates to all four levels of intentional consciousness: experience, understanding, judging and deciding. The whole man is thus evoked. And aside from conversions one has breakdowns or derailments, distortions (see Lonergan 1957, 243-71). In any single consciousness all three types of conversion may be present or lacking; any one may be present or two or all three of them. Conversion manifests itself in deeds and words. Conversion consists in a radical revision of formerly held opinions, beliefs or positions and "transforms the concrete individual" completely (Lonergan 1957, 338).

Conclusion

To finish, fullness takes us beyond flourishing (ordinary happiness) and conversion issues in joy. For Taylor, Lonergan and Voegelin, the fullness of joy is found in an encounter with the divine Ground of being, who reveals Himself as Ground and Goal, origin and end. In this alone is humanity's (final) fulfilment. Taylor uses this term "fulfilment" in a broader sense than the ordinary word which is usually used to describe whatever fulfils my own personal needs or self-satisfactions. He explains: "I want to extend it to whatever realizes (what we see as) the highest and fullest form of life, even if this demands the sacrifice of personal 'fulfilment'" (Taylor SA 838, n.9). Writing about such fulfilment, in *Man's Search for Meaning*, Frankl, who managed to find meaning in a concentration camp, wrote that a thought transfixed him and it was this: that for the first time in his life he saw the truth that had been expounded by the poets and philosophers of all times, that love is the ultimate goal to which the human spirit can aspire, that life is about meaning and not happiness, that man's salvation is in and through love. Let me conclude with his words:

> I understood how a man who has nothing left in this world still may know bliss, be it only for a brief moment, in the contemplation of his beloved. In a position of utter desolation, when man cannot express himself in positive action, when his only achievement may consist in enduring his sufferings in the right way—an honourable way—in such a position man can, through loving contemplation of the image he carries of his beloved, achieve

fulfilment. For the first time in my life I was able to understand the meaning of the words, "The angels are lost in perpetual contemplation of an infinite glory". (Frankl 1959, 49).

References

Buber, Martin, 1952. *Eclipse of God*. New York, Humanity Books.
Costello, Stephen J. (ed.), 2002. *The Search for Spirituality: Seven Paths Within the Catholic Tradition*. Dublin: The Liffey Press.
Frankl, Viktor, 2004. *Man's Search for Meaning*. London-Sydney-Auckland-Johannesburg, Rider.
Griffiths, Bede, 1979. *The Golden String*. London: Fount.
Havel, Vacel, 1988. *Letters to Olga*. New York: Knopf.
Hederman, Mark Patrick, 2000. *Manikon Eros*. Dublin: Veritas.
Lonergan, Bernard, 2005. *Insight: A Study of Human Understanding*. Toronto: University of Toronto Press.
—. 1971. *Method in Theology*. Toronto: University of Toronto Press.
Mallarmé, Stéphane, 1994. *Stéphane Mallarmé: Selected Poems*, trans. Henry Weinfield. Berkeley: University of California Press.
Rieff, Philip, 1966. *The Triumph of the Therapeutic*. New York: Harper and Row.
Rilke, Rainer Maria, 1976. *Poems 1906 to 1926*. Trans. J. B. Leishman, London: Hogarth Press.
Taylor, Charles, 1989. *Sources of the Self: The Making of the Modern Identity*. Cambridge: Cambridge University Press.
Walsh, David, 1989. *The Third Millennium: Reflections on Faith and Reason*. Washington, D.C.: Georgetown University Press.

OUR "ETHICAL PREDICAMENT": GETTING TO THE HEART OF *A SECULAR AGE*

JOSEPH DUNNE

Reading Taylor: A Context of Engagement

When I confessed to a colleague that I hadn't yet finished reading this book, on which I'd soon be presenting a paper, his reply was at once reassuring and unsettling: "Has anyone? Will anyone ever?" What he was alluding to of course was the book's *size*, its gargantuan word-count in what is only a little shy of a thousand pages—and the affront of this in a culture of the sound-bite and an academy where we scramble to produce the next puny article. I wouldn't be the only reader to feel that, less being more, all this could have been said more tersely—and that a properly alert editor at Harvard University Press would have been far more active with her red pen or erase key, ensuring that we got a leaner, fitter, and more reader-friendly volume.

But this has been only a partial reaction, offset by a ready concession that such mass is not out of scale with the heroic ambition and sweep of this work: its attempt to offer a comprehensive and in some respects quite revisionist interpretation of the mainline development of western culture over the past seven hundred years; its unabashed commitment to telling a very grand narrative when this genre is supposed to be passé or subject to proper "incredulity";[1] its overarching attempt to discern the fate of religion and theology in an age widely taken to be post-religious; its multi-disciplinary range and in particular its development of large historical, sociological and philosophical perspectives that are inter-penetrating and mutually informing; its "take" on the scientific project that has increasingly shaped our dominant world views; its easy summoning of authors and texts across huge swathes of the artistic and literary canon, sometimes, for example, in close readings of individual poems in French and German as well as in English; and in all this, its intention, not just to tell a story about our past, but, rather, in doing this, to help us to understand who and where we are now.

Moreover, this ambition and scale of the work are themselves matched by the erudition and gifts of the author: this is a magisterial book and one is truly in the hands of a master. Faced with the daunting task occasioned by this fact, I take comfort in knowing that other chapters in this volume take up the kind of task that Taylor envisages for other scholars in his preface (and that I do not attempt here): that of "developing, applying, modifying, and transposing" his argument in the book. More modestly, I want to identify and attempt to bring out a central theme running through his book that I find especially interesting and important. I will focus, in the second part of the paper, on his conception of the *ethical*. Having clarified this conception, as it is elaborated in earlier works as well as in *A Secular Age*, I will go on, in the third and final section, to discuss, more particularly, his analysis in this book of what he calls our "*ethical predicament*". But first, since a primarily expository intention—to fasten on an aspect of what Taylor is saying—may seem to mute my own voice, or to be insufficiently engaged (an incongruous response, surely, to a philosopher who has been such a trenchant critic of the disengaged stance in philosophy and in other disciplines), let me conclude these introductory remarks by confessing why this book speaks to me in a way that may make it worthwhile to try to write about it now.

"To do philosophy", Iris Murdoch says, "is to explore one's own temperament, and yet at the same time to attempt to discover the truth" (Murdoch 1983a, 68). I find this a congenial characterisation of philosophy's task (though "identity" might perhaps be a better term here than "temperament"—evoking more the meanings rather than just the peculiar combination of genes that make one who one is); and in my own attempts to carry it out, few, if any, authors have been more helpful companions than Taylor. All of us are, in his well-known expression, "self-interpreting animals" (see Taylor 1975a, 45-76); and in trying to interpret myself, I find the field of interpretations opened by his work resonant and suggestive. I take it that this may well *not* be the case for others formed in a cultural or social milieu different from mine, or indeed for people of a younger generation in today's Ireland. But let me say something briefly about why it *is* the case for me, in a way that seems to make it worthwhile to write about it here.

The starting point for Taylor's book is the fact that in 1500 it was almost impossible for anyone in Europe to be an unbeliever. Well, this seemed *still* to be the case in Tipperary during my childhood there in the 1950s. Moreover, the "enchantment" that Taylor goes on to write about as the condition of an earlier world, now firmly displaced, was still palpable to me then as a child: I well remember the fascination with which I listened to my father's stories—told to adults more than to us children—about "pisheogs", various dark arts through which, for example, a farmer might have blighted his neighbour's crops or made his cows run dry, bagging or bucketing these forfeited yields for himself.

As a child then I also had the experience—though I know that many of my contemporaries did *not*—of having my sense of the good shaped by an inspiring religious presence (particularly through two older nuns in whom I encountered what I can only remember as a kind of saintliness, the radiance of embodied goodness); and I find articulated in Taylor's work not only the defining significance for anyone of this sense of the good, and especially the highest good, but also its formation primarily through meeting and witness and only secondarily through argument and discourse.[2]

I began post-primary schooling in 1960, going on to university in the second half of that decade. When I spent my undergraduate years as a seminarian, I was living through (though I could not have known it at the time) the last high fling of what in this book Taylor calls the "Age of Mobilisation"—that period through the nineteenth century and well into the middle of the twentieth century when churches around the world, and perhaps nowhere more successfully than in the case of the Catholic church in Ireland, were forming themselves into highly cohesive organisations, with a hierarchically ordered and tightly controlled leadership, enlisting cadres of middle-line clerical officers, enclosing their ordinary members in thick bonds of identification and allegiance, prescribing for them what to believe, and how to—or how not to— behave and feel, fusing religious belief and practice with senses of national identity and civilisational order, policing boundaries with non-members, and indeed extending the ranks through disciplined and vigorous outreach. The inner strains and contradictions of this kind of church organisation, as Taylor points out, were brought to the surface at Vatican 2; and in any case, as he also points out, it was "perfectly set up for a precipitate fall in the next age which was beginning to dawn at mid-century" (SA 472).

This next age was of course the "Age of Authenticity",[3] and having left the seminary in 1968, I immediately began to catch its heady whiff in the hugely liberating atmosphere of late 1960s University College Dublin, still ensconced in Earlsford Terrace, with the Iveagh Gardens and Stephen's Green commodiously adjacent, where I went on to do philosophy as a post-graduate student. This period was a defining one in my life—so that I cannot help responding warmly to Taylor's frequent and, I think, invariably sympathetic advertences to it. For those of us who were then coming of age intellectually, Marxism was inescapable—and often enough in an uncompromisingly hard-line version. But I think that Taylor is right when he reads the 1960s more as the last—or at least, up to now, the most recent—attempt to reanimate the spirit of Romantic protest.

When I recall now and try to understand what opened up, and meant so much to me, at that time, I find especially illuminating his invocations of Schiller, and especially *Letters on the Aesthetic Education of Man*, invocations that recur rhythmically throughout *A Secular Age*. Here we find the canonical critique of the dissociation of reason and feeling and the suppression of desire by moral injunction; and the definitive statement of that higher integration in which rationality and feeling, morality and appetite are aligned in the fullest form of unity, a form which realises the beautiful and is expressed through play. This is a vision of harmony *within* a human being but also of wider harmony *between* humans and indeed between humans and Nature, a Nature that surges through and finds its own highest expression in them.

You might suppose that the 1960s ended for me when I got my first (and only) teaching job in 1970. But they didn't really. After all, for me they had only begun in 1968—so that I had some catching up to do; and anyhow for everyone didn't the "sixties leak into the 'seventies"? Allow me, then, to recall another significant presence from that time. I began to read and teach the work of Ivan Illich (*The Celebration of Awareness, Tools for Conviviality, Medical Nemesis*, as well as *Deschooling Society*), inspired by the experience of attending a seminar he gave in Newman House *circa* 1972—the most electrifying intellectual encounter of my life, before or since. I was to meet Illich again when he returned to Dublin nearly twenty years later, by which time he was wracked by an illness for which he would not undergo surgery and his work had already been marginalised by the same engines of academic fashion-making that had earlier made him a cult-figure. Given my first excitement at Illich's work, and my later sadness at his ostracism, I was moved—and surprised—to re-discover him featuring as a crucial figure, engaged with complete sympathy, in the nicely surprising company of Peguy and Hopkins, in the final chapter of Taylor's book.

Illich's fate was only one symptom of the fact, so well registered by Taylor, that in the decades after the 1960s and 1970s we have been living in post-Utopian times. Politically, this fact was sealed by the election of the Thatcher government in 1979 and the collapse of communism a decade later. Philosophically, it has been most apparent in the huge revival and advancement, in place of the Romantic vision, of post-humanist or anti-humanist thought: an intense preoccupation, pervasive across so many disciplines now, with a dark underside to Being, a formless Will or Will to Power, beyond good and evil, licensing assertion and excess, energised by violence and unchecked by benevolence, swallowing beauty in the Sublime and even the monstrous. The philosophers who engaged us most in the sixties included Rousseau, Hegel, Marx, Heidegger, Sartre, and Merleau-Ponty. For us, at least, Nietzsche's star had not then risen: post-modernism had not yet emerged to claim him as prophet.

How things have changed! What Taylor calls the "post-Schopenhaurian turn" has erupted into philosophy since the eighties—in the reception of thinkers such as Bataille, Lacan, Foucault, Lyotard, and Deleuze. One has felt a strong resistance in Taylor to this line of thought—evident for example in an early critical essay on Foucault, motivated by the sense that any coherent basis for an emancipatory project was voided in his work (Taylor 1975b). At the heart of Taylor's own work *is* a concern for emancipation, however defined, on whatever terms, however meliorist, or at whatever pace—"the long march" is a key phrase in *Modern Social Imaginaries* and *la lotta continua*, the struggle goes on, is a chapter title in *The Ethics of Authenticity*.[4] This has led some commentators to regard him as an upbeat thinker: in a review of *Sources of the Self*, Judith Shklar said that Taylor "dwelled on the sunny side of the street" and spoke for those "who fear scepticism more than evil"—a remark not intended as a compliment to anyone writing towards the end of what Shklar took (rightly in so many respects) to be an appalling century (Shklar 1991). Taylor mentions Shklar in *A Secular Age*, noting the "deep wisdom" in her liberalism of fear (SA 685). He realises how well grounded this fear is. But he's also aware of the cost to our shared life if we succumb too readily to it. And so his effort here is to take its full measure. Hence, his introduction of the whole post-Schopenhaurian turn—or the "immanent counter-Enlightenment" as he now calls it—and the seriousness with which he engages it: our capacity for violence, unrestrained sexuality, and indeed for charged combinations of both, is a deepening preoccupation throughout the book.[5]

The Ethical

Having just said something (not too self-indulgently, I hope) about how and why Taylor's work speaks to me, I want to go on now to focus on a specific feature of this book. I refer to its concern with, and understanding of, the ethical—or as one might better say, and as he sometimes himself says, the ethical-spiritual. Since its subject is secularity and secularisation, clearly religion and the great stand-off in our age between belief and unbelief is the major topic of the book. But though Taylor does not disguise where his own ultimate sympathies lie, only a very cursory reading of *A Secular Age* suffices to show how devoid it is of polemical intent—or, at least, how very far from traditional apologetics. Taylor's chief concern is not to demonstrate the epistemic superiority of religious belief or, more specifically, that of Catholic Christianity. For his attention is less on the deep disagreements *between* it and exclusive humanism in its various versions, including gung-ho materialism, than on the ambivalences, tensions and "cross-pressures" *within* each of these positions. Now the tensions and cross-pressures he explores all stem from what he calls our "ethical predicament"—a predicament that faces *all* of the contending parties, that we all share, inescapably, whichever side of the debate we find ourselves on. I want to go on to look briefly at his analysis of this predicament. But first let me focus a little more broadly on the ethical and its central place in this as in so many of Taylor's other works.

The ethical is crucial, for example, to Taylor's denial of the claim in standard secularisation theory that exclusive humanism or "the death of God" demonstrably follows from the scientific revolution in train since the seventeenth century. He acknowledges of course that the achievements and successes of modern science, as well as the disengaged perspective on the universe and on human beings ingrained in its methods of inquiry and explanation, now motivate very many people to regard religious belief as fatally discredited. But for him this conclusion is not at all the result of a valid argument; its undoubtedly strong appeal stems from a narrative which casts modern human beings as outgrowing a state of childish tutelage, foregoing consolation and illusion, and courageously facing the bleakness of an indifferent universe in which they willingly assume responsibility for human survival and welfare. The real force, the clinching factor, is not epistemological but ethical.

Taylor's focus on the ethical is of a piece with his interest in the texture of *lived-experience*, an interest that might warrant the characterisation of him as a phenomenologist.[6] But he avoids the standard charge levelled at phenomenology— that it naturalises experience, failing to register the profound structural transformations that can only be disclosed through more genealogical inquiry. Taylor offers us his own account (not too different from Foucault's) of massive shifts that have taken place since 1500, sinking into our world at a deeply experiential level and radically changing the nature of agency and selfhood, our comportment towards the world and others, and our sense of ourselves. He shows how, unlike our ancestors of some centuries ago, we are "buffered selves", much less porous to an encompassing world because our sense of agency and initiative is firmly anchored within an inner, mental space. This is a space with depths to be explored in a new kind of privacy and interiority; but it is also subject to massive discipline arising from a newly disengaged stance to the life of embodied passions. This stance extends inward the instrumental attitude already adopted to cosmic and social orders shorn of inherent significance or purpose and standing over against us as modern *individuals*—individuals, moreover, enclosed in a flat temporal structure where time, like space, has become linear and homogenous, one more resource to be managed instrumentally.

You couldn't say that we experience all this; rather it's become second nature to us, so lodged in the frame through which our experience is formed that it's not itself available to be experienced within this frame. We have lost the sense of how novel it is, how unlike other modalities through which human beings have experienced the world and their own lives within it, and how little, therefore, it can be taken as simply the basic default template of human nature itself—once the encumbrances of enchantment, superstition, etc., have been sloughed off. Taylor calls it "the *immanent frame*" and he sees it as the one within which all of us live and operate in western modernity. It's very easy to take it, and indeed it very often is taken—nowhere more extensively and assertively than in the secular academy—to carry exclusive humanism as its necessary corollary. But it's just this construction of it, or spin on it, that Taylor wants to contest; or rather he wants to show that it is just that—a *spin*. His use of the word "spin" here is not too pejorative; it aligns with Wittgenstein's idea of "a picture that holds us captive", a viewpoint that has become so habitual that we fail or forget to see it *as* a viewpoint, taking it to be just blindingly obvious. It's this illusion of obviousness that Taylor wants to dispel. Otherwise, he doesn't mind conceding that belief, as well as unbelief, arises out of "an overall take on human life" or "a general sense of things", that our viewpoint here is based not on knock-down arguments built from outside it but on an "anticipatory confidence" that arises within it. If "full lucidity" is available to us here it resides in acknowledging this fact.

I'm relating Taylor's concern with the ethical to the primacy that he accords to lived experience over intellectually formulated positions, or theories that are to be proved or disproved by the force of rational argument. But this primacy shouldn't obscure the fact that his book is itself a formidable intellectual articulation, or that he doesn't treat exclusive humanism as argumentatively derived mainly because he thinks that the arguments on which it's putatively based are such bad ones—a claim for which he thinks he himself produces a *good* argument. Nor does it cancel the other ironic fact that much modern experience is very theory-prone; that we tend to live in our heads; that we are products of a prolonged process of "excarnation" that makes it difficult for us, for example, to feel compassion as a movement in the guts (of the kind attributed to the Good Samaritan in the gospel story); that we tend to trust only what can be established from a spectatorial stance that is, in Taylor's own phrase, "experience-far"; or that, in his strong "Desdemona analogy", we are apt, like Othello, to allow third person evidence to trump what we have learned as an "I" related to a "you" (SA 567-68).[7]

Having linked the ethical to changes in our modes of experience, I need to elaborate a little on its more specific import for Taylor. Nowadays "ethics" tends to be used interchangeably with morality—a fact reinforced by the recent growth in professional ethics in many fields, including medicine, business and indeed academic research. But this fact sets us up to misunderstand what Taylor means by the term. For he means something quite different from morality—at least as this has been identified and theorised in the dominant schools of moral philosophy in recent decades (especially utilitarianism or Kant-inspired deontology). For these have been concerned exclusively with right and wrong—with what I *ought* to do or not to do. And this is regulated by rules and decision-procedures, which are to be derived from principles, the principles themselves and the derivations from them being worked out by rational argument—argument that can be conducted disinterestedly and, as it were, on neutral ground. Taylor's unease with morality, thus conceived, runs like a *leitmotif* throughout *A Secular Age*. It's related, for instance, to his alertness to the suppressed underside of the civilised personality produced by disciplinary regimes that have been increasingly internalised from the Renaissance onwards; in his sympathy for outbreaks of this underside in the carnivalesque and the festive (Bakhtin); and in his related sensitivity to the anthropological insight (of Victor Turner) that "anti-structure" is the necessary and ineliminable compliment to "structure". It appears too, in his resistance to the way in which, as in medicine, "objectified knowledge begins in modern culture to take over ethics", so that "what you need is the sharpness to follow the logic of an argument", allied to a strong will that can enforce argumentatively derived conclusions in the teeth of powerful instinctual resistance. And it motivates his antipathy to the "code-fixation" (or "nomolatry") that increasingly regulates the mores of secular liberal societies—extending from the academy into mainstream political and moral life and "providing the charter for new and more powerful forms of paternalism" (SA 501)—an antipathy underwritten by an incisively analytical argument as to why our ethical lives can never be "decanted into a code" (SA 704-07).

In a few places in *A Secular Age*, Taylor points to the huge difference between this kind of modern morality and Aristotelian ethics, where "'phronesis' doesn't allow us to separate a knowledge component from the practice of virtue" (SA 501) and where virtue itself is conceived, under the image of a "soul in harmony", as a form "already at work in human nature which the virtuous person has to help emerge, rather than... a pattern imposed ab extra" (SA 112). In company with some of his philosophical contemporaries, notably Alasdair MacIntyre and Bernard Williams, Taylor has wanted to embrace this kind of ethics, focused on the kind of actions and dispositions that are worthwhile because they enhance a whole life, bringing human fulfilment or flourishing. But while he has certainly made this move, he has wanted to take a further step—a step, one might say, that brings ethics not just beyond morality but towards spirituality.[8] This further step is one that Taylor credits Iris Murdoch with having already taken, in arguing, for example, that modern moral theory is based on what she called "far too shallow and flimsy an idea of human personality" (Murdoch 1983b, 43). And this view aligns with Taylor's own in *Sources of the Self*, where he repeatedly calls attention to a "cramping" or a "stifling" of the spirit endemic in the naturalistic temper of a great deal of modern culture including its philosophy.[9]

The kind of double movement beyond morality that I describe here can be linked to three related images that Taylor offers in an essay he contributed to a *Festschrift* for Murdoch.[10] The "corral", he suggests, symbolises a restricted field in which the concern is with duty or obligation, *what it is right to do*, rightness here being equated with justice, which is itself equated with fairness (this is the domain of morality, in the modern narrow sense*)*; the "field" symbolises a more ample space in which the concern is not with what one ought to do but rather with *what kind of human life it is good to lead* as conducing or contributing to one's human flourishing (here Aristotle, rather than Kant, or Bentham or Mill, is the exemplary philosopher); while the "forest" symbolises a further opening in which the possibility arises of self-transformation through responsiveness to *what can most fully inspire one's love*—a supremely high good that is irreducible to a rich or satisfying life (happiness as conventionally conceived and lived) and may lead one voluntarily to endure suffering or even death. Taylor's conception of the ethical makes him attentive both to the field and the forest, and to the liminal space lying between both and leading from one to the other.

This imagery does not recur in *A Secular Age*, but the ethical-spiritual terrain marked out by it appears in the very first chapter under the rubric of "fullness" and plays a crucial role in the subsequent argument, especially in the later chapters of the book. The concept of fullness, as the very term suggests, aims high in terms of the possibilities that it holds open for a human life. Taylor does not of course deny that lives can be humdrum and mediocre, consumed by the daily grind—and beyond that can be terribly warped or wasted. It's rather that terms such as "humdrum" and "wasted" can have the meanings they do only by implying some contrast notion of a truly fulfilled life, one that is admirably rich and rewarding. This is not necessarily a judgement that needs to be passed by a third person; rather, a person herself recognises it by way of felt frustration, lack, disease or ache. This feeling indeed is available to all of us. For we live most of our lives in the middle register of a more or less satisfactory quotidian round in family, work or play. But this sense of the adequacy of our lives is sustainable, Taylor seems to suggest, only against the horizon of something higher, more meaningful, more intrinsically worthwhile, with which we can have some contact—even if it is only to be haunted by it. Taylor mentions breakthrough experiences of particular individuals—early on, of Bede Griffiths and, later, of Vaclav Havel—sudden and brief epiphanies that brought an enlarged dimension to their whole subsequent experience. And he suggests that, though this kind of dramatic conversion is rare, we all have moments of intimation when some sense of what ultimately counts in our lives opens to us and remains both as a potential source of empowerment and, because of this, a pole of orientation: we are drawn toward it, and when nearest to it can experience life at its best, most integrated, most generous, or self-forgetful; just as, when far from it, we feel divided, estranged, empty. When thus put—which is pretty close to the way that Taylor himself puts it in the Introduction to the book—this may sound like the "flow" or "zone" much canvassed in contemporary "positive psychology";[11] but that it is more and other than this become apparent in later chapters. As Taylor then brings out, it's at the core of our "ethical predicament", a predicament that he analyses in terms of the key historical developments that, as he sees it, have defined our contemporary spiritual landscape.

Our Ethical Predicament: Dilemmas of Fullness

The post-axial religions have offered us visions that involve some break with ordinary human flourishing—a kind of renunciation of ordinary human desires—as the condition of reaching for real fullness. Christianity, particularly as subject to a continuous reforming drive from the late Middle Ages onwards, has most influentially inscribed this vision in western culture. But one of the most defining moves in modernity has been a principled rejection of the Christian disparagement or denial of the ordinary satisfactions of this life, here in the world and the flesh. As Taylor has often pointed out, this critique *of* religion arose first as a critique *within* religion: he traces it to what he calls the "affirmation of ordinary life", the according of a new dignity to life in the family and at work which was part of the Reformation's reaction against the older Catholic valorisation of celibate vocations and the monkish virtues.[12] But this was later to be generalised into a critique of *all* religion and absorbed into the bloodstream of modern atheism. This great divide between religiously inspired and atheistic world views, which was opened up in the eighteenth century and deepened in the nineteenth, is now very firmly settled. But analysing the issues implicit in it is, in Taylor's view, still essential if we are to understand not just attractions or repulsions around the two polar positions (monotheistic religion and exclusive humanism) but also what now inspires the huge array of spiritual dwelling places or paths that proliferate in the "super-nova" of a post-Durkheimian culture characterised by "galloping pluralism on the spiritual plane" (SA 300).

Taylor is fully alive to what motivates the anti-religious animus of modern humanism: "a pox on all transcendence" is his pithy formulation of it. And his response to this is typical of his whole hermeneutical approach, or philosophical style, in this book. "Faced with this slogan," he writes, "the reaction ought to be complex, including the following elements: a) the slogan is wrong, b) but it comes from a real and important experience which should not be denigrated, and thus c) one must resist it, but can't simply stigmatize it as total error" (SA 629). Very Taylorian! The "real and important experience" is of the need for wholeness in life, the integral place of bodily desire and its satisfaction in such wholeness, and the consequent "mutilation" incurred when this satisfaction is foresworn in the name of some supposedly "higher" purpose. Taylor fully acknowledges the validity of this experience of unspectacular flawed everyday loves, or "the homecomings to the ordinary" symbolised at the very beginning of western culture by Ulysses' return to Penelope and still celebrated by Joyce in the persons of Bloom and Molly three millennia later.[13] He also gives reasons for claiming that the body is *not* depreciated by Christianity, pointing not only to the Protestant affirmation of ordinary life, but to the fact that, as a religion of Incarnation, its eschatological vision is of reconciliation of the human with the divine in the resurrected *body*. Moreover, he shows that renunciation implies no depreciation—to the contrary it's precisely because these satisfactions are real and valuable that it can count as *renunciation*. And anyhow renunciation is only for the sake of doing God's will; and it's God's will that humans flourish—a fact borne out in the many stories of feeding and healing in the gospels as in the ministry of countless renouncers in the subsequent history of the church. It's related to all this, then, that the death of Jesus is utterly unlike that of Socrates and, *pace* Nietzsche, Christianity is not a vulgarised Platonism. But this is only a part, and not the most important part, of Taylor's "complex" response.

He goes on to point out that the charge of mutilation against Christianity has not precluded the very different charge of bowdlerisation: that, actually, Christianity cannot face the refractory elements of the human condition that give rise to irresolvable tragedy, and so tidies everything up in a consoling spiritualist phantasy. Moreover, these two charges, from apparently opposite directions, can be brought together to impale Christianity on the horns of a dilemma: to avoid the charge of mutilation it can soften its message and lower its demands (the tendency of "liberal" Christianity)—and thereby open itself all the more to the bowdlerising, sanitising charge; or, to escape the latter, it can raise the bar and toughen the task (the tendency of strict, especially Calvinist theology)—thereby impaling itself on the other, mutilating, horn. Taylor does not try to extricate Christianity from this dilemma. His response, rather, is to elucidate it *as* a dilemma and, in doing so, to show that humanist critics who bring it forward are also themselves intricated in it—this being neither to their discredit nor surprising since, in his story, they, like their contemporary Christian counterparts, are products of the long Reform and thus, as he puts it, 'brothers under the skin'.

A good deal of standard Enlightenment humanism, Taylor points out, is open to both the bowdlerisation and the mutilation charges. For while its conception of "normal" civilised life is taken to be untroubled and conflict-free, in fact it presupposes and for the most part hides a great deal of discipline (here the mutilation charge kicks in). In cases where this discipline has broken down, in dealing with delinquents and deviants, it openly appears. But even here, when it doesn't resort to manifest coercion, it passes itself off as therapy or re-education, targeting respectively pathology and faulty development. Humans are taken to be malleable, with strong but quite straightforward drives—ultimately around pleasure and pain—which are amenable to training and redirection. With the right conditioning, good habits will be inculcated and disaffected youths will end up being nice to old ladies. But here of course the bowdlerisation charge becomes apposite; the fulfilled life is assumed to be the normalised life. There is huge underestimation not only of the strength of the instincts to be subdued (especially in many young males) but also of their meta-biological character, the fact that, outside the objectivising, reductive stance, they may have important human significance and thus be inextricably caught up in a person's being and vision as well as their desire.

At a political level a similarly cost-free assumption is evident in the neo-liberal belief that, with globalisation and the spread of the market-economy, the world will naturally settle into democracy and peace. But this "end of history" thesis has not seen recent history any less marked by violence and war—and so is one further bowdlerisation.

But there is of course a higher and more exigent humanism, implicit in the morality and politics of liberalism (as espoused, for example, by Martha Nussbaum), with its commitment to human rights, very exacting standards of justice and equality, and ambitious programmes of welfare and aid. As is well known, Taylor fully shares these liberal aspirations. However, he first points out that, aiming very high, they imply a great deal of self-transcendence on the part of those who would live up to them (for him they are a "colossal extension of a Gospel ethic to a universal solidarity" (SA 695)). And second, he asks what can inspire people actually to live up to them, by what *sources* can they be empowered and sustained in doing so?

The least reductive humanist answer (with a conspicuously Kantian inflection) is: a sense of my own dignity—I would have to think less of myself as a human being if I did not set these standards for myself, nor can I impute any less dignity to other human beings. Here Taylor retorts that abiding by the standards entails a great deal of internal discipline. And this becomes especially strained when the actual human beings with whom I have to deal turn out to be distasteful or refractory, "parodying or betraying" the dignity with which I credit them. Here, he suggests, inner discipline all too easily slips and, fuelled by contempt, is externalised in the harsh treatment and abuse that I visit on those who are my supposed beneficiaries. It goes without saying that this dynamic has recurred throughout Christian history. But Taylor is asking whether the successor culture of exclusive humanism is really proof against it. Mustn't it too carry its own forms of mutilation (through the severe inner and/or outer discipline that it cannot but impose)? Or, if it answers 'no', does it not then succumb to its own form of bowdlerisation, covering up the depth of human intransigence that it may have to confront, and therefore the difficulty of the task that it has to assume?

Here Taylor complicates and greatly enriches his analysis by introducing the anti-humanism of the "immanent counter-Enlightenment" as the now no longer excluded third protagonist at the table with Christianity and exclusive humanism.[14] Nietzscheans can make hay, as Taylor points out, with the discomfiture of both of these viewpoints in facing the dilemmas just posed. The great strength of their position lies in its unflinching readiness to overthrow the Crucified and no less the civilised restraints supporting the egalitarian and democratic aspirations of "noble" forms of humanism—and ruthlessly to expose the *ressentiment* seething beneath their respective asceticisms.

Nor is this overcoming of mutilation purchased at the cost of any bowdlerisation: to the contrary, it embraces the Dionysian depths, valorising violence and excess—and thus reclaiming, one might say, the numinosity invested in them by pre-Axial forms of religion. Taylor takes very seriously the challenge here, finding in modern anti-humanism too a valid experience that must not be simply denigrated. Still, the very consistency and strength of this position exacts its own cost: jettisoning the highest spiritual aspirations of the mainline western tradition, ancient and modern. And how many of us could really countenance paying this cost?

In relation to all this, Taylor formulates what he calls "the maximal demand" ("maximal" here returns us to the notion of "fullness"): "how to define our highest spiritual and moral aspirations for human beings, while showing a path to the transformation involved which doesn't crush, mutilate or deny what is essential to our humanity" (SA 639-40). And he asks the question whether trying to meet this demand, or resolve the deep dilemmas implicit in it, is simply "mission impossible". He certainly wants to avoid answering yes to this question. His attempt to do so entails sketching, in some of the final sections of the book, a Christian anthropology and theology that intriguingly hews to orthodoxy (the central mysteries of original sin and atonement are still in place) while at the same time pointing discreetly to the need to re-open questions (not least about sexuality) often considered to be foreclosed in the moral teaching of the Church. It is beyond the scope of this paper to explore Taylor's answer here; my more limited concern has been to introduce and delineate the question.[15]

References

Archer, Margaret, 2004a. Models of Man: Admissions of Transcendence. In M. S. Archer, A. Collier and D. V. Porrora, eds., *Transcendence, Critical Realism and God*. London: Routledge, 63-81.

—. 2004b. On Understanding Religious Experience: The Challenge of St. Theresa to Social Theory, in Archer, Collier and Porrora, eds., op cit., 138-54.

Csikszentmihalyi, Mihaly, 1991. *Flow: The Psychology of Optimal Experience.* New York: HarperPerennial.

Dunne, Joseph, 2003. After Philosophy and Religion: Spirituality and its Counterfeits. In D. Carr and J. Haldane, eds., *Philosophy, Spirituality and Education.* Oxford: Blackwell, 194-204.

Kiberd, Declan, 2009. *Ulysses and Us: The Art of Everyday Living.* London: Faber.

Lyotard. J-F., 1984. *The Post-Modern Condition: A Report on Knowledge.* Minneapolis: University of Minnesota Press.

Murdoch, Iris, 1983a. On "God" and "Good". In S. Hauerwas and A. MacIntyre, eds., *Revisions: Changing Perspectives in Moral Philosophy.* Notre Dame and London: University of Notre Dame Press.

—. 1983b. Against Dryness: A Polemical Sketch. In Hauerwas and MacIntyre, eds., op cit, 43.

Shklar, Judith, 1991. Review of Charles Taylor, *Source of the Self.* In *Political Theory,* 19:1, 105-109.

Taylor, Charles, 1964. *The Explanation of Behaviour.* London: Routledge and Kegan Paul.

—. 1975a. *Philosophical Papers 1. Human Agency and Language.* Cambridge: Cambridge University Press.

—. 1975b. Foucault on Freedom and Truth. In *Philosophical Papers 2. Philosophy and the Human Science.* Cambridge: Cambridge University Press, 152-84.

—. 1975c. *Hegel.* Cambridge: Cambridge University Press.

—. 1979. *Hegel and Modern Society.* Cambridge: Cambridge University Press.

—. 1991. *The Ethics of Authenticity.* Cambridge MA: Harvard University Press.

—. 1992. *Sources of the Self: The Making of the Modern Identity.* Cambridge MA, Harvard University Press.

—. 1993. Engaged Agency and Background in Heidegger. In Charles Guignon, ed., *The Cambridge Companion to Heidegger.* Cambridge: Cambridge University Press, 317-36.

—. 1995. *Philosophical Arguments.* Cambridge MA.: Harvard University Press.

—. 1996. Iris Murdoch and Moral Philosophy. In Maria Antonaccio and William Shweiker, eds., *Iris Murdoch and the Search for Human Goodness.* Chicago and London: University of Chicago Press.

—. 1999. A Catholic Modernity? In James Heft, ed., *A Catholic Modernity?* Oxford: Oxford University Press, 13-38.

—. 2004. *Modern Social Imaginaries.* Durham NC: Duke University Press.

DEISM, SPINOZISM, ANTI-HUMANISM

IAN LEASK

Charles Taylor's attitude towards Deism—or, more precisely, towards its historical significance—was already made abundantly clear in *Sources of the Self*: "understanding the motives for Deism is so important", Taylor declared, "[because it] promises, or threatens, to give us the key to the whole modern development which we gesture at with the word 'secularization'" (Taylor 1989, 309). With *A Secular Age*, the same conviction about Deism's significance is consolidated and even intensified: now, we are told, Deism can be taken as "The Turning Point" in the (quasi-tragic) unfolding of secular modernity; in particular, Deism comes to be regarded as the foundation of that "exclusive humanism" which, for Taylor, radically reorients our ontic commitments and renders transcendence severely attenuated (or worse).

To an extent, what follows, below, will serve to bolster Taylor's wider thesis regarding the relationship between early modern thought and the wider dissemination of naturalistic, immanent, principles. However, the main purpose here is not to corroborate Taylor's claims, but, instead, to raise a crucial, critical issue—namely, that, by failing to account for the *Spinozism* that (at the very least) informs so much Deism, Taylor faces serious difficulties in substantiating his claim that Deism effectively founds the "exclusive humanism" of the modern, secular world. As we shall see, the "Deists" upon whom Taylor himself focuses—Tindal and Toland—can be regarded as promulgating and intensifying the radical naturalism of Spinoza (rather than some version of Lockeanism[1]); as such, the "Deism" they present is more like the demotion, rather than the promotion, of any "special status" for humanity (as a supposed "kingdom within a kingdom").[2] In short, the claim here is that, by neglecting the Spinozistic infrastructure of Deism, Taylor's asserted correlation between Deism and humanism is rendered highly problematic.[3]

To make its case, this chapter consists of four main sections: 1) a summary of Taylor's account of Deism; 2) a survey of Spinoza's naturalism; 3) attention to Tindal and, especially, Toland, *qua* Spinozism; and 4) some concluding remarks.

Taylor on Deism

The overall narrative of Taylor's *A Secular Age* is now familiar enough: through a vast "subtraction story", Taylor suggests, a kind of Whig version of history (as Progress) has become accepted as the one and only truth; as a result, a so-called "immanent frame" (a notion unique to *A Secular Age*, apparently) has become universalized, and so, in turn, the cosmos has become increasingly conceptualized without any reference to the transcendent. Of course, there is still the possibility of opening certain "windows" to transcendence, within this wider regime of immanence; nonetheless, the trend depicted is towards a definite hegemony of the secular. What is more, an attendant (or intrinsic) element of this hegemony is the emergence of an "exclusive humanism"—in other words, the emergence of a kind of putative autonomy or self-sufficiency for humanity which, in turn, comes to verge on hubristic self-inflation à la Heidegger's "subjectification of Being" (albeit in a more domesticated depiction).

Part of Taylor's project, it seems, is to try to delineate the necessary conditions for the possibility of secular modernity's emergence. Accordingly, he will stress that his is not just a kind of disembodied academic exercise; instead, the (thoroughly Hegelian) task he wants to pursue—especially in chapters Six and Seven of *A Secular Age*—is to sift through the "sedimentations" (SA 268) that constitute us, and our contemporary, secular age, in order to construct some wider, historically substantiated, self-understanding. And what this phenomenological recapitulation (of the inner form of our cultural history) aims to lay bare is that the "exclusive humanism" of today depends crucially on the particular attitude of early modernity—an attitude that Taylor configures as *Deism*.

Taylor employs "Deism" as something close to a catch-all term designed to explain a reduction, or shrinkage, in the scope and domain of religion (and in this respect, at least, his understanding seems wholly consonant with so much of the contemporary critical reaction to Deism in its initial appearances). Thus Deism, in Taylor's hands, involves something like the following concatenation:

> the reformulation of "living a holy life", in terms reducible solely to moral maxims (which are located immanently, within the self);
> the (corresponding) decline in soteriological devotion to Christ, in prayer and devotion, and in the general practices of holiness;
> the reformulation of providence—so that God's purposes do not transcend *humans*' good;[4]
> the diminution of the significance of transcendence;

the undermining of the fundamentality of grace (in terms of the "call" to some super-natural good);

the undermining of a Trinitarian stress on the Holy Spirit as bridging finite and infinite;

the consolidation of the (bourgeois) stress on industry, discipline and productivity, according to which godliness becomes further desacralized.

Overall, it seems, Deism creates something like the necessary "spiritual" conditions for the naturalism that will spawn modern scientific rationality; as such, it becomes a root cause of the "self-sufficient framework" and "buffered identity" of the modern epoch. (As Taylor puts it, "[t]he sense that there is a further vocation for human being, beyond human flourishing, atrophies in the climate of 'Deism'" (SA 242).) Deism, for Taylor, is thus the beginning of a downward slide—away from God, and towards a vastly inflated, idolatrous, notion of "Man"—that characterizes modernity. It is one of the great, fateful, perhaps even destinal, moments of human history.

For sure, Taylor's treatment of this "Deistic humanism" is a *tour de force*, full of his usual, insightful, brilliance. Nonetheless, and perhaps inevitably (given the vast, synoptic sweep of Taylor's thesis), there are still important critical questions that we can ask here. One issue that arises immediately concerns the slipperiness of what precisely "Deism" stands for. Thus, it may be an exaggeration to designate it as merely the invention of Leslie Stephen, the Victorian historian of ideas; nonetheless, and as contemporary scholarship has established fairly convincingly, Deism is a multiform and far from straightforward affair. Herrick, for example, prefaces his account by stressing the sheer difficulty in defining Deism (Herrick 1997, 22-24); Lund insists that "Deism" had no determinate and settled meaning in the 18th century itself (Lund 1995); while Hudson, stressing that "Deism" and "Deist" are "vague terms of shifting import... [which] can encourage over-unified interpretations of particular texts" (Hudson 2009, 3), makes it a central hermeneutical principle that we should "avoid monolithic patterns of interpretation which reduce [Deist writers]... to resting points in a teleological history of secularization" (ibid., 1). Taylor, it seems, has a confidence about the univocal status of Deism that more recent historiography hardly supports.

However, the issue I want to explore here concerns Taylor's correlation of humanism and Deism—specifically, the possibility that the "shift to exclusive humanism" might be too easily posited as somehow intrinsic to the Deistic "revolution" (and so one of "the facts of the case"

(SA 259)). As we shall see, it seems that the more carefully we investigate some of the original Spinozistic formations of Deism; and the more we appreciate the way in which, as Louis Althusser has put it, Deism provides one of the "sites" (*lieux*) in which "the history of philosophy's repressed Spinozism... unfolded as a subterranean history" (Althusser & Balibar 2009, 114), the less evidence we find of the kind of exalted status for "man" that Taylor takes to be automatic, or even axiomatic. Put otherwise: appreciating Deism's Spinozistic inspiration serves to destabilize a casual characterisation of Deism as humanism.[5]

To begin to address this cluster of issues, we might focus initially upon the materialist implications of Spinoza's naturalism—for this will provide the key to our critical questioning of Taylor's account of Deism. Specifically, and as we shall see, Spinoza's naturalism finds, not just a continuation, but an intensification in the work of John Toland, the most philosophically substantial of the so-called Deists.

Spinoza's Naturalism

Spinoza's substance-monism, his rejection of teleology and "final ends", and his identification of God and nature, are all familiar enough fare (in general terms, at least); similarly, the "critical-historical" method of interpretation he offers in the *Theological-Political Treatise* is broadly understood as a crucial landmark in the modern reception of Scripture. However, what remains far less appreciated—and perhaps even obscured and distorted by a Romantic appropriation of Spinoza—is the extent and implications of Spinoza's naturalism. Anything like full treatment of this massive topic is obviously beyond our present scope; however, we can still highlight certain features that have particular relevance for our study.

First, there are the implications of Spinoza's "parallelism", or his positing of Thought and Extension as the corresponding attributes of a single substance. (Thought and Extension are ultimately one and the same, Spinoza tells us: they are *attributes*, not separate substances themselves.) As well as being a convenient mechanism for overcoming Cartesian dualism, this monism also means that—*contra* Descartes—the soul or mind is refused any eminence or special status.[6] Descartes may posit a (thinking) subject outside of nature (which it, the subject, then "thinks"); and he may thus assume that, as Spinoza puts it, "the mind has absolute power over its actions" (Spinoza 2002, 277).[7] But for Spinoza, not only is there is no gulf between humanity and the rest of nature; concomitantly, there is no substantial "self" somehow outside of nature. *Contra* Descartes, Spinoza is adamant that "[t]he being of substance does not pertain to the essence of man; i.e., substance does not constitute the form of man [*formam hominis*]" (ibid., 249).[8]

Furthermore, as well as refusing any primacy to the mind, Spinoza's "parallelism" adumbrates a naturalism far greater in extent than that which the *Ethics* establishes explicitly.[9] For Spinoza will ultimately stress the *autonomy* of the physical: given that the mind is a mode of thinking;[10] and, given that modes cannot exceed their attributes, so it follows that "the mind [cannot] determine the body to motion or rest, or to anything else (if there is anything else)" (Spinoza 2002, 279).[11] The motion-and-rest of the body must arise from *another body*; "it cannot arise from the mind" (ibid., 279).[12] In turn, this same autonomy must necessarily undermine any claim made on behalf of the putative primacy or "special status" of the soul:[13] Spinoza is not merely suggesting a limit to what role the mind might play *vis-à-vis* the body; he is suggesting that the mind plays *no role at all* in determining the body. He is fully aware that this will appear counter-intuitive—paintings and temples, for example, seem impossible to understand without reference to plans, intentions, and ideas. Nonetheless, as far as he is concerned, such counter-intuitive assumptions are themselves more like indices of our ignorance: they do not explain *how* the mind might have primacy; and they can be met with counter-examples, also drawn from experience, such as the complexity of the non-purposive, or non-conscious, actions of sleepwalkers (*somnambuli*). In short, contemporary knowledge of nature is simply not adequate: "nobody as yet knows the structure of the body so accurately as to explain all its functions", and "no-one knows in what way and by what means the mind can move body" (Spinoza 2002, 280).[14] Accordingly, Spinoza suggests, there can be no *a priori* justification for ruling out the possibility of a far wider "physical" understanding of human beings.

Spinoza, then, is committed to a radical naturalism.[15] He explicitly denies the priority of mind (and so, *pari passu*, negates any conception of "man within Nature" as some kind of "kingdom within a kingdom [*imperium in imperio*]" (Spinoza 2002, 277)[16]); and he also raises the possibility that—notwithstanding a supposed equiprimordiality[17]—corporeality may have a kind of foundational status,[18] and thus that consciousness is more like a *function* of the body.[19] The more that the mind comes to know about nature, it seems, the fewer privileges it can give itself. Accordingly, we could say that Spinoza's naturalism contains nothing like the promulgation of some "buffered selfhood": early modern materialism may well be crucial in establishing an "immanent frame"; in Spinoza's case, however, it is not at all clear that a radical naturalism can also be equated with any kind of humanism. Indeed, Spinozistic immanence is more like an *anti*-humanism—probably a far more rigorous anti-humanism than any of its late 20th century counterparts:[20] Spinoza will insist,[21] after all, that we need to rid ourselves of the various anthropomorphisms that cloud our thinking, and that lead to ridiculous assumptions that the cosmos is ordered according to some "final cause", or that we have a special place in the universe, or that God has a kind of personal interest in humanity (and even took human form[22]).[23] It seems that—in the case of Spinoza, at least—any correlation between immanence and humanism is far too casually assumed: where, for Taylor, modernity means "a humanism accepting no final goals beyond human flourishing" (SA 18), Spinoza's thought rules out both humanism and final goals.[24]

Deism

Moving our focus more directly towards Taylor's treatment of Deism, the broad principle that guides our subsequent discussion is that, although in no way acknowledged by Taylor himself, the Deists upon whom he will concentrate—Tindal and, more particularly, Toland[25]—can both be understood as profoundly Spinozistic thinkers. For sure, this principle is strongly influenced by Jonathan Israel's case for taking the radical Enlightenment as a whole to be profoundly Spinozistic;[26] as such, it might seem open to the same kind of critical responses that Israel's work has engendered (from, for example, Piet Steenbakkers, Theo Verbeek, or— especially— Margaret Jacob[27]). However, it is worth stressing, initially, that the scholarly authority invoked here is by no means restricted to Israel. For one thing, Leslie Stephen had declared as early as 1876 that

> The whole essence of the deist position may be found in Spinoza's *Tractatus Theologico-Politicus*. A few of the philosopher's pages have expanded into volumes and libraries of discussions; but the germs of the whole discussion are present. (Stephen 1991, 33)[28]

More significantly, though, close textual analysis can establish an even stronger case in favour of Deism *qua* Spinozism than any scholarly authority (even *Radical Enlightenment* itself). Thus any debt to Israel that this thesis owes is—hopefully—in no sense exclusive: if anything, the principal claims made here regarding Deism and Spinozistic anti-humanism have been *neglected* elsewhere.

Although the question of "humanism" is our main focus, nonetheless, our survey can still benefit from following Taylor's own Deistic exemplars: considering Mathew Tindal's thought first, we can establish important context by examining the general imprint that Spinoza leaves;

and by then giving more focussed attention to John Toland, we find that the engagement with Spinoza becomes so profound that Toland's thought is more like an attempted "consummation" of Spinozistic naturalism (and its correlative anti-humanism). In other words: the two great Deists to whom Taylor himself gives explicit attention can provide us with what, crucially, Taylor seems to ignore: 1) a general indication of Spinozistic influence, and 2) a very particular "case study", in which the full implications of Spinozistic naturalism become more apparent.

Tindal

Tindal, the apostate Oxford don and disseminator of dissent, would draw heavily on Spinoza for the kind of "deconstruction" of Church authority that he proposed—in works ranging from *The Rights of the Christian Church Asserted* (1706), through to his most famous piece, *Christianity as Old as Creation* (1730). In part, this influence was formal and methodological: following Spinoza's *Theological-Political Treatise*, Tindal offers a critical-historical account which treats Scripture as a datum in need of explanation (like any other textual product), and which separates the *meaning* of Scripture from its supposed truth.[29] But it was also manifest—more obviously and more dramatically—in terms of so much of the content of his work, especially *Christianity as Old as Creation* (a text which would prompt over a hundred contemporary critical responses). For, whether it was stressing that true happiness meant "living up to the Dictates of Nature" (Tindal 1995, ch.3), depicting revealed religion and nature to have the same end (ch.6, ch.7), asserting that God acts *necessarily* (ch.10), or differentiating superstition and "true religion" (ch.13), *Christianity as Old as Creation* displayed a clear and unambiguous Spinozistic imprint.

Regarding the identity of nature and the substance of religion, for example, Tindal's formulation becomes something like a Spinozism subjected to prolix refashioning:

> Belief in the Existence of a God, and Sense and Practice of those Duties, which result from the knowledge, we, by our Reason, have of him, and his Perfections; and of ourselves, and our own Imperfections; and of the Relation we stand in to him, and to our Fellow-Creatures; so that the *Religion of Nature* takes in every Thing that is founded on the Reason and Nature of Things. (Tindal 1995, 13)

Similarly, he will urge humanity always to employ its reason, in order to overcome superstition and its political exploitation: not adhering to rational notions provides "the Occasion of all Superstition, and those innumerable Mischiefs that Mankind, on the Account of Religion, have done either to themselves, or one another"; and, what is more,

> Nothing can be more absurd than to suppose God has taken this Power… and plac'd it incontroulably in the Hands of Men, who, having an Interest in corrupting it, do, generally speaking, so manage Matters, as if Religion was the Means, and their Power the End, for which it was instituted. (Tindal 1995, 107)[30]

Elsewhere, he upholds what he takes to be the moral core of Scripture as providing rational maxims that are not just compatible with, but identical to, their secular equivalents. He denies the possibility of there being a theological truth somehow *above* reason, lambasting "the Absurdity of not being govern'd by the Reason of things in all Matters of Religion" (Tindal 1995, 73).[31] And he condemns the pervasive anthropomorphism of religion: "imput[ing] human Parts… and human Passions, even of the worst kind, to God" (ibid., 225) can only result in "[the] Absurdity of debasing God, and cloathing him with our Infirmities" (ibid., 73).[32]

For sure, Spinoza is hardly Tindal's only source: he will also draw deeply, if unevenly, from the Cambridge Platonists, Locke, Bayle, Cudworth and Toland himself (amongst so many others). Nonetheless, given our main focus here, we should note, not just the general stamp of Spinozism indicated above, but also that this same mark was thoroughly apparent to Tindal's contemporary opponents. A celebrated, anonymous, 1735 tract, for example, would depict Tindal's work as being wholly derivative of an impious "club of Deists and Atheists", with Spinoza featuring prominently amongst them: the (supposed) result was Tindal's commitment to the (supposedly) Spinozistic notion that there is "one only extended or material substance differently modified".[33] William Carroll, in his *Spinoza Reviv'd* (1711), would depict Tindal's destabilizing Deism as being founded upon a "Spinozerian atheism"; and he would catalogue, in parallel columns, correspondences and "similarities" between Tindal's works and a variety of Spinoza's texts.[34] George Hickes, in his *Preliminary Discourse* to Carroll's treatise, would accuse Tindal of the wholesale plundering of Spinoza's texts (all for the cause of destroying religious authority); he would make explicit mention of the pernicious effects of failing to distinguish *natura naturans* and *natura naturata*. And Abel Evans, in his polemical poem *The Apparition* (1710), would include the following, damning, lines:

> Spinoza Smiles, and cries—The *Work* is done,
> T[indal] shall Finish; (*Satan's* Darling Son)
> T[indal] shall Finish, what *Spinoza* first Begun.[35]

In short: whether or not Tindal was an original philosophical force, he was recognized by his contemporaries—whom we can follow today, in this respect—as being one of the general disseminators of the "execrable principles" within Spinoza's work.

All of which cannot be said to establish that Tindal is necessarily committed wholly and clearly to a Spinozistic anti-humanism. Nonetheless, it does establish important context—overlooked by Taylor himself—for understanding the formation and articulation of Deism. This context becomes even more significant when we consider the far fuller, and more appropriate, case-study that John Toland provides—for (as we have already noted) Toland is not only a more substantial and original thinker than Tindal, he is also explicitly concerned with what we might term the *intensification* of Spinozistic immanence. As we shall see, this same intensification means, necessarily, the further, naturalistic, "reduction" of humanity's supposed eminence.

Toland

For sure, Toland's best known work, *Christianity Not Mysterious* (1696), seems to demonstrate a thoroughly Lockean thinker at work. However, we need also to consider, not just that the main structuring principle of that work is, of course, the Spinozistic rejection of any distinction between what is contrary to reason and what is above reason;[36] and not just that the young Toland had studied in Leiden with Spinozistic scripturalists like Spanheim, Le Clerc and Van Dale; but also—and more significantly—that his most explicitly metaphysical work, the Fourth and Fifth of his *Letters to Serena*, of 1704, provides a sustained engagement with Spinoza's immanent ontology (and its various implications).

The central metaphysical issue in the *Letters to Serena* is, in effect, how Spinoza might explain motion without betraying that same ontological immanence. After all, in the so-called "Physical Interlude" of the *Ethics*, Spinoza seems to end up caught in an aporetic circle of his own making: we are presented with the principle that "a body in motion will continue to move until it is determined to rest by another body, and a body at rest continues to be at rest until it is determined to move by another body" (Spinoza 2002, 253)[37]—and yet, even if any transcendent source of movement (such as "God's Will") is ruled out *tout court*, there seems to be no attempt to justify this principle immanently by appeal to the axioms, definitions or propositions provided previously in the text. Spinoza *asserts* that bodies at the "horizontal" level must be subject to some kind of "vertical", kinetic, regulation; but there is no clearly established deductive chain to justify his claims. Thus, even if he may want to avoid bringing in the arbitrary fiat of some non-immanent God, something supposedly external to natural necessity, to "explain" motion (and thus individuation); what he leaves us with, as an alternative, is presented as a kind of *fait accompli*, or brute fact, without being deduced rationally from axioms and definitions. Emilia Giancotti has summarized the problem thus:

> [Why] does motion not belong to the essence of substance as it is expressed under the attribute of extension, remaining situated at the level of effect, whereas it defines modality itself as the accomplishment of the causality of substance insofar as it is extension? A clear vision of the role of motion would perhaps have led Spinoza to a "radicalization" of what on the contrary remained simple 'aspects' of materialism. (Giancotti 1997, 57)

In effect, Toland will seek to provide precisely this "radicalization" by extracting core elements from the thought of *Leibniz*, the philosopher with whom he would have so much direct contact at the start of the 18th century.[38] For it is Leibniz's metaphysics (and physics)—completely shorn, needless to say, of their original, theological, coefficients—that will allow Toland to develop his clear commitment to the notion that bodies contain their *own*, inherent, motive force (and thus to "radicalize" Spinoza's already heretical ontology).

Briefly, we could say that, by the 1690s, Leibniz's increasing concern with (or, rather, development of) dynamics leads him to the fairly settled *metaphysical* convictions[39] 1) that "behind" the fact of any local motion, a principle of Action, or Force, is necessary for any adequate account of reality, and 2) that this Force, in turn, must be seen as applying to (or within) each individual substance. Regardless of the efficacy or success of Leibniz's distinction between metaphysical principle and physical "phenomena", a crucial point for us is that, by the time of his encounters with Toland in Berlin and Hanover, at the start of the 18th century, Leibniz has a well honed and well established position: each substance, he is now convinced, embodies a force of action or "cause of change [*causa mutationis*]" (Leibniz 1969, 393); and so each substance is—to some extent, at least—*self*-moved.[40] Reality can be understood as (unextended) energy; and substances are, fundamentally, fields of forces, or "centres of activity"—centres that can maintain and propel themselves by themselves. The universe is in no sense a collection of inert stuff activated *via* some ongoing miracle.

Of course, Leibniz will also depict these laws of motion as being derived from a *theological* principle of perfection and order—in other words, as the effect of the choice and the wisdom of God. For it is God who places active natures in the things of the world, which itself is created by Him as the best of all possible worlds, governed, as such, by the rational principles which determine physical laws.[41] Mechanical principles are thus the consequence of God's benevolent choice and design (and thus confirmation of a wider, pre-established harmony): for Leibniz, the principle of Force serves ultimately to deny naturalism, to reinstate the ontological supremacy of the soul, and to confirm the (operational) presence in the world of "the monarch of the divine city" (Leibniz 1969, 652)[42]—God Almighty.

Toland's daring move in the *Letters to Serena* is entirely to extract the Leibnizian principle of Force from its theological setting, in order to provide the "radicalization" of Spinozistic materialism noted above: Force will now be taken to be *its own, immanent, source*, rather than the indirect expression or manifestation of some transcendent or transitive cause. In other words, Leibnizian insight is put to work for the kind of naturalistic purpose that Leibniz would simply not countenance: motive Force bolstering the sheer autonomy of the material world. Hence the central metaphysical contention in the *Letters to Serena*—namely, that movement is an intrinsic element in the "stuff" of the cosmos, that "*Motion is essential to Matter*,[…] as inseperable from its Nature as Impenetrability or Extension, and that it ought to make a part of its Definition" (Toland 1976a, 148-9). Force, Toland insists (*contra* Spinoza), must be considered an *attribute*, rather than mode; the basic units of the Tolandian cosmos are to be taken as centres of self-initiated activity. But of course, this same Force is to be treated entirely on its own terms and not (*contra* Leibniz) as the manifestation of God. What becomes apparent, as a result, is the centrality of the principle of "Action"—and thus the truth that "no part of Matter… [is] without its own internal Energy" (ibid.). Stressing the fundamental, attributive, status of Force allows Toland to expel any possible residue of crypto-occasionalism, and so to "consummate" Spinozistic immanence. The notion of an "independent" soul is banished; and the material world needs no extra- or supra-material principle for its operation and its explanation.

Accordingly, we can understand Toland as propogating a naturalism that is even more forceful (or, perhaps, more "scandalous") than its Spinozistic source.[43] For example, we find an important convergence between section 15 of the Fourth of the *Letters* and the Scholium to Proposition 39 of Book Four of the *Ethics*, regarding the dissolution of the dead body and its subsequent metamorphosis: where Spinoza "do[es] not venture to deny that the human body... [can] assume another nature [*aliam naturam*] quite different from its own" (Spinoza 2002, 342), Toland, describing "the total Dissolution of our System at death", writes that

> [we] become Parts of a thousand other things at once; our Carcases partly mixing with the Dust and Water of the Earth, partly exhal'd and evaporated into the Air, flying to so many different places, mixing and incorporating with innumerable things. (Toland 1976a, 189)

Both seem to agree that, although there is life after death, this is not the (immaterial) continuation of "my" personal identity:[44] rather, it is that state in which the "parts [of the body] are so disposed that they acquire a different proportion of motion and rest to one another" (Spinoza 2002, 342); the parts that once made up "me" continue—but "without me", as it were. Spinoza is reluctant to pursue the issue too much further, for fear of "afford[ing] material for the superstitious to raise new problems" (ibid.); Toland has no such misgivings.

Or, again, we have Toland's suggestion, at the end of the fifth of the *Letters*, that *conatus* is already an unconscious identification of the "intrinsick and essential Action of Matter" (Toland 1976a, 237). To be sure, Spinoza's physics (or "proto-physics"[45]) might have it that finite modes are subject to ongoing, *extrinsic* determination by some infinite, "vertical" principle; yet with the psychology of *Ethics* Book Three, Spinoza will argue that striving is "nothing but the actual essence of the thing itself" (Spinoza 2002, 283); and that singular entities are *inherently* active—not so much (passive) vehicles for God's expression, more the active *expressing of* God. (Singular things, Spinoza tells us, are that "whereby [God] is and acts" (ibid.).) Accordingly, and assuming that Spinoza's later discussion of *conatus* presupposes some foundation in the physics of bodies, it seems that Toland is seeking to treat universally Spinoza's famous claim that "*each* thing [*unaquaeque res*], insofar as it is in itself, endeavours [*conatur*] to persist in its own being" (ibid.). It suits Toland's purpose only too well to project the later claims in the *Ethics* regarding the inherent or self-sourced power of and within particular things onto the earlier assertion that finite modes are subject to *extrinsic* determination: foundational activity can thus replace constitutive passivity; and Force can thus "become manifest" everywhere.

However, what seems most significant of all, in terms of Toland's radicalized Spinozism (and its subsequent "anti-humanist" materialism), is the clear commitment he expresses, in a kind of first draft of the *Letters*,[46] that it is as a result of the body and "corporeal things" that the soul, or self, is what it is, thinks what it thinks, and does what it does: "C'est par le corps, et par les choses corporelles, que l'âme est ce qu'elle est, qu'elle pense ce que pense, et qu'elle fait tout ce qu'elle fait", he states. Leibnizian intellectualism may make extravagant claims about a "pure" reasoning without the senses, Toland observes; but he remains insistent that there can be nothing in our thoughts which does not originate in our senses, and that, ultimately, the soul, or self, is nothing but "le résultat de l'impression que font les choses sensibles sur le cerveau", the result of sense-impressions on the brain.[47] (Essentially the same position will be articulated even more robustly 16 years later, in Toland's *Pantheisticon*, where he tells us that "Thought… is a peculiar Motion of the Brain, the proper Organ of this Faculty; or rather a certain Part of the Brain continued in the Spinal Marrow, and in the Nerves with their Membranes, constitutes the principal Seat of the Soul, and performs the Motion both of Thought and Sensation" (Toland 1976b, 22); and that "Ideas [are] formed in the Brain (which Organ, as it is corporeal and very complex, it can produce nothing but what is corporeal)" (ibid., 24).[48]) Plainly, then, Toland is committed to a radical materialism,[49] one that is so "remorseless"[50] that any kind of humanism simply cannot feature; indeed, as the Toland scholar Pierre Lurbe would have it, the Tolandian system means nothing less than "la mort du sujet".[51] It seems, accordingly, that any claim which takes Toland's thought to exemplify the supposed identity of Deism and "exclusive humanism" is rendered profoundly unstable, if not unsustainable.

Conclusion

Bearing in mind all of the above, and in summary, we could construct a syllogism along the following lines:

P1 Deism is profoundly Spinozistic
P2 Spinozism is not a humanism
t Deism is not about the promulgation of "exclusive humanism"

To be sure, this itself is far too neat. After all, Deism in general could have been profoundly influenced by Spinoza without every thinker branded "Deist" accepting the full extent of his philosophy (in particular, his anti-humanism): not every Deist can be taken to have concurred with Spinoza's apparent relegation of "man" (and his assumed special status). And, perhaps more importantly: to emphasize a Spinozistic imprint upon early modernity is, in one sense, to do nothing but confirm Taylor's wider claims regarding immanence, naturalism and the growth of secularity. Thus there can be no question that identifying the Spinozistic infrastructure of (some elements within) Deism means that, in turn, Taylor's thesis somehow falls apart. Far from it.

However, what we have seen, above, is surely still indicative of a certain over-hastiness on Taylor's part, a kind of pre-determination to make the scholarly "facts" fit a pre-ordained frame (or Frame). Earlier in his career, Taylor had acknowledged how "Spinoza was the great philosopher of the anti-subject, the philosopher who more than any other in the Western tradition seems to take us beyond and outside of subjectivity" (Taylor 1975, 16); 30 years later, however, the lack of attention Taylor affords the Spinozism which informs Deism—and, more particularly, the Deists whom he himself singles out—renders deeply problematic his pivotal contention that Deism provides "the context for the leap into exclusive humanism" (SA 257). Even if Taylor is proposing "a certain interpretative grid" (SA 275) rather than a precise scholarly analysis, it seems that Deism—Deism understood in the Spinozistic terms set out here, that is—simply cannot perform the central role that Taylor asks of it.

All of which, in turn, may gesture to a far more significant point—namely, that, whatever the undoubtedly inflated role given to the subject by the various Idealisms of modernity, it is *naturalism* that has presented, and continues to present, the most radical challenges to "transcendence". After all, Idealisms may deify "Man", *via* what Pierre Macherey has recognized as "merely an impoverished and inverted theology" that installs "Man... [as] god over himself" (Macherey 1978, 66); but naturalism seems to deny the possibility of any deification whatsoever.

References

Althusser, Louis & Étienne Balibar, 2009. *Reading Capital*, trans. Ben Brewster, London: Verso.
Giancotti, Emilia, 1997. The Birth of Modern Materialism in Hobbes and Spinoza. In *The New Spinoza*, Warren Montag & Ted Stolze eds., Minneapolis: University of Minnesota Press, 48-62.
Herrick, James A., 1997. *The Radical Rhetoric of the English Deists: The Discourse of Scepticism 1680-1750*, Columbia: University South Carolina Press.
Hudson, Wayne, 2009. *The English Deists. Studies in Early Enlightenment*, London: Pickering & Chatto.

Leibniz, G.W., 1969. *Philosophical Papers and Letters*, trans. & ed. Leroy Loemker, 2nd ed., Dordrecht: Reidel.

Lund, R.D., 1995. *The Margins of Orthodoxy: Heterodox Writing and Cultural Response, 1660-1750*, Cambridge University Press.

Macherey, Pierre, 1978. *A Theory of Literary Production*, trans. Geoffrey Wall, London: Routledge & Kegan Paul.

Spinoza, Baruch, 2002. *Complete Works*, trans. Samuel Shirley, ed. Michael Morgan, Indianapolis: Hackett.

Stephen, Leslie, 1991. *History of English Thought in the Eighteenth Century*, facsimile reprint of 1902 edition, Bristol: Thoemmes.

Taylor, Charles, 1975. *Hegel*, Cambridge University Press.

—. 1989. *Sources of the Self. The Making of Modern Identity*, Harvard University Press

Tindal, Mathew, 1995. *Christianity as Old as Creation*, in John Valdimar Price (ed.), *History of British Deism*, 8 vols., London: Routledge/Thoemmes Press, vol.5.

Toland, John, 1976a. *Letters to Serena*, London, 1704; facsimile reprint, New York & London: Garland.

—. 1976b. *Pantheisticon*, London: 1720; facsimile reprint, New York: Garland.

ESTABLISHING AN ETHICAL COMMUNITY: TAYLOR AND THE CHRISTIAN SELF

MARY SHANAHAN

In this chapter I want to consider Taylor's analysis of the fragmentation of society and its lack of shared projects in the light of Plato's philosophy of friendship. My chief concern shall be to show how, when we read aspects of Taylor's work in conjunction with Plato's, we can come to view ethics as the fundamental shared project of humanity. To illustrate my claims I shall draw upon Plato's *Phaedrus*, with some reference to the *Symposium*, and Taylor's *Ethics of Authenticity*, *A Secular Age* and his Marianist Award Lecture "A Catholic Modernity?" Beginning with Plato's philosophy of friendship, and focusing exclusively upon its ethical import as a model of ethical co-development, I shall then move on to assess Taylor's comments on the fragmentation of contemporary society.

Plato's "Philosophy of Friendship": Ethical Co-Development

The theme of friendship is explored on numerous occasions in Plato's *oeuvre* and is, accordingly, intrinsic to the development of his philosophical worldview. Although Plato sets his explorations of friendship within an erotic context,[1] he attempts to recast this relationship in ethically educational terms in order to transcend the boundaries of such a traditional Greek practice.[2] In effect, what Plato does, whilst openly recognising the libidinal drives that can provide the impetus for entering into such a relationship, is to shift the focus away from a love of the purely sensual (a love of sexual gratification and fulfilment) towards an openness to the love of the sensible (a love of wisdom: philosophy). Let us begin by focusing upon the ethical impetus that Plato contends such relationships should be driven by.

In the Platonic schema, a philosophical life is also an ethical life which simultaneously affects one's friendships, one's (political) community and one's self-understanding. The *Phaedrus* provides us with just such "full" account of philosophical being, for in this dialogue education, desire, ethics and philosophy are linked together *via* friendship. According to this curiously "divided" dialogue,[3] the lover and beloved can, provided that they are able to keep their chaotic souls in order, grow together philosophically.[4] To put it another way, rather than setting up an "either/or" dichotomy in which it is *either* the lover (*erastes*) *or* the beloved (*eromenos*) who gains, Plato attempts to sketch an ethical situation in which the lover *and* the beloved can develop, or "gain", in ethical terms.[5] Although the account is not without its problems, not least the unequal status of the two parties concerned, the value of the underlying notion that friendship leads to the mutual ethical, philosophical and educational growth of both individuals is not to be underestimated. Consider, for example, 256a-c where Socrates comments:

> Now if the victory goes to the better [*beltio*] elements in both their minds, which lead them to follow the assigned regimen of philosophy, their life here below is one of bliss and shared understanding [*homonoetikon*]. They are modest and fully in control [*egkrateis*] of themselves now that they have enslaved [*doulosamenoi*] the part that brought trouble into the soul and set free [*eleutherosaotes*] the part that gave it virtue... *There is no greater good* [*meisdon agathon*] *than this that either human self-control or divine madness* [*theia mania*] *can offer a man*. [My emphasis, M.S.]

Inserting the proviso that the true benefits of this perfect, philosophical friendship can only be attained through a de-sexualised relationship, and hence recasting a more traditional understanding, Plato has Socrates note that, in effect, friendship is a divine gift, the benefits of which far outweigh the difficulties of attaining and maintaining self-control in the face of over-whelming beauty (such are the terms in which the beloved is described by Plato). True and loving friendship is thus the most beautiful experience that we can have in the physical world but, more than this, its effects reach out beyond this world (or life) and towards the next. This key human experience brings together, according to Plato, the physical and metaphysical aspects of our being and it is this which is the unique feature of our desire for ethical relationships. Thus, one might well contend that the "Phaedrean" account of friendship appeals to what one might term our "metaphysicality".[6]

Throughout Socrates' second speech, Plato insists that the relationship between the lover and the beloved results in the improvement of *both* of their souls. In particular, his focus on the lover presents the notion of reorienting one's concerns away from the egocentric and towards the ethically intersubjective. Thus, the Platonic account of friendship can be viewed as developmental because the relationship develops by aiming itself at the ethical (the Good).[7] At the same time as the relationship *per se* is reorienting itself towards the Good, the souls of the friends develop likewise by reorienting themselves towards the Good. Thus, as the souls reorient individually towards the Good, their joint effort to reorient their relationship towards the Good manifests itself as a co-development of their ethical and philosophical potential.

At 255a-b Socrates remarks of the beloved: "[A]s time goes forward... he allows his lover to talk and spend time with him, and the man's good will is close at hand, the [beloved]... is amazed by it..." There has been a "courtship", to use an antiquated phrase, which has given both parties an opportunity to grow in love and respect for one another. Most importantly, and this is not a feature of either the Lysian or the first "Socratic" accounts of the lover which precede this speech in the dialogue, the lover has been "inspired by a god". Friendship-love pursued in the name of wisdom has both a divine origin and a divine destination—a "divine teleology"—and this is what sets it apart from other, lesser forms of "friendship". Important for my claims is the fact that such an argument concerning both the developmental nature of friendship and its divine *telos* is not restricted solely to the *Phaedrus*; on this note I would like to turn briefly to the *Symposium*.[8]

Noting that coming to be ethical is a developmental process by use of his well-known staircase analogy, Plato writes that: "So when someone rises by... stages, through loving... correctly, and begins to see this beauty [*kalon*], he has almost grasped his goal... which is learning of this very Beauty..." (211b-c). Like the *Phaedrus* (and also the implicit message of the *Lysis*) the emphasis falls on loving *correctly* (what I have referred to already as Plato's "desexualising" of the relationship) in order to harness one's ethical being.

Plato chooses to highlight the benefits of loving correctly by providing a detailed description of a failed relationship; I am referring, of course, to the relationship between Socrates and Alcibiades. Brazen entrance aside, Alcibiades will show himself to be a man who is in love. Moreover, he will show himself to be a man who does not know what to do with these feelings of love. The man whom he loves, Socrates (who appears to love him in return), is not beautiful (certainly not in the classical Greek understanding of the term), and does not make him feel validated (he claims that Socrates makes him feel ashamed of himself).

On the other hand, Alcibiades, though classically handsome, cannot be considered Platonically beautiful, because he has little to offer by way of virtue. He is not open to the ethical potential of his life with Socrates, nor does he wish to be (for example, he admits to covering his ears to avoid hearing Socrates' wise words). He has no inclination to move beyond "beautiful bodies" to "beautiful practices", and so on, yet Socrates loves him dearly (and in a desexualised manner). The problem, from Plato's standpoint regarding true friendship, is that it cannot be deemed to be a co-developmental ethical relationship if both parties are not equally committed to a strong desire for the ethical or the Good. Such a relationship entails being committed to facing up to and overcoming the struggles that will be encountered along the way and, most importantly, committing to such together.

To refer back to the *Phaedrus* for a moment, its charioteer analogy (though which the human soul is depicted as a tripartite composite of moderation, *hubris* and reason) depicts not only the internal struggle in the lover's soul but also the joint struggle, within the relationship, to continually aid one another's ethical development. For example, the descriptions at 254d-e and 256a-b highlight both the continuing struggle for moderation and the merits of that apparently necessary struggle.[9] Just as the internal elements of the soul must work together to produce harmony within the individual so too must the lover and the beloved work together in order to attain and maintain a harmonious (ethical) relationship.

Returning to our consideration of the *Symposium*, it must be noted that, for Plato, human love is imperfectly beautiful (though, of course, it is made possible because of the pre-existence of perfect Beauty *per se*). However, because it is imperfect, human love always has the potential to become, to develop, insofar as it is "deployed" within the context of the ethical. At its core then, Plato's account of love is committed to the imperishable "bettering" potential of love. The tragedy of Socrates' love for Alcibiades is that it can never be developed in an ethical framework because both parties are not both equally committed to this (that is, Socrates is, but Alcibiades is not). It is only Socrates who comprehends the necessity of altruism and ethical co-development for true friendship and, ultimately, Alcibiades' failure to appreciate this will cost him dearly.[10]

Plato views love, as exemplified in the philosophical friendship, as essential to one's ethical development. Furthermore, one cannot develop ethically if one is alone; one must be an active partner in an ethical (philosophical) love relationship.[11] However, Plato also realises that human love, because it is imperfect and incomplete, does not necessarily lead us to a philosophical counterpoint who wishes to be such (this is what his account of Socrates and Alcibiades purports to show). Human love is an imperfect but necessary means of realising and developing the ethical potentiality of one's soul and this is precisely what Plato is at pains to show in his philosophical account of friendship-love.

As I have stated, what the Platonic accounts of friendship attempt to demonstrate is the inextricable link between philosophy, ethics and friendship. In effect, we might say that, for Plato, ethics and friendship, and, further to this, philosophy and education are, in fact, all part of one and the same phenomenon (hence the dialogues referred to posit a link between these facets of human living). But, most striking of all in my view is the appeal to ethical co-development. For Plato, the ethical drive is also an intersubjective one and so ethics (and philosophy, and education, and friendship, and so on) is *necessarily* a shared project. This notion that a shared project can be of lasting benefit to the individuals involved in attempting to realise that project is precisely what Taylor notes has been, or is being, lost in contemporary society (albeit contemporary Western society).[12] Of course, we must note that whilst Plato writes from the perspective of an ancient Greek, Taylor writes from that of a modern Western Catholic which, of course, leads to points of divergence between the two thinkers. Nevertheless, the fact that their outlooks are not completely reconcilable with one another does not mean that they have nothing constructive to "say" to one another. On this note, I turn to my analysis of Taylor.

The Fragmentation of Secularity: Taylor's Call for a Return to Shared Projects[13]

Taylor's philosophical project has been moulded by his commitment to Christianity and, more specifically, to Roman Catholicism.[14] However, it has also been informed by his detailed studies of a plethora of influential philosophers.[15] Now, it is not, of course, my project in this chapter to present an analysis to each and every one of the many factors that have influenced Taylor's thinking. I shall instead, for the purposes of clarity, limit my comments to just one element of this thinking: the fragmentation of contemporary society.

In *A Secular Age* Taylor argues that in our "culture [that is] informed by an ethic of authenticity... The focus is on the individual, and on his/her experience" (SA 507). The result is a spiritual quest without a specifically religious frame of reference.[16] Not only this but, as he further highlights, one of the worrying features of modernity is its appeal to an apparent "self-centredness". Human beings thus find themselves at the centre of all meaning and there is thus no longer any need, nor place, for a higher meaning. As Taylor puts it: "...the general understanding of the human predicament before modernity placed us in an order where we were not at the top" (SA 15). Like Plato, Taylor is wary of a social outlook in which the transcendent (and, we might add, the metaphysical) is not attested to at an intrinsic level. What seems to matter is "me, right now" rather than, for example, "us and our community" (which, of course, includes the "me" but in a co-developmental rather than an isolated sense). Also, like Plato, he is very much of the view that the community needs to be a cohesive ethical unity; hence his concern with the loss of shared projects.[17]

Stepping away from *A Secular Age* but remaining with the themes of fragmentation and shared ethical projects, I wish to turn to another of Taylor's well-known works: *The Ethics of Authenticity*. In this text, Taylor outlines his position as follows:

> A fragmented society is one whose members find it harder and harder to identify with their political society as a community. This lack of identification may reflect an atomistic outlook, in which people come to see society purely instrumentally. But it also helps to entrench atomism, because the absence of effective common action throws people back on themselves... Successful common action can bring a sense of empowerment and also strengthen identification with the political community. (Taylor 1991, 117-118)

Taylor's position is as such that, so far as he understands it, without shared projects, or "successful common action", humanity is effectively condemned to a fragmented existence.[18] Thus, for Taylor, fragmentation is most certainly not a merely convenient philosophical notion that captures the imagination of his many readers.[19] With the idea of fragmentation he identifies what he deems to be a core feature of contemporary society: the loss of a sense of the transcendent in our newly "buffered" identities.[20] Furthermore, he notes that our lack of shared projects is a highly dangerous feature of society due to its effective ability to inhibit the development of a sense of community.[21] Taylor writes that:

> The danger is not actual despotic control but fragmentation—that is, a people increasingly less capable of forming a common purpose and carrying it out. Fragmentation arises when people come to see themselves more and more atomistically,... as less and less bound to their fellow citizens in common projects and allegiances. (Taylor 1991, 112-113)

Taylor's concern here reflects the solidarity that all Christian persons are called to and, as such, is bound up with the call to ethical responsibility.[22] If we look to the *Catechism of the Catholic Church* we can see this view precisely articulated at paragraph 1939 which states that: "The principle of solidarity, also articulated in terms of 'friendship' or 'social charity', is a direct demand of human and Christian brotherhood". If we do not value shared projects (such as friendship, education and social justice movements), we are also, as a direct consequence, in danger of losing a sense of the need for social solidarity. The Christian message is undoubtedly one of ethical co-development because we are all called to aid one another along the very tricky way that is the path of virtue.[23] We will certainly slip-up, we will fail, but we can also get up and continue to move along the way.

Also important for Taylor is the view that our communities should be respectful of diversity. However, Taylor does not hold that the establishment of shared projects would require each individual involved to be the same as the other.[24] In fact, for Taylor, our diversity is an essential feature of the society that is built upon the foundations of shared ethical projects that are expressions of what he refers to in 'A Catholic Modernity?' as "unity-across-difference" (Taylor 1999, 14). Thus our shared projects are not reductive enterprises in which each individual is simply like all of the others, rather, they are communal events in which each person is ethically co-developed and commits her/himself to this. In ethical shared projects, we achieve:

> [T]he oneness of diverse beings who come to see that they cannot attain wholeness alone, that their complementarity is essential, rather than of beings who come to accept that they are ultimately identical... (Taylor 1999, 14)

Taylor is not asserting that contemporary society is an entirely lost and immoral one (he has many positive things to say about the interface between modernity or secularization and religion). However, what he does contend is that it is losing its sense of the transcendent. Thus, a return to, and a reapplication of, Gospel values is needed if the Christian vision of life is to be retained. This can happen through shared practices that are rooted in the core Christian values such as a genuine love of one's neighbour.[25] Thus he notes that:

> We live in an extraordinary moral culture, measured against the norm of human history, in which suffering and death, through famine, flood, earthquake, pestilence, or war, can awaken worldwide movements of sympathy and practical society... Somewhere along the road, this culture ceases to be simply Christian-inspired— although people of deep Christian faith continue to be important in today's movements. (Taylor 1999, 25-26)

It is indubitable that such movements are carried out in the spirit of an ethical shared project and it would be entirely remiss of me to contend anything to the contrary simply because such movements are not always of an exclusively Christian character (in fact, it would go against the principle of "unity-across-difference"). Consider, for example, the immense value that I am arguing should be placed upon Plato's pre-Christian call to ethical co-development.

However, what Taylor is attesting to is the fact that all Christians are universally called to solidarity, to respect for the other person and to ethical co-development through attempting to build a community which will work towards the realisation of the Kingdom of God.[26] In a sense, Taylor is stating that whilst the continued ethical impetus of society (the development of the UN charter of human rights for example) is to be applauded and encouraged, care needs to be taken that the aim of such action is not located away from the transcendent (as I have noted, Plato is also very much concerned with 'aiming' at the transcendent). If we operate within a purely "immanent frame of reference" then we are in danger of missing the many gifts that Christian life offers us, and so Taylor advises us, like Plato before him, that we must "turn to transcendence... through the full-hearted love of some good beyond life" (Taylor 1999, 28-29).[27]

Concluding Remarks: Building an Ethical Community by Aiming at the Transcendent

For both Plato and Taylor, an "other-centric" approach towards what Brendan Purcell has aptly referred to as "co-personal oneness" (Purcell 1996, 266) is of critical importance in our increasingly fragmented society. According to both thinkers, a transcendent frame of reference is essential for the establishment of shared projects which will manifest themselves in the ethical co-development of those participating in such projects.

Through the example of Plato's philosophy of friendship, I have tracked the educational and philosophical merits of choosing such a path of educational co-development. Paying particular attention to the *Phaedrus* and *Symposium*, I argued that Plato's model of friendship could be viewed as an ethical micro-community which, in turn, would benefit the macro-community of the *polis*. Turning to Taylor, and thus an explicitly Christian context, I assessed his comments on the fragmentation of society and his call for shared projects. Ultimately, I have argued that Taylor, like Plato, also calls us to ethical co-development through participation in shared projects.

Essentially, I took Platonic friendship as an example of a shared practice (the practice of ethical living) which led to the ethical co-development of the two parties involved. That is not to say that there are no examples of Christian thinkers who write on the ethical value of friendship (as a case in point, Thomas Aquinas is a good example). However, by bringing Taylor and Plato together, the following shared insight has been highlighted: the value of the community, at both the micro- and the macro- level, should not be forgotten and it is our responsibility to ensure that this does not happen.

Both Taylor and Plato attest to the difficulty of human life as lived, even if Plato is not writing in a Christian atmosphere. Taylor points to the fractures in our society (our "slip-ups", if you will) which could, in part, be overcome through shared projects; Plato highlights how our potentiality for goodness can be overshadowed by our immense potentiality for badness if we do not have a loving philosophical friend to guide us along the way.[28] For both thinkers, the 'sinfulness' (this, of course, is not a term that Plato would use although it is a notion that he may be considered as having been quite sympathetic to) of humanity is a very real problem but it is not the end of the matter. They both recognise that, even in the face of adversity (perhaps even more so), our potentiality for goodness can shine through. For both, shared projects (even if they do understand them differently) can encourage and sustain a real and lasting commitment to goodness. The establishment of such shared projects, then, is in our hands.

References

Abbey, Ruth, 2000. *Charles Taylor*, Princeton & Oxford: Princeton University Press.

Abbott, Walter M., 1966. *Documents of Vatican II*, London: Geoffrey Chapman.

Barnes, Jonathan, ed., 1984. *The Complete Works of Aristotle*, Princeton: Princeton University Press.

Chapman, Geoffrey, ed., 2002. *Catechism of the Catholic Church*, London: Continuum.

Cooper, John. M. ed., 1997. *Plato: Complete Works*, Indianapolis & Cambridge: Hackforth.

Crombie, I.M., 1964. *Plato: The Midwife's Apprentice*, London: Routledge & Kegan Paul.

Donne, John, 2004. *Devotions upon Emergent Occasions*, Montana: Kessinger Publishing.

Dover, K. J., 1978. *Greek Homosexuality,* London: Duckworth.

Ferrari, G.R. F., 1987. *Listening to the Cicadas: A Study of Plato's*

Phaedrus, Cambridge: Cambridge University Press.
Gallagher, Michael Paul, 2003. *Clashing Symbols: An Introduction to Faith and Culture,* Mahwah, N.J.: Paulist Press.
Gutman, Amy, ed., 1994. *Multiculturalism: Examining the Politics of Recognition*, Princeton, N.J.: Princeton University Press.
Hannoosh, Michele, 1987. Metaphysicality and Belief: Eliot on Laforgue. *Comparative Literature* 39.4 (Autumn): 340-351.
Kastely, James L., 2002. Respecting the Rupture: Not Solving the Problem of Unity in the *Phaedrus. Philosophy and Rhetoric* 35. 2 (July): 138-152.
Levinas, Emmanuel, 1985. *Ethics and Infinity: Conversations with Philippe Nemo*, trans. Richard Cohen. Pittsburgh: Duquesne University Press.
—. 1987. *Time and the Other*, trans. Richard Cohen. Pittsburgh: Duquesne University Press.
—. 1998, trans. Alphonso Lingis. *Otherwise than Being or Beyond Essence*, trans. Alphonso Lingis, Pittsburgh: Duquesne University Press.
MacIntyre, Alasdair, 1981. *After Virtue: A Study in Moral Theory*, London: Duckworth.
—. 1999. *Dependent Rational Animals: Why Human Beings Need the Virtues,* Illinois: Open Court Publishing.
Piper, Josef, 2000. *Enthusiasm and Divine Madness: On the Platonic Dialogue Phaedrus,* trans. Richard and Clara Winston. South Bend, Indiana: St. Augustine Press.
Peperzak, Adriaan T., Simon Critchley & Robert Bernasconi, (eds.), 1996. *Emmanuel Levinas: Basic Philosophical Writings*, Indiana: Indiana University Press.
Plato, 1986, trans. C. J. Rowe. *Phaedrus*, Oxford: Aris & Phillips.
—. 1998, trans. C.J. Rowe. *Symposium*, Oxford: Aris & Phillips.
—. 1999, trans. Christopher Gill. *The Symposium*, Harmondsworth: Penguin.
—. 2003. *Republic*, Oxford: Oxford University Press.
Pope Benedict XVI, 2009. General Audience: 2nd December 2009. http://www.vatican.va/holy_father/benedict_xvi/audiences/2009/docu ments/hf_ben-xvi_aud_20091202_en.html.
Purcell, Brendan, 1996. *The Drama of Humanity: Towards a Philosophy of Humanity in History*, Frankfurt am Main: Peter Lang.
Taylor, Charles, 1989. *Sources of the Self: The Making of the Modern Identity*, Cambridge, M.A.: Harvard University Press.
—. 1991. *The Ethics of Authenticity*, Cambridge, M.A.: Harvard University

Press.
—. 1999. *A Catholic Modernity? Charles Taylor's Marianist Award Lecture*, Oxford: Oxford University Press.
Vlastos, Gregory, 1981. *Platonic Studies*, Princeton: Princeton University Press.

Part Two:

Applications and Explorations

THE CHASTE MORNING OF THE INFINITE: SECULARIZATION BETWEEN THE SOCIAL SCIENCES AND THEOLOGY

MICHAEL A. CONWAY

Introduction

When you work in a small department on a Theology Faculty it can happen that a colleague may go on sabbatical or move on to a new job and, before you know it, you are timetabled to teach an undergraduate course on something about which you know very little or even, in the worst case scenario, absolutely nothing at all! With the opening class looming and a firm resolve to remain at least one lecture ahead of the students, I reach inevitably in this situation for a good encyclopedia article. Usually I find that after doing some basic research in this way, I can relax somewhat, and, at least tell myself that I will manage the situation. And so in this tried and tested spirit I looked up the word "secularization" in the *Catholic Encyclopedia* of 1912; it's the online version, which means that it is the easiest to consult! If you do this, you will see that the entire entry is dedicated to two very important issues: firstly, the process whereby those in religious vows (both solemn and simple are mentioned) are returned, willingly, to the lay state; and secondly, the process in which Church property is transferred, unwillingly I might add, to lay ownership (as happened, for example, under Henry VIII or during the French Revolution).

If you are somewhat perplexed by this and look up the word again in the *New Catholic Encyclopedia*, this time the revised edition from 2000, you will be surprised to see that there is no mention whatsoever of either vocation or of land! In its place you read: "Secularization: A social and cultural process by which nonreligous beliefs, practices, and institutions replace religious ones in certain spheres of life."[1] It would appear that for the editors of the dictionary at least the term had undergone a radical change in the intervening years.

This change would appear to have taken place during the latter half of the nineteenth century, where in the first volume of the avant-garde *Fine*

Arts Quarterly Review of 1863 a secularization of Art was identified with "[throwing] off the conventionalism of the cloister, and instinctively [turning] to the study of nature." (Bond 1863) Indeed, the Irish historian W.E.H. Lecky referred, two years later, to a "general secularization of the European intellect" and, in particular, to "a secularization of politics," observing that "theological interests gradually ceased to be a main object of political combinations... and... the basis of authority was secularized" (Lecky 1865, I, 21; II, 36).

This shift in terminology would go hand in hand with the development of a new discipline, particularly in France, that has its roots in the positive tradition and was directed towards social reform. It turned its attention to the study of society as a positive science, and one of its founding fathers, Auguste Comte, designated the discipline with the neologism "sociology" (from the Latin *socius*, meaning companion, and the Greek *logos*, meaning word).[2] Very soon this emerging discipline would detect a significant dynamic in a multiplicity of social contexts, whereby religion and religious influences were removed steadily from the socio-cultural order through a process of "differentiation", as alternative agencies and personnel took the place of clergy and religious and, in that sense, Church control.

In its most extreme form the secularization thesis held that religion was doomed as a social and cultural reality, since its dwindling social significance would in time lead to its total disappearance from the public square. This prognosis, as we now know, proved to be somewhat inaccurate, or at least to be a little too hasty, so that by the time that the entry was drafted for the *New Catholic Encyclopedia* of the year 2000, you could argue that "secularization" had come and gone. (See, for example, Berger 1999.) But that is to be somewhat off the mark, and, in any case, for many social scientists the process of secularization is still read as an integral component of inevitable social change.

If you read this dictionary entry in the light of Charles Taylor's *A Secular Age*, it is difficult to be entirely happy with its account: of the three significations of the term outlined by the Canadian philosopher in his introduction, only one is dealt with in the entry, namely, the first that implies the shift in the cultural centrality of religion, manifested in the separation of the religious sphere from other social spheres; there is no allusion to the second, that expresses the decrease of levels of belief and religious practice, or to the third, the more interesting one from Taylor's perspective, which refers to the free character of the option to believe and to the growing difficulty of professing faith in the Western environment. This is the change in the conditions of belief: "from a society in which it was virtually impossible not to believe in God, to one in which faith, even for the staunchest believer, is one human possibility among others" (SA, 3). One might claim that—beyond the now obvious issue of the legitimate separation of Church and State—that theology has not been too interested in secularization, which begs the question if secularization as a macro process is an issue at all for theology, and if it is, then what exactly is the nature of this issue?

Secularization: The Revision of a Theory

The secularization thesis is a theoretical proposal from within what we might call historico-sociology. It claims to describe an observable socio-constellation that has to do with religion in the present and to offer an explanation of the socio-cultural processes that have led to this constellation. Not only that but on the basis of a socio-historical analysis of religion, thus understood, it projects certain determinations about religion onto the emerging future. Secularization as evidenced by this social differentiation is a slow and largely irreversible process, whereby we are witnessing an autonomization of various spheres of existence. It is to this that historians and social scientists have been paying so much attention. The classical secularization thesis would claim that this process would eventually lead to the disappearance of religion as such, and the prevailing prognosis, up to recently, was the arrival, if not of a general atheistic society, then, at the very least, of an agnostic one. This was written into the very fabric of the socio-historic development of so-called advanced societies.

This, however, did not quite go to plan and the "theory of secularization" had to be revised and reformulated, and this, from within the social sciences themselves. In many ways Charles Taylor's *A Secular Age* is part of this reappraisal and may well be a landmark study of the conditions of belief and religious practice. He has revisited the secularization debate and presented an analysis that is more competent philosophically, and more historically rooted, than earlier discussions, and is better equipped in terms of its categories to deal with what is a fascinating and enigmatic phenomenon. In the major work that is *A Secular Age* he has retrieved single-handedly entire matrices for our times that were at least neglected in cognizant discussions of the dominant culture, such as the emotional and communitarian dimension of the person, the inextinguishable demand for transcendence (albeit perhaps questionable), and the historical roots of various constructs of contemporary life (Oviedo 2008). Taylor has contributed more than most in describing secularization's historical origins, suggesting its limitations, and elaborating a precise diagnosis of the cultural matrix within which a contemporary religious decision is inscribed, and he has done this largely from within the boundaries of historico-sociology.

It is now clear that secularization is increasingly viewed, even by social scientists, as a problematic process and with time the degree to which it clarifies issues is also the degree to which the theory itself must be modified. This is not to say that it is a redundant way of approaching the issues at hand; in general it can still be argued that it is a normal development of an advanced society that says something profound about its self-understanding. Whereas the earliest stages in the development of the secularization thesis were indeed hostile to religion, treating it as either infantile (Comte) or backward (Weber), with time, and not denying the process itself, dilemmas, paradoxes, and perhaps dangers have appeared on the horizon, not just for believers, but for all of society, that have effects, that are not always welcome, on cultural expression, and, most significantly, on the realm of values. One would not wish that secularization would emerge as an initial stage in a counter-movement to the achievement of Western civilization, a kind of de-civilization. In spite of the clearly recognizable progress that has been made (such as the legitimate separation of domains) as part of the process, we are still far from understanding its consequences. One could mention, as an example, Jürgen Habermas' concern about what he calls the "derailing secularization of society" (*entgleisenden Säkularisierung der Gesellschaft*), his acknowledgement of the place of believers in society, and the role that religion might play in under-girding the moral matrix of contemporary culture (Irlenborn 2008).

Social Theory and Theology

Most of the now classical discussions of the secularization thesis understand the phenomenon to be a reality that is historically conditioned and characterized as a development in a particular period of time. This temporal dimension is essential to the narrative and is the overriding factor in all discussions and the one that is agreed on: secularization is a process that has a history. There is a story and Taylor, for example, challenges the subtraction version of this story:

> I will be making a continuing polemic against what I call "subtraction stories". Concisely put, I mean by this stories of modernity in general, and secularity in particular, which explain them by human beings having lost,

or sloughed off, or liberated themselves from certain earlier, confining horizons, or illusions, or limitations of knowledge. (SA, 22)

For brevity, let me call this *horizontal secularization*. Here the theorist—historian, social scientist, cultural anthropologist, sociologist, or even theologian—trawls through the past and constructs a socio-politico-cultural narrative on a principle of alleged continuity. I say alleged, because that is the strongest statement that can be made. The most you can hope for—or claim—is a general agreement that there is continuity. Indeed, the plurality of versions of the secularization thesis, the multiplicity of readings and interpretations of the same material, and the divergent forms it takes on separate continents confirm this indirectly. It can never be established that the continuity is absolute or ontological for those who might wish to read the dynamic in realist metaphysical terms.[3]

This, however, is precisely the problem for the theologian: not a problem of faith, but, ironically perhaps, a problem of reason. Sociological theory can never make a claim that goes beyond its phenomenological description; it can certainly tell us something, even something important, about social reality, it is not blind; but it cannot make any claim on the absolute, either in, or beyond, the empirical order. It has strictly speaking no purchase on anything that might be deemed permanent. This is why, like all discourse, it is utterly helpless in predicting the future. It may point to significant factors at play in society that in turn have an impact on future development, but it cannot describe categorically the future of our social reality. Between a description of what might be in the future and definitive prediction there is the chasm of the infinite. If it attempts to bridge this chasm—as it has—it goes beyond its own capacity and violates the principles of the discipline itself. It will also, of course, be surprised to find itself surprised by life! This is why some social scientists got it so utterly wrong in the 1970s when they predicted the utter demise of religion (Berger, for one, admits this).[4]

The essential problem was not with the unpredictability of religion or religious life, or, indeed, the contingency of life, but with taking a legitimate discourse abstracted from life and then setting it above life, so as to make claims that could in no way be justified, as though one had finally eaten of the tree of knowledge! No sociological discourse, as indeed no scientific discourse, stands above or independent of the very life from which it is itself abstracted. The abstraction itself puts definite limitations on what may be justifiably concluded from any results that might be established. Not only that, but the abstraction is a contingent one that can, and does, take a multiplicity of forms, none of which can claim in any way to be definitive.

But there is a second more serious problem with the use, or indeed misuse, of social theories for theology and for a consistent discourse on religion. In a technical sense no definitive judgment can be made on such shifting grounds: a multiplicity of narratives of secularization with different parameters (in terms of origins, process, and possible outcomes) cannot be the ground on which a decision is made for (or indeed against) the transcendent. Just as the dynamic of hermeneutics may take us around a vicious circle to infinity, the horizontal narratives of secularization open up a new infinity, namely, the infinite regression or progression (depending on how one views this process) of ever "thicker descriptions" (Clifford Geertz), any one of which, at any point, may proffer material that will radically re-cast the religious landscape for a new generation. Taylor's work now stands among the more substantial of such narratives.

This would appear to leave only one option, in this context, for religious faith: that is to jump across this abyss and simply believe! Take a leap of faith, which you might even designate as "anticipatory confidence". But, and this is the sting, that would be an heretical thing to do! Take for example, John Paul II's Encyclical, *Fides et Ratio*, on faith and reason, which states:

> Even if faith is superior to reason there can never be a true divergence between faith and reason, since the same God who reveals the mysteries and bestows the gift of faith has also placed in the human spirit the light of reason.[5]

Jumping and leaving the forum of reason behind is not an option for the theologian, even if it might be acceptable for the historian or the social scientist subject to some idea of possible subsequent falsification. This is a path that the theologian cannot take, not, mind you, because of faith, but for the sake of reason. And Weber was incorrect in his discussion of the process of disenchantment (*die Entzauberungsprozess*) in claiming that there was only one avenue open for the person of faith, and this entailed the supposedly inevitable "sacrifice of the intellect (*das Opfer des Intellektes*)" (Weber 1917).[6] So what are we to make of this?

Vertical Secularization

At the outset it must be said that horizontal secularization, which is largely a politico-socio-cultural description, cannot do justice in its presuppositions to the reality of religion and the life of faith. It studies religion only by abstracting from it, which, if taken subsequently as representative of religion, can only be a distortion of it. What it studies is not religion *per se*, its contours, its development, its future, but a trace of religion—that which is left behind, can be measured, analyzed, and written up. Religious faith cannot be reduced to a positive determination and, strictly speaking, the social sciences do not deal with religion or religious faith. In using these terms, they benefit from a common familiarity with these categories, but what they treat is only an aspect, and it is not even an essential one. Horizontal secularization is much more an archaeology than a living science of religion. This is not to denigrate the discipline as a legitimate and important study (even for theology), but rather to relativize appropriately its preoccupation and mark the corresponding lacunae of its methodology from the perspective of theology. What it studies, *historia*, is remnants, deposits left in the wake of a living reality, whose life is always elsewhere and otherwise. This is congenital to the discipline: it cannot study this life as part of its competency because at its origin, in its very presuppositions, it must effect what I will term a *vertical secularization* in order to begin its study, which, strictly speaking is a positive empirical enquiry. This is a necessary requirement of the methodology of the social scientist, as it is of any science (be it physics, politics, economics, etc.). To paraphrase Alistair Cambell, Tony Blair's Press Secretary: it must not do God! Technically, social science does not, and cannot, do religion because, as it is practised (that's social science, not religion), it must not. Taylor's attempt to date may well be the most ambitious—which, no doubt because of his Hegelian background, strives to take the processes of history seriously—but it falls squarely within the tradition.[7]

It is vital that these boundaries are not only clearly marked out and respected, but also that the ensuing limitation on whatever results may follow is acknowledged. The synthesis that is religious faith includes, of course, objective factors (transmitted through tradition and witness and open to positive enquiry), but, it also integrates as essential into this same synthesis, not only personal motives that give faith its most secure foundation, but also the supernatural witness that is given interiorly. Socio-cultural analysis cannot, and indeed ought not, take this complexity into account. It does not even attend to these possibilities. This limitation is an a priori option that must be taken; it is not necessarily the only legitimate one. From a theologian's perspective it is not even the most reasonable one! The initial rejection of the transcendent that is required in a positive methodology (that is limited to attending to the empirical) haunts the entire discourse of horizontal secularization, no matter what the outcome is to which one aspires.[8]

Nietzsche and the Historical

In his powerful essay on the use of history for life, someone who is always worth listening to, Friedrich Nietzsche, opens his discourse with a quotation from Goethe:

> Uebrigens ist mir alles verhasst, was mich bloss belehrt, ohne meine Thätigkeit zu vermehren oder unmittelbar zu beleben. (Besides, I hate everything that merely instructs me, without increasing or directly invigorating my activity). (Nietzsche 1874, 241)

Here the contrast between instructing and invigorating is interesting, between the process and the moment, between the horizontal and the vertical, the archeological and the genealogical. It is, of course, typical of the early Nietzsche: Apollo or Dionysios, the scientist or the mystic—as they say on *Big Brother*: you decide!

What Nietzsche realizes is that life ought not to be subsumed into the straightjacket of any narrative and, particularly, in this case, the historical one. Not only is it illegitimate in the sense of going beyond what is justifiable in terms of reason, but it also reduces or stunts life itself in the very moment. It secularizes it: draws it fully into the epoch, into the narrative of time past and, in doing so, violates it.[9] And this, Nietzsche underlines is not just for an individual, but for a people, and even for a culture: "There is a degree of sleeplessness, of rumination, of the historical sense, which is harmful and ultimately fatal to what is living, be it a man, or a people, or a culture."[10]

For Nietzsche, to inhabit the present, to experience it, to know it, we must be able, to some degree, to forget the past, the sixteenth century, the Enlightenment, the sixties, last year, last week, and even this morning! He terms this the unhistorical: "the unhistorical is like a surrounding atmosphere within which alone life can germinate so as to disappear again with the destruction of this atmosphere."[11] This cannot, of course, be a matter of exclusivity: without history, there would be no identity, personal or communal; but when all is subsumed to history, we are no longer dealing with life, but with a simulacrum. Not only that, but, when the totality of life is framed in the categories of historical narrative, we imprison ourselves in the phrases and opinions of others and cut off our very creativity, both as an individual and as a culture. For Nietzsche, history is always subservient to life and life is always more than history. He observes that "the study of history is salutary and future-promising only in the wake of a mighty new current of life, of an evolving culture, for example, that is to say only when it is dominated and lead by a higher force and does not itself lead and dominate."[12]

Vertical Secularization and the Life of Faith

But why is it that life *per se*, the present moment, the unhistorical (in Nietzsche's sense) is so important for a discourse on religion? What exactly is it that that, which I am calling vertical secularization, has savagely limited to the detriment of a discourse on religion? Vertical secularization prejudges the very matter that it wishes to explore, namely, the relationship that religion maintains in a particular culture with its own internal structures and with the individual *per se*. At the outset vertical secularization claims firstly to know what "religion" is and defines it from an alien perspective that is indebted to an "objective" methodology borrowed for the most part from the natural sciences. Claiming to treat religion, or to be able to treat religion, in a purely theoretical, objective fashion, and claiming to reserve judgment until the end of one's exploration of the phenomenon itself that is religion, is to totally denature the very substance—if I may use that term—of what one wishes to explore.

If faith, religion, religious practice, rites, sacramental realities, liturgy, and sacred texts (I have found all of these spoken of in textbooks of the social sciences) are to be studied in their particular character and specific distinction from other phenomena—and they can be studied as phenomena: i.e., not as revealed realities, but as realities that might be revelatory—then precisely a reductive theoretical reflection is utterly inadequate in determining them *in their specificity*. On the one hand, effectively, one cannot truly know such phenomena except to some degree in living them (they are congenitally personal) and one cannot live them without first having judged them as livable. This means that the normative preoccupation is neither external, nor subsequent, nor accessory, but is constitutive of the fact itself. This applies equally to freedom or to morality: it cannot be known merely on the theoretical plane, one has to act.

The understanding of religion that is adopted by the social scientist is only valid in retrospect, for the past, for what is already *accomplished*: whereas religious life itself is completely suspended (like the moral life) from what is to be realized, to future realities that are always singular with respect to a thinking person gifted with freedom.[13] It is fundamentally personal and creative of the world, and there is always the ulterior in it. In a very perceptive comment on Taylor's book, Peter E. Gordon of Harvard remarks:

> If the typical modern believer (and perhaps Taylor himself) truly finds the possibility of *his own* disbelief 'inconceivable,' then *that* belief is not optional at all. But then modern belief in *this* sense seems no *less* 'axiomatic' than pre-modern belief. It is a pity that Taylor does not address this issue. (Gordon 2008, 655)

In many ways this points to the Achilles' heel of the entire enterprise that is *A Secular World* in terms of how it deals specifically with faith and religion. It is the direction in which Taylor does not go, and, at least from a theologian's perspective, it really would have been the most interesting!

In making the mistake of assimilating the religious in its totality to the domain of positive facts that can be studied physically, empirically, statistically, historically, politically and so on, one is exposed—no matter how one wishes to respect the evident originality of this fact, and no matter how one searches a rule of understanding for the future—to falling into a sort of socio-cultural idealism that remains impotent in clarifying, in directing, or in justifying the socio-religious nisus itself: a history of the religion of yesterday would not, no matter how legitimate and how useful it is, suffice to constitute any religious phenomenon, or proffer the rule of its future, which we might seek to clarify.

Beyond a Reductive Positive Methodology

How is one to contend with this vertical secularization? Is it simply necessary at a methodological level? How is one to treat any religious phenomenon according to a veritable positive spirit that is not, from the outset, radically reductive in its methodology? Is this even possible? Is it possible to study religion at all in the analytic positive framework, so that reason maintains a critical function in examining religious belief, practice, and social structures?

For this paper, I will limit myself to two brief points: firstly, indicating a possible way forward in dealing with this particularly complex matter; and secondly, pointing to the enlargement of perspective that this might proffer over against the more traditional framing of these issues.

In his clash with Émile Durkeim over a cognate matter, Maurice Blondel is the one Catholic philosopher who dealt explicitly with these issues from *within* the positive tradition and opened an avenue for a critical engagement with theology (see Blondel 1893 and 1906). It is extraordinary that Taylor, a Catholic and a Francophile, does not draw on any of his philosophy. Blondel suggests that rather than examining such issues from within the subject/object dichotomy of a necessarily reductive positivism, we ought to ask how to define the immanent relation of the implicit to the explicit in human action.[14] The issue then becomes that of how one is to realize the progressive (and indeed critical) adequation of what are fundamental and obscure exigencies of human consciousness with the normal satisfactions of life and the ends to which one aspires. It is a matter of examining how the immanent desire in human consciousness is satisfied through ever-expanding moments of the phenomenological order that are inevitably willed and integrated as constitutive of the real. The significant issue is that this can still be done critically and from within the positive methodology (see Conway, 2000). It is clear that the religious impulse (its primary beliefs, its social structures, its dogmatic tenets, its specific practices, etc.) is a given that is as real as any other positive fact and is open to the same critical analysis in terms of its ability to respond to, to explain, and to make explicit that which is implicit in human action.

This is to reframe the entire problematic and facilitates a deeper dichotomy than that, say, between the "background" and the "buffered self." To render the background entirely discursive in one's investigation (as, say, Taylor does) is to prejudge the normative spontaneity, not only of individual life, but also of the social life of the community, its structures, its dynamics, its hierarchies, etc. Human action harbours powers and energies that cannot be comprehensively rendered in theory abstracted from its origin in practice. That is why the level of practice *per se*, which can never be subsumed into thought, no matter how comprehensive it strives to be, is vital in understanding religion.

Taylor and Theology?

Theology, as a discipline, has been less radically affected by the rise of the reductive version of the positive methodology than many other disciplines. This is so since, on the one hand, in its own desire to overcome the reductive scholasticism that had come to dominate theology (at least in Catholic circles) towards the end of the nineteenth century, it already had to deal with many of the issues that have emerged in the positivist tradition in science and philosophy. On the other hand, it has always maintained its continuity with the medieval theological tradition that kept alive the issues to which I am drawing your attention under the rubric of final causality. The language and register may now be dated, but the issues, at once philosophical and theological, will not go away. And the social sciences only escape them to the degree that they remain an abstract study.

One could argue that Christian theology has always been concerned with this vertical secularization, albeit in a range of differing categories that depend on any particular historical period. St Augustine in his controversy with Pelagius debated the vertical secularization of human action by means of the language of grace. Various discussions span the centuries and have, as one might expect, at every stage impacted on horizontal secularization. Curiously, Taylor avoids any substantial discussion on this vertical plane: there is little engagement with, for example, twentieth century theology per se, no mention of Barth, Bultmann, Chenu, Lonergan (a fellow Canadian), Metz, Newman, Rahner, Schillebeeckx, and, the most surprising of all, no engagement with De Lubac's monumental work in historical theology.[15] There are occasional references, among others, to Congar, Daniélou, Tillich, and Von Balthasar, but mostly for non-theological arguments. This is a rather perplexing state of affairs: that one would write a major work on religion (albeit in another register) and never really consult the theologians! Does this say something, implicitly, about contemporary academic discourse on religion? I do wonder!

The Autonomy and Diversity of Domains

The significant achievement of enlightenment rationality in that region that is concerned with religion and the related secularization process has been the recognition of distinct domains of competency that remain relatively autonomous: the most obvious one being the separation of Church and State. The separation of domains covers a wide spectrum of disciplines and areas of specific competency: physics and economics, for example, are deemed to be independent of, say, religion or psychology. No one would seriously question this in the terms of the disciplines: one does not include religious considerations in attempting to solve Einstein's Field Equations! Yet this separation needs to be carefully clarified if we are to avoid an absolute fragmentation of our world and leave unfettered more sinister dynamics in society. No autonomous domain can be left entirely to its own devices: perhaps it is only now that we are fully aware of the risks of so-called self-regulation. The autonomy itself that spheres of life enjoy must be carefully and clearly delineated. This goes, of course, for religion too as a social reality.

To clarify more precisely the diversity and separation of domains that is so important to contemporary politics, economics, education, medicine, religion, and so on, one first needs to recognize that the autonomy of the various spheres of life is grounded fundamentally *only* with respect to the facts themselves that constitute the individual domains. They are autonomous in the region marked out by their initial specifications and determinations. They each have their own procedures, their own working data, and their own internal logic; within this domain they each aim at a reasoned analysis and a coherent presentation of their results. But beyond or outside this region they have no special competency whatsoever. It is only through an initial *abstraction* that they come to be separate domains of study and achieve their theoretical status. Not only that, but, the range of facts that constitute any autonomous area is always in the process of becoming, of being updated, of being added to, and of being restructured.[16] They do not even need to be internally coherent.[17] There is nothing substantial or essential about such epistemological regions: they never enjoy an ontological status in the strict sense of the term. There is no direct grasp or apprehension of the real; in particular they are not fragments of an ontology that might in some way be added together to make up the totality of the real.[18] It is precisely because of this limited bearing that they cannot, rightly, tolerate any outside interference. And for this reason in a strict sense religious faith does not overlap with these respective domains. Of course they are *all* always subservient to a total end that inevitably lies outside the series of the fragmentary investigations that they undertake. In this sense each domain is dependent on the totality of concrete life and practice to which it is always answerable.

If one is to conduct an intelligent, rational dialogue on, for example, the interaction between the social sciences and religion it is essential to be critical in the face of premature conclusions, conscious of the partial and subaltern character of one's determinations, and indeed modest in the face of the complexity of the very life one wishes to explore. To speak in this context of falsification, as Peter Berger does, is highly misleading (see, for example, Berger 2008, 10). It is not a matter of attaining a falsified theory as though one moved incrementally (or even exponentially) towards a true theory that would finally be un-falsifiable. It is rather a matter of a better theory that explains more comprehensively a set of contingent positive facts. Social theories can (and indeed will) be developed to infinity: they will emerge in different ages, according to different concerns, to explain differing sets of initial data. By its very genesis all socio-cultural theory, because of the various levels of contingency operating within it, is limited and, therefore, can be "falsified" in the positive sense. The social sciences are not in a position to make a comprehensive judgment on the concrete and total reality out of which they themselves have emerged. Their initial data is always hypothetical; their results are always provisional, and their subject matter will change *ad infinitum*: there will always be a new generation of social scientists, who will always have something new to say!

Theology and the Social Sciences

It would now seem that we have come to a crossroads in our discussion of secularization, particularly when viewed from the interface between the social sciences and theology. The achievements, determinations, results, of the social sciences do not, indeed cannot, stand in contradiction to the life of faith. Rather these very achievements give to faith a better account, not only of the intimate solidity of its certitude, but also of the varied expanse of its natural supports. We should indeed continue to put energy into ever-denser narratives of horizontal secularization that will continue to bear fruit in helping us understand our past so as to prepare for our future, and, in this, the social sciences have a lead role to play. However, we now need this horizontal research to be accompanied by a series of equally important studies that critically clarify the limited nature of their achievement and that restores to our intellectual endeavour that vertical exploration that will not only clarify the precise boundaries that are inherent in any study of the immanent order, but also proffer principles of delineation and re-establish legitimate domains of research in the exploration of concrete life. A new conception of the solidarity *beyond* the abstract autonomy of the particular spheres (education, politics, economics, medicine, law, religion, etc), of their collaboration, and their inter-independence is required that will overcome the radical separation of domains that in no small way contributes to socio-cultural decay.

It can be said that secularization as a process is in fact a Christian phenomenon. All discussion on, and in relation to, secularization is a parasitic logos whose host is Christianity and every statement—positive or negative—is ultimately a statement too about Christianity. If there is a newfound freedom it is of a Christian origin; if there are inherent fears then they are Christian fears. If modernity (or postmodernity) looks over its grown-up shoulders at its aged Christian parent and declares that it is a myth, irrational, obscurantist, and oppressive, then surely it begs the question of how this teenager is to explain that something so mature, rational, and healthy could have come from such a naïve or even unreal source? (See Valadier 2007, 256-57)

The freedom that has been procured for institutions, for areas of research, for various orders in society, and so on, is to be acknowledged and welcomed as part of the goodness of the created order. Indeed, the Second Vatican Council calls for respect for the autonomy of earthly affairs (*Gaudium et spes*, 36). It belongs at the very heart of a theology of creation and redemption and more specifically to the economy of grace and freedom. From the perspective of theology, it cannot be read as something purely negative, or, for that matter, as a threat to religion and to life lived in liturgy with the transcendent.

However, the so-called desecularization process is not now without its dangers for society and for religion, and it is incumbent on theology, in particular, to reflect carefully on this post-Enlightenment re-enchantment of the world. The achievement of the Enlightenment and the concomitant process of secularization—in particular the legitimate autonomization of various domains—must not now be threatened. It must, rather, be integrated firmly into a theology that speaks critically to this re-enchantment in the light of the lessons learned since the Enlightenment. In short, religion must not be allowed to re-emerge in a fundamentalist (or indeed fideist) register.

It is for this reason that I am now suggesting that we must turn to a careful study of vertical secularization, so as to clarify more carefully and consistently the boundaries, legitimate powers, and healthy decision-making structures, which might guide this new phase in the socio-political development of the West. The technological, scientific, economic-driven world that is now to the fore in human consciousness needs to be re-integrated in a humanistic, value-centered, and even sacral cosmos if we are to preserve an equilibrium within which the human person might, to use Taylor's word, flourish. It is only along the vertical axis that this can be achieved; and it is also this axis that opens again for the Western mind the legitimate question of religion and the possibility of an engagement with the dawn of the infinite.

I would like to finish with a poem by Les Murray called 'The Blueprint':

The Blueprint

Whatever the great religions offer
it is their afterlife their people want:
Heaven, Paradise, higher reincarnations,
together or apart—
for these they will love God, or butter Karma.

Afterlife. Wherever it already exists
people will crawl into ships' frameworks
or suffocate in truck containers to reach it,

they will conjure it down
on their beaches and their pooled clay streets,
inject it, marry into it.

The secular withholds any obeisance
that is aimed upwards.
It must go declaratively down,
but an "accident of consciousness
between two eternities of oblivion"—
all of us have done one
of those eternities already, on our ear.

After the second, we require an afterlife
greater and stranger than science gives us now,
life like, then unlike
what mortal life has been.

References

Berger, Peter L. 1999. The Desecularization of the World: A Global Overview. In Berger, ed., *The Desecularization of the World: Resurgent Religion and World Politics*, 1-18. Grand Rapids, Michigan: Eerdmans.

Berger, Peter, Grace Davie, and Effie Fokas, eds. 2008. *Religious America, Secular Europe? A Theme and Variations*. Bodmin: Ashgate.

Blondel, Maurice. 1906. Lettre à la Société Française de Philosophie concernant le rapport de E. Durkheim, « Détermination du fait Moral ». In Maurice Blondel, *Oeuvres complètes*. 1997. vol. II, ed. Claude Troisfontaines, 571-78. Paris : PUF.

—. 1893. L'Action. Essai d'une critique de la vie et d'une science de la pratique. In Maurice Blondel, 1995. *Œuvres complètes*, vol. I, ed. Claude Troisfontaines. Paris : PUF. For the English translation, see Maurice Blondel, *Action. Essay on a Critique of life and a Science of Practice*. 1984. Trans. Oliva Blanchette, Notre Dame: Notre Dame Press.

Bond, Edward Augustus. 1863. Description of an Illuminated Latin Psalter. *Fine Arts Quarterly* 1: 77-96.

Conway, Michael A. 2000. *The Science of Life: Maurice Blondel's philosophy of action and the scientific method*. Frankfurt a.M.: Peter Lang.

—. 2006. A Positive Phenomenology. The Structure of Maurice Blondel's Early Philosophy. *Heythrop Journal* 47: 579-600.

Gordon, Peter E. 2008. The Place of the Sacred in the Absence of God: Charles Taylor's *A Secular Age*. *Journal of the History of Ideas* 69: 647-73.

Hegel, Georg Wilhelm Friedrich. 1821. Grundlinien der Philosophie des Rechts. In G.W.F. Hegel, *Sämtliche Werke*, ed. H. Glockner. 1950. Vol. 7, Vorrede. Stuttgart: Frommann Verlag.

Irlenborn, Bernd. 2008. Religion und öffentliche Vernunft: Zur Bedeutung des christlichen Glaubens bei Jürgen Haberman.*Freiburger Zeitschirft für Philosophie und Theologie* 55: 380-400.

Lecky, W.E.H. 1865. *History of the Rise and Influence of the Spirit of Rationalism in Europe*, 1910, vol I & II. London: Watts and Co.

Nietzsche, Friedrich. 1874. Unzeitgemässes Betrachtungen, Zweites Stück: Vom Nutzen und Nachteil der Historie für das Leben. In Friedrich Nietzsche, *Nietzsche Werke: Kritische Gesamtausgabe*, ed. Giorgio Colli and Mazzino Montinari, 1972, Vol. III.1, 239-330. Berlin: De Gruyter.

Oviedo, Lluis. 2008. I Cristiani in un Mondo Secolarizzato: La Proposta di Charles Taylor. *Antonianum* 83: 511-23.

Störig, H.J. 1965. *Kleine Weltgeschichte der Wissenschaft*. Berlin: Kohnhammer.

Taylor, Charles. 2007. *A Secular Age*. Harvard: Harvard University.

Valadier, Paul. 2007. *Détresse du Politique, Force du religieux*. Paris: Du Seuil.

Weber, Max. 1917. Wissenschaft als Beruf. In Max Weber, *Gesammelte Aufsätze zur Wissenschaftslehre*, ed. Johannes Winckelmann, 1985, 582-613. Tübingen: J.C.B. Mohr.

Translating Taylor:
Pastoral and Theologial Horizons

Michael Paul Gallagher

When Charles Taylor was 29 and completing his doctorate in Oxford, he published an article entitled "Clericalism" in a quarterly edited by the Benedictine monks of Downside Abbey. This youthful piece voices a sometimes angry critique about the marginal role allowed to lay people in the Catholic Church. He had been reading, he says, such French theologians as Congar, Chenu and de Lubac who were to be such key figures during the Second Vatican Council, an event still two years in the future. Here was a brilliant young Canadian Catholic, who was finding intellectual nourishment for himself in theology, and offering early indications of his future interest in the question of the secular. On the first page he offered this blunt judgement: "In many churches the faithful are systematically excluded from any active or indeed conscious participation in the liturgy" (Taylor 1960, 167). Notice the words "system" and "participation". Later in life he will become a great discerner of cultural systems and he will also become a fighter not only for political participation in Canada, but, more to our purposes, he will come to see Christian faith in terms of a participation in God's own loving.

This 1960 article goes beyond complaining about the clergy robbing the laity of power. Clericalism, it argues, had been responsible for isolating the Church from cultural developments of recent centuries. It embodied a rejection of humanism and a downgrading of human freedom, attitudes rooted in an image of God as utterly separate from history. So the secular world, the world of lay Catholics, was seen as ultimately unimportant and the Church of a merely closed or defensive clericalism assumed a ghetto stance against modernity. Instead, according to the young Taylor, believers can and should embrace the adventure of history with "energy, devotion and courage" (Taylor 1960, 179). Why? Because an Incarnation in history "requires that there be a humanism" and because it is through history that we move towards God (Taylor 1960, 180).

This remarkable article, prophetic of Vatican II in ways, can serve as an overture to the symphony of Taylor's thinking that I want to summarise here. It is evidence of his early passion for religious themes, a dimension that was never absent in his writings, but one which often went quiet, or stayed in the background, only to come to the fore again in the last decade. To take a more recent example: in 2008 Taylor wrote a short reflection on the barriers between intellectuals and religion today. Nearly half a century after that Downside piece, his critique now is directed against a more secular suppression, against an academic form of clericalism, whereby philosophers, sociologists and historians find it perfectly normal to ignore the spiritual dimension of life as unworthy of attention. Because of this exclusion, Taylor argues these disciplines render themselves incapable of exploring vital issues of today. In the secularised world of today "the result is that people forget the answers to the great questions of life. But what is worse is that they even forget the questions" (Taylor 2008, 31). It is typical of Taylor to fight excesses or simplifications on various fronts.

With that background I come to my plan for this essay, which aims to provide an introduction to Taylor for those engaged in religious education. I propose to explore five major dimensions of Taylor's thought, all of them touching on the culture that conditions faith today. This presentation will not focus on Ireland, but let me briefly mention two relevant themes in Taylor. He occasionally comments directly on Ireland, remarking in *A Secular Age* that when the "link between national identity and Catholicism" disappears, a falling off in faith can happen "with a bewildering rapidity" (SA 491)—surely a comment that is finding a surprising verification in recent times. Concerning still more painful issues, the closing pages of *Sources of the Self* acknowledge the "terrible record" of "appalling destruction wrought in the name of faith", adding that, in spite everything believers try to hold onto, a promise of "a divine affirmation of the human, more total than humans can ever attain unaided" (Taylor 1989, 521). In a similar fashion, responding to commentators on his *A Catholic Modernity*, he recognises that "there is a lot of hostility out there", adding that we need to be "aware of what anger is doing for us". And he ends with this comment: "changing the tone might be the essential prelude to changing the content" (Taylor 1999, 123-125). As will be seen, on many issues he invites us to deepen the agenda and to develop more complex versions of our situation and our story.

Five Dimensions

Five important themes in Taylor's work offer both light and challenge to people concerned about religious education. The plan is to explore his key positions on modernity, secularisation, religion in general, Christianity in particular, and forms of faith for today. By doing so we can also appreciate his goal to understand "what it is to live in an age of secularity" (SA 678).

A constant concern of Taylor's has been to discern the complex *impact of modernity*. He is famous for his defence of the ideal of personal authenticity born from modernity. But again and again he voices his worry about how this high human goal can descend into individualist self-closure, or a subjectivism that "would tend towards emptiness" (Taylor 1989, 507). In typical fashion, he asks, how we are to "rescue admirable ideals from sliding into demeaning modes of realisation" (Taylor 1999, 37). What was "great" in modernity can so easily become "shallow or dangerous" (Taylor 1991, 120). As one commentator has put it, "the pre-modern understanding of identity is no longer tenable, but neither is the modern understanding. The subjectivism of modernity is a dead end" (Braman 2008, 30).

In various texts Taylor situates his own position between the camp of the "knockers" and of the "boosters" of modernity. One group laments about everything modern, whereas the other exalts the achievements without any recognition of shadows. "The cultural pessimism of the knockers is not only mistaken, it is also counter-productive" (Taylor 1991, 79). In this light Taylor wants us to acknowledge the shrinking of our human horizons and hopes when a "soft relativism" becomes the dominant lifestyle (Taylor 1991, 21, 45), or when self-fulfilment forgets commitments to the fulfilment of others. In short, achieving authenticity will always involve a struggle against trivialising and reductive images. The pertinence of all this for religious formation seems obvious: it implies that in contemporary circumstances we cannot simply transmit faith or be satisfied with a neutral description of religious positions. Taylor would indicate a more subtle and ambitious aim, whereby we help young people to recognise the battle zones of our culture, to sift out the sources of silliness from the sources of a fullness worthy of our hopes. Surely education can offer skills of discernment and decision—trusting, as he says, that our freedom is not zero and that we can, if we really want, "remake the conditions of our own existence" (Taylor 1991, 100-101).

Secondly, there is his insistence that a deeper story needs to be told concerning *secularisation*. Here he invites us to look beyond sociological externalism or determinism: in his view it is superficial to talk simply about the decline of religious practice, or of an inevitable loss of faith in an age of science and technology. He resists the master narrative of much sociology whereby religion inevitably retreats when instrumental modernity enters the scene. In his view a deeper and more significant secularisation happens on the level of our self-images and dispositions, in those less conscious zones that constitute our "social imaginary". "The interesting story is not simply one of decline" but of "new ways of existing both in and out of relation with God" (SA 437). "Modernity is secular... in the fact that religion occupies a different place" (Taylor 2004, 194).

In this way he refocuses the debate from visible and measurable social changes, important in themselves, to the more delicate movements of our spiritual or moral sensibility. Or as Seamus Heaney says in one of his poems ("Out of this world") about an eclipse of faith: "the loss occurred off stage", hence away from the glare of controversy or media debates or without much explicit thinking. For Taylor, too, secularisation involves much more than quantifiable changes of behaviour. He invites us to talk less about explicit loss of beliefs and to focus more on our "background of unformulated understandings", where we live on an "embodied" or "symbolic" level of "habitus" (Taylor 1995, 28-29). He calls us to deepen the agenda from outer and explicit factors to the zone of our shared images and often hidden assumptions about life. He moves our attention from the merely sociological to the spiritual sensibility of a whole generation, giving particular emphasis to the crucial area of community roots: "without a framework, one falls into a life that is spiritually senseless" (Taylor 1989, 18).

Once again he would seem to challenge religious education to develop tools for a more subtle cultural reflection, because if secularisation entails a "disembedding" of individuals from older roots of belonging, what is at stake is not simply a social development but an "identity shift" on the level of our imagination. On this last point Taylor's approach could fruitfully be situated in a rich tradition of exploring our pre-conceptual dispositions, ranging from John Henry Newman (whom he never seems to mention) on the "religious imagination" to Paul Ricoeur on imagination as our prophetic threshold of possibility and of action.

Our third area concerns the *role of religion* in this cultural battleground of human meaning, values and images. Let me highlight one of Taylor's asides that caused surprising reactions among my theology students in Rome during a discussion of his book. It has to do with his rejection of the claim "that the main point of religion is solving the human need for meaning" (SA 718). In its context in *A Secular Age*, this theme arises when Taylor is asking himself about a certain flatness of horizon provoked by modern culture. Can we perhaps suffer from a "malaise of immanence" due to the "eclipse of transcendence" (SA 308-309)? If so, one response would be to propose religion as meeting that gap. About this Taylor has serious reservations. He is unwilling to let a functional or Durkheimian approach to religion have a monopoly (as it often does in sociological writing). To assume that the "essence of religion" lies in answering our human need for meaning is to accept as "the final truth on things" what he calls the "view from here" (SA 718), where "here" can imply one of the unquestioned biases of modernity, whereby an individualist perspective shapes our sense of what is real or what is unreal. Thus unexamined subjective perceptions become the measure of truth, including religious truth, as expressed in statements like "I feel comfortable with that" or "It makes sense to me right now". Taylor declares his unease with all this, and his unwillingness to accept that religion exists simply to satisfy the quest for a significant life. In place of this anthropocentrism he insists on religion as a source of graced transformation. In fact "the perspective of a transformation of human beings" takes them beyond what "is normally understood as human flourishing" (SA 430). Ultimately, faith is a question that links truth with freedom because it involves "choosing ourselves in the light of the infinite" (Taylor 1989, 449). This is the peak of our self-transcendence.

If one seeks to connect this emphasis with the field of religious education, Taylor can be seen as touching a sensitive and controversial area, sometimes summed up in the contrast between theology and religious studies. The former insists on grounding itself in a faith commitment, whereas the latter prefers to describe religion phenomenologically, from outside any existential involvement. Taylor would seem to favour theology in the stricter sense and to echo a long line of theological thought about the subtle temptations of modernity. To mention just two famous examples: John Henry Newman wrote eloquently and ironically about what he called "religion of the day", in other words the tendency of the comfortable British Empire at its peak to cultivate a tame version of the gospel for inner consolation. In more recent times the German theologian Johann Baptist Metz has written with similar energy about a "bourgeois" reduction of Christianity, without passion, without drama, without disturbance and keeping a safe distance from the suffering all around us.

That over-humanising temptation is inevitably present in our culture of religious education today: we want to make faith real for people, and that is an admirable and passionate hope. But in our desire to communicate faith in a comprehensible way, to become all things to all kind of people, as St Paul advised, there lurks the subtle danger—that we rob the gospel of its disturbing beauty and uniqueness. Of course we have to go into people's hearts by the doorway of their imaginations and perceptions. Of course religion gives meaning to life, but it does so much more, and it can be difficult to find the right language for that so-much-more. As Taylor has quipped, distancing himself from Marcel Gauchet, "a purely cultural account of religion would be like Hamlet without the Prince" (Taylor 1997, xv).

That brings us to Taylor's occasional but numerous comments on *Christianity* as he understands it. What he sees as specific to Christian faith is captured in this sentence from *A Secular Age*: "God's initiative is to enter, in full vulnerability, the heart of the resistance, to be among humans, offering participation in the divine life" (SA 654), and in this light "we have to struggle to recover a sense of what the Incarnation can mean" (SA 753). As a philosopher Taylor often seems hesitant to elaborate on these more theological insights, but what is striking is his repeated emphasis on Christian revelation as empowering and transforming us through a sharing in God's own life and love. In an eloquent passage in *A Catholic Modernity*, he wonders whether we can imagine such a high source of love as a reality for human beings. Here are his own words (in a somewhat complex sentence): "our being in the image of God is also our standing among others in the stream of love which is that facet of God's life we try to grasp, very inadequately, in speaking of the Trinity. Now it makes a whole lot of difference whether you think this kind of love is a possibility for us humans. I think it is, but only to the extent that we open ourselves to God" (Taylor 1999, 35).

Once again the stimulus for religious educators seems evident. There are many convergences that unite various religious traditions, and yet we need to find both intellectual and spiritual ways of communicating the differentness of Christianity, its specific identity and call. If some of our students are going to be atheists, let us hope that their religious education will have awoken them to the grit and drama of a gospel they are unable to believe, thus saving them from the shallower unbelief of a merely fashionable distaste for Church.

Our fifth and final dimension has to do with how Taylor discerns some new *forms of faith* emerging for today's culture. In many writings he has insisted that cultural change spells not the death of faith as such but a challenge to older embodiments or languages of faith. As early as 1965 Bernard Lonergan, the most distinguished of Canadian theologians (whom, strangely, Taylor never mentions), had remarked that what is called a crisis of faith is more often than not a crisis of culture, where older assumptions fragment and older expressions lose their impact.

Taylor would add that a time of cultural upheaval can in fact purify our expressions of faith where our previous images of God were "too simple, too anthropocentric, too indulgent" and he adds, that faith "has survived... by evolving" (Taylor 2002, 57, 104). More pastorally he suggests that our different cultural sensibility requires a different spiritual formation for future believers. Although he does not quote Karl Rahner in *A Secular Age*, his approach seems in tune with a famous but often misunderstood Rahnerian claim that the believers of the future will have to be mystics or else they will not be believers. The meaning of "mystic" here is not the high sense of the contemplatives but a capacity to recognise God's presence and guidance in our ordinary human experience. Taylor also suggests that "we are just at the beginning of a new age of religious searching, whose outcome no one can foresee" (SA 535), but what seems sure is that faith commitment today need to be less "collective" and "more personal", "more christocentric" (SA 541), and also a path of gradual discovery (or mystagogy to echo Rahner again), because in Taylor's words "God is slowly educating mankind, slowly turning it, transforming it from within" (SA 668).

In this light we can see the catechetical potential of the final chapter of *A Secular Age*, entitled "Conversions", where Taylor explores narratives of transformed lives where people open unexpectedly to the surprise of God. His narratives of grace range from Francis of Assisi to Bede Griffiths or Jean Vanier, and include poets such as Péguy and Hopkins. The implicit argument here is that we need some kind of religious experience or "epiphany" to ground our believing today and that awakening the spiritual imagination is a key moment in preparing fragmented moderns for the word of God. In Taylor's own words, "a new poetic language can serve to find a way", in order to let "the work of God" retrieve "experiential reality" (SA 757). To stress the power of narrative and of symbol, of biography and witness, is not a novelty in the world of religious education. What is fascinating is to see Taylor also arriving at this emphasis at the end of his lengthy study of the secular.

An Imaginary Monologue

As a closing section of this paper, I want to change wavelength and to risk a little experiment in imagination. I wonder what might Charles Taylor say to those involved in religious education today. And so I have tried to create a monologue in his voice, so to speak. What might he say?

First of all learn to take on board the hugeness of the cultural revolution you have experienced, and continue to experience. It involves much more than a set of easily explainable social changes. It entails more than a different set of ideas. In place of a seemingly stable identity, people find themselves in an ocean of cross currents, of multiple identities on the move. For many the emerging context has meant a painful and even sudden uprooting on the level of their religious self-images. In particular it has displaced Church-based religion from its previous centrality: forms of religious belonging and expression that then seemed so secure have come to appear unreal, out of touch or even oppressive. Previously religious belief was the default option, and now unbelief or at least a large-scale unchurching has taken its place. The cultural context has swung from one of smooth pre-modern inheritance of meaning through a fast "disembedding" along "modern" lines, with an ambiguous individualism becoming dominant, to a later situation of confusion, fragmentation, dispersal, or drifting that some people call post-modern. And so the agenda of faith, and the whole context of our receiving and deciding, has changed radically.

For years I have insisted that the real theatre of secularisation is not found in sociological statistics of religious diminishment. A deeper erosion occurs in our often unformulated but shared images of our spiritual identity. Is the external horizontal life everything or are there higher vertical invitations for us beyond what we glimpse with our empirical eyes?

Faced with such enormous change, it is vital to discern well and to remember that our freedom to respond creatively is never extinguished. As regards definite lines of faith formation, don't expect me to give up directives. I'm just a philosopher with a passion for exploring the deeper shifts of history, of our self-interpretations and how we live them. But I am also a Catholic, increasingly inclined to ponder the emerging forms of faith today and indeed the whole issue of the future of Christianity—all in the light of the converging insights I have accumulated through the years.

I sometimes speak of my religious "hunches", and perhaps that word is understandably tentative, because a philosopher today is not meant to wear his faith on his sleeve in academic circles. In old age I have been rebelling more frequently than before against that self-censure. What are some of these hunches that over time have strengthened into strong convictions? That religion is a key universal dimension of our humanity, and that to suppress or avoid this quest and possibility is to risk not just a spiritual but an anthropological impoverishment. Moreover, I have come to see that a neutral approach to religion is reductive. If Christianity, for instance, is true, it offers more than an answer to my hunger for anchors in a confusing world: it is rooted in an extraordinary event of God in history that continues to happen in us. It involves an almost incredible sharing in God's love rather than just institutional belonging or believing. Christ is our source of transformation now rather than just a founder of a tradition in the past. The historical and functional interpretations of religion are valid approaches but they should not monopolize our vision. To echo the gospel, there is something more than Solomon here.

For years people in theological and religious circles have been saying that nowadays faith has to be a decision, not just a passive transmission (a terrible word more suited to car engines). That stress on choice is valid but it is not enough. The decision is not about a religious truth but about a whole way of life, a different vision of everything, ultimately about learning, or better, receiving a different divine love, called *agape*. Don't ask me for help about how to communicate this to a new generation. My hunch, to repeat that word, is that it is always easier to "teach religion" functionally and historically, and no doubt that is needed. However, there is another drama of spiritual conversion to be prepared and pointed towards, if people are to arrive at a livable faith for today and tomorrow. Modernity has taught us to value neutrality, or a certain kind of objectivity, to such an extent that we can become afraid of going any further or facing a path of more costly commitment. I have been a constant defender of the positive achievements of modernity, in particular its ideal of personal authenticity and its commitment to human rights. But we should not ignore or deny the tendency to reduce the personal to the merely individual, to shrink authenticity into self-fulfilment without conscience, and we need to discern and critique these cultural forms of a drifting existence as more undermining of Christian faith in practice than the intellectual attacks of angry atheists.

My hunch is that religious formation today needs to be doubly discerning. It needs to be critical of the dehumanizing factors in the culture that rob people of spiritual depth. This is not a matter of scapegoating the dominant life-styles but of asking the right questions about their impact on our self-horizons. And secondly there is a call for Christians to be honestly and humbly self-critical of their own structures and their own reductions of the grit of the gospel. Christian history is marked by terrible scandals that can make one despair of our Church and of ourselves. My own hesitant hope is that after facing the darkness, slowly and in a spirit of mourning, we can become more ready for new light on our always fragile choices and new creativity in our always inadequate embodiments of faith.

For years I have been fascinated by our longing for fullness and for human flourishing in its many forms. Although I recognise, with deep respect, the genuineness of non-religious versions of fullness and flourishing, I am convinced that the religious road is both more true and more blessedly in tune with us. Here, at least for Christians, fullness and flourishing come as gifts in a relationship, not simply as a self-achievement, but as "something they receive... in something like a personal relationship from another being capable of love and giving" (SA 8).

In other words, I have come to hold the real source of our goodness and of our loving has to be larger than us. I worry that the unanchored individual—isolated from others, from a tradition of meaning, can be deprived of this possibility of religious faith as the most credible source of our transformation towards love.

If ever I were to write more explicitly about Christian spirituality, perhaps the epigraph of the book could be from the opening of John's Gospel: "from Christ's fullness we have all received", but I would want to evoke also the fragilities of faith, its darknesses and dangers, and the ever-changing adventure of trying to make that vision reachable, more through incarnate living than through my long journey of reflection on it. Because, in short, believers are receivers who are being gradually liberated by God to live out a love that seeks to transform our whole shadowed history.[1]

References

Braman, Brian J. 2008. *Meaning and Authenticity: Bernard Lonergan & Charles Taylor on the Drama of Authentic Human Existence*. Toronto: University of Toronto Press.
Taylor, Charles, 1960. Clericalism. *The Downside Review* 78, 167-180.
—. 1989. *Sources of the Self: The Making of the Modern Identity*. Cambridge, MA: Harvard University Press.
—. 1991. *The Ethics of Authenticity*. Cambridge, MA: Harvard University Press.
—. 1995. Two Theories of Modernity. *Harvard Center Report* 25 (2), 24-33.
—. 1997. Foreword to Marcel Gauchet, *The Disenchantment of the World: a political history of religion*. Princeton: Princeton University Press, ix-xv.
—. 1999. *A Catholic Modernity?* Oxford: Oxford University Press.
—. 2002. *Varieties of Religion Today: William James Revisited*. Cambridge, MA: Harvard University Press.

—. 2004. *Modern Social Imaginaries*. Durham: Duke University Press.
—. 2008. La secolarizzazione fallita e la riscoperta dello spirito, *Vita e Pensiero* 91 (Nov-Dec), 29-33. My translation.

Ireland: A Secular Age?

Patrick Hannon

Among the many reviews of *A Secular Age* is one which appeared in the London *Spectator*, on the 10th of October 2007, by the English church historian Edward Norman. Norman's review begins as follows:

> Here is a book which the theological establishment will doubtless fall upon as an obese child might reach for a packet of crisps. Not that they will understand much of it: for this is a universal explanation of things, written from a philosophical perspective, and which, despite the homely illustrations to which philosophical writers are sometimes given, is densely composed and at times difficult to follow. It is also nearly 1,000 pages of fine print.

As one who might be supposed to belong to a theological establishment (and who is as partial to a packet of crisps as the next), let me assure you that I stand warned. Norman may have exaggerated the bulk of *A Secular Age*—it's not quite "1,000 pages of fine print"—but he didn't exaggerate its density, and it would be a foolhardy member of any establishment who claimed to have comprehended it all. Fortunately our purposes now don't require us to have comprehended it all.

But of course it's only right to acknowledge at the outset that Taylor's work is indeed congenial to anyone whose trade is Catholic moral theology. General reasons for this are obvious, and chiefly that there is a fit between his thinking and some ideas which are familiar to a practitioner of the discipline of Christian ethics in a natural law tradition. Here is someone in whose background lie the Greeks and Augustine and Aquinas, but who is at home with Hegel, Kant and Heidegger; who is imbued also with Judeo-Christian ideas about human being and human destiny; and who writes in and about our world, or at any rate our western world; whose insights illuminate areas of experience and of reflection on experience that are concerns of Christian moral theology too.

More particularly, it can't be surprising that in seeking to explicate

Catholic social doctrine one might call in aid someone whose political thinking is communitarian in temper, even if he doesn't list himself among the communitarians. For although Catholic teaching—I should probably say official Catholic teaching—declines to tie itself to any one political philosophy or programme, it works with ideas about the person that insist very strongly upon human relationality, whether that relationality is thought of in terms of Aquinas's view of humanity as social, or more fundamentally—more theologically, as some might want to say—in terms of the *imago* of a Trinitarian God, as grounding the equal dignity of each woman and man.

It's not difficult to list the themes and emphases of Taylor's political thinking that make for this kind of congeniality. *Sources of the Self* and *The Ethics of Authenticity* provide the background for his account of more particular topics, for an overview of which one need go no further than the table of contents of his *Philosophical Arguments*. There is, for example, his critique of atomism and of methodological individualism; his account of "irreducibly social goods"; his development of a "politics of recognition"; his insistence on the dialogical character of human self-understanding; his views about civil society, and about liberal politics in the public square. Taylor's work contains much to challenge as well as to illuminate the social ethics that emerge from Christian tradition.

But of course the work of Charles Taylor which is the focus of the proceedings of this volume has to do with concerns that range far beyond the conventional boundaries of social theory and political philosophy. Consistently with a significant strand in Taylor's earlier thinking, *A Secular Age* invites the reader into the domain of the metaphysical and of the explicitly religious, and invites converse with theologies and theologians as well as with philosophers and philosophies of religion. Although—as he himself observes—the world his book surveys is that of Latin Christendom, with a narrative of secularisation shaped above all by western modernity, his account of the "new" secularity has implications for all the faiths, including "faiths" that are avowedly non-religious.

Wondering how to enter the conversation today, and mindful of the presence of specialist expertise in philosophy and economics, politics and social theory (and not to mention theology), I thought I might have recourse to two strategies that are familiar now across the disciplines. I thought first that an observer from the field of Christian ethics might be allowed a naïve reading of Taylor's texts, naïve in the technical sense, and if naïve also in the usual sense, this will surely come to light. And I thought, second, that I might adopt an approach that could be called narrative, and recount in brief a story which invites construal in terms of

Taylor's secularities 1, 2 and 3. My own interest in Taylor's work stems from an interest in the general question of religion and public life; an interest especially, granted the "establishment" from which I come, in Catholic understandings of church and world, and of the future for the *ekklesia* in the *polis,* a polis that is now, of course, in so many ways a cosmopolis. I hope it's not parochial to have assumed that a gathering such as this, in a location in which *akademia* and *ekklesia* intermingle and fuse, will have an interest in the bearing of its concerns on the Irish scene.

Of course, the question of the place of religion in public life has latterly become actual in many other countries, in the EU as in the US, in Canada as in Australia, to list only places in which "western" forms of the question are to be met. It is without doubt a large and complex question, inflected, as Taylor might say, according to the very varying contexts in which it is being lived. Even at this distance we got a sense again of the US experience in the last presidential election. From time to time we're reminded of its various European versions: France and the banning of the headscarves, Germany and periodic murmurings against the *Kirchensteuer,* Italy and the crucifix in the schoolroom. And of course there is the question of the role of religion in the European Union, in so many ways epitomised in the debate about whether a reference to Christianity should be included in a European Constitution.

The question's Irish inflection has most commonly been in terms of the relationship of church and state, and there are still issues that may be framed in those terms, even if—or especially because—we have a Constitution that guarantees freedom of religion and provides against the establishment of any religion; even though, that is, it has constitutionally been the case that we can be construed in terms of Taylor's Secularity 1. And because Catholicism is the denomination of the majority, church-state debates on this island have been conducted mainly in terms of relationships between the Catholic Church and the state; "state" understood as the government and institutions of the Republic especially, "church" understood also mainly as institution and governance. The history of those relationships has been well studied, John Whyte's *Church and State in Ireland* being still, from the point of view of our interest here, the most comprehensive authoritative account.

Whyte's book studies that history as it unfolded in the fifty years that followed the State's foundation in 1922; but, of course, church-state relationships since that time have not fossilized, either as regards the law or in fact. And you could express what's been happening as a steady erosion of various traces of the influence of Catholic teachings on the Constitution and the law. The erosion was signalled by a constitutional amendment in 1972 whereby the "special position" of the Roman Catholic Church was no longer acknowledged, but it was effectively initiated by a decision of the Supreme Court in 1973 which declared that a ban on the importation of contraceptives, going back to a statute of 1935, was unconstitutional. Later there was an amendment of a constitutional provision which prohibited the enactment of divorce legislation; later again, repeal of a law of 1861 which criminalised sexual relations between consenting males. There have been other evidences of the waning of institutionalised influence, but these are the main markers, and I hope they give a sufficient indication of what is meant by speaking of an erosion of traces of Catholic influence on the law of the Irish Republic.

The background of social change against which these developments took place is a story of the "modernising" of Ireland, and that's a story that I won't attempt to summarise here. Our story-within-a-story—the story of the erosion of traces of Catholic influence in the law and in the Constitution—is itself in need of some qualifying detail, for in 1983 there was a constitutional amendment which provided some entrenchment of existing law concerning abortion; and that provision and its subsequent history is evidence of a persistent Catholic influence at the level of constitutional law. There is the fact also that the Preamble to the Constitution invokes the Trinity, and that a reference to Jesus Christ is of an obviously Catholic provenance; and that certain Directives for Social Policy are drawn from what in 1937 was the official Catholic position of the Catholic Church on the matters to which the directives refer.

But on the whole it's fair to say that in the decades since the foundation of the State, Irish society is progressively more describable in terms of what Taylor calls Secularity 1. What of Secularity 2? Impression and observation are enough to warrant saying that over the past decade especially there has been a dramatic decline in regular church attendances. One would have to qualify this of course, distinguishing between urban and rural, distinguishing too between different areas of our main cities; distinguishing perhaps between Northern Ireland and the Republic; remembering also such phenomena as an apparently enduring interest in the relevance of liturgy and ritual to all that's summarised in the phrase births, marriages and deaths. Yet we are undoubtedly in a time of declining attendance, and we have certainly moved beyond the time when it was unnecessary to convince young people that they ought to attend Mass each Sunday.

How or whether Ireland fits in the narrative of the emergence of Secularity 3 is an immensely complex question, hardly less complex than the task of assessing the validity of Taylor's thesis which is the focal concern of this Colloquium. For present purposes perhaps it's enough to say that if the core of the thesis is that religious faith is now only one option, viable no doubt, but no more viable than unbelief, there's little evidence that Ireland differs greatly from her neighbours to the east or to the west. And if a contributory factor in the emergence of secularity 3 is a pluralism of faith as well as an ethnic pluralism, one has only to remark the fact that during the past few decades Islam has acquired a significant presence in Ireland. More problematic for Ireland's religious leaders is what the title of a recent book by Jesuit sociologist Micheál Mac Gréil calls the challenge of indifference.

MacGréil's book carries the findings of a survey carried out between November 2007 and March 2008 which aimed to measure the religious attitudes, behaviour and beliefs of a national sample of 1,015 Irish Adults of 18 years and older. The results disclose a situation in some respects unsurprising, most notably a drop in regular church attendance to 42% once a week (43% for Roman Catholics) from 79% in 1988-9. Yet 86% reported a "closeness" to God, and over 70% said they pray at least once a week, 50% once a day or more often. What suggested his book's title to MacGréil, however, was mainly the discovery that among those whose attendance at church had declined, 68% replied that they couldn't be bothered, and that as regards handing on the faith a quarter thought that children should be left to make up their own minds.

In a *Commonweal* essay on *A Secular Age* Peter Steinfels asks whether "this growing penumbra of the less committed" is a stable aspect of the modern secular age or whether it's transitional, "an intermediate stage on the way to that disappearance or marginalization of religion the traditional theorists of secularization anticipated?" And he sketches questions for Catholic leadership in particular:

> Suppose we try to imagine a Catholic identity capable of confronting an unprecedented array of religious and spiritual options that cannot be easily dismissed, capable of living with greater doubt and uncertainty, and likely to undergo crucial formation in early adulthood rather than childhood... [I]s such an identity really possible without a quantum leap in theological knowledge, intellectual openness, and spiritual guidance compared to the past? Will it be found in homilies, parish life, Catholic educational initiatives?" (vol. CXXXV, No. 9.)

Steinfels's words could serve as an introduction to a programme for renewal in the Catholic Church in Ireland as elsewhere in the world of which Taylor's narrative of secularisation speaks. But in Ireland as elsewhere the energies of Catholic Church leadership are for some time now being absorbed in coping with the fall-out from revelations of child sexual abuse by priests and religious, and the failure of the leadership to deal with the abuse. In Ireland too is there evident a massive problem of credibility for the current leadership, with an impact yet to be measured on the leadership's capacity to influence the shaping of Irish society.

As to what that capacity has hitherto been, we have already seen something of the ways in which it has played out in the field of law and legislation. It may be of interest to notice that since the early seventies the Catholic bishops, whenever they have intervened in public debate about social morality, have always explicitly recognised that legislative change or constitutional amendment are matters for the personal conscience judgment of lawmakers and citizens respectively. This recognition has invariably been accompanied by a clear statement of Catholic teaching on the substantive moral issue—contraception, for example, or divorce or abortion—and the bishops have also always argued for their own view of a contemplated measure. The influence of their interventions on the outcomes of the various debates has varied, and in most instances has not been easy to estimate with precision, given that there have generally been other factors which might have contributed to the result.

Still, it will hardly be maintained that "the church's" position has played no role in the evolution of the law in Ireland during the past several decades, albeit the direction of that evolution is generally characterised as toward the "liberalisation" of Irish society. Of course, a Catholic influence on Irish life hasn't been confined to the realm of law, for there has also been a very strong church presence in primary and post-primary education, and at third level in the management and staffing of the several colleges of education; and there has been a highly significant presence of the religious orders in the sphere of health, even if latterly, with dwindling numbers of vocations to religious life, their influence is sustained mainly by way of ownership or patronage or management, and the promotion of an appropriate ethos.

But what of the future? I have been speaking so far mainly about the Catholic church and the tasks of Catholic leadership, so perhaps the first thing to say at this point is that if the Christian churches wish to take a constructive part in the making of modern Ireland they will need to explore the possibilities for common Christian witness more thoroughly and with more commitment than has up to now been the case. They will need indeed to give due weight to the emergence in Ireland of a religious pluralism, recognising for example that Irish society now includes a significant Islamic population, and recognising that there is also a non-religious secular voice which has every entitlement to be heard in Ireland's *agora* now.

It is perhaps this last aspect of modern Irish life that must give most difficulty for the religious communities and their leaderships, for the secular voice is often presumed to be not just non-religious but anti-religious, as indeed it sometimes is. So perhaps the second thing to be said is that Ireland needs a debate in which the very idea of secularisation or of secularity is explored and clarified. It's likely to come as a surprise to some that Catholic theology is not negative about the process of secularisation per se. Karl Rahner, for example, has written of "worldliness of the world which has been brought about by a long process of development by Christianity itself, a de-numinization and de-sacralization which is in accordance with the nature of Christianity itself", contrasted with "a secularism which is at basis identical with atheism and is the mortal enemy of Christianity itself" (Rahner 1974, 168). Even a more "Augustinian" reading such as one finds in the writings Benedict XVI, whilst repudiating a naturalistic secularism closed to the possibility of faith in a transcendent God, acknowledges the validity of a secularisation that allows for what Vatican Two described as the rightful autonomy of earthly affairs (GS 36).

But perhaps it will be a surprise also to discover that a leading European philosopher who is religiously agnostic could find common ground with the then Cardinal Ratzinger when in 2004 they discussed the place of religion in the secular liberal state. In the course of an interchange about the "pre-political" foundations of the modern democratic state, Jürgen Habermas wrote:

> The neutrality of the state authority on questions of world views guarantees the same ethical freedom to every citizen. This is incompatible with the political universalization of a secularist world view of the world. When secularized citizens act in their role as citizens of the state, they must not deny in principle that religious images of the world have the potential to express truth. Nor must they refuse their believing fellow citizens the right to make contributions in a religious language to public debates. Indeed, a liberal political culture can expect that the secularized citizens play their part in the endeavours to translate relevant contributions from the religious language into a language that is accessible to the public as a whole. (Ratzinger and Habermas 2006, 51)

Of course, debates about the place of religion are rarely general or simply abstract but arise from concrete situations in which one or other party feels threatened or aggrieved by what is seen as the imposition of a world-view on those who don't share it. That has been the case in the Irish debates about the legal changes to which I've referred above but—though the abortion debate is likely to recur, as is perhaps the question of gay marriage—the world of (especially) primary education is likely to be the arena of most public controversy in the future, as critics continue to question the propriety of denominational schooling. Critics are also likely to consider that there is some unfinished business in the sphere of health, given some differences between an ethos shaped by Catholic teaching on bioethics and an ethos not so shaped.

It would be impossible, even if I were competent to do so, to address in detail here the particular challenges that the evolution of Irish society is bringing in these areas. And—to cite a current controversy—the kind of point made in the Rahner and Habermas passages quoted earlier must seem remote to parents who are exercised about what should be done regarding religious education in the "third type" of primary school recently introduced in county Dublin. Yet I would want to maintain that for the future health of Irish society, civic education, whether of adults or of children, whether of religious provenance or not, needs to open people's minds to the dimensions intimated in passages such as these. This is not simply in aid of enabling more intellectual depth in public debate about matters of the utmost social importance, but in the hope that some of the bitterness which too often surfaces can be countered in a broader view.

I would want to maintain too that in Ireland there is a need for debate within the academy about religion and public life, interdisciplinary, and faithful to the academy's conventions regarding freedom of thought, and to the canons of scholarship. Obstacles to this kind of debate are numerous, not least that until recently there was a statutory impediment to the provision of theology as a subject in the colleges of the National University of Ireland. Nor are the prospects for a respectful hearing for Roman Catholic theology's potential contribution helped by the perception that the thinking of Catholic theologians is constrained by an official orthodoxy and controlled by the Vatican.

Doubtless it would be possible to hold a debate about religion and public life without the participation of Catholic theology, but the undertaking must seem extremely odd in a country such as Ireland, in which Catholicism is still the religion of the majority, and in which Catholic traditions of devotion and of morality have exercised so strong an influence. There is a whole literature in the Irish language which is unintelligible apart from a knowledge of Christian beliefs and practices, and so of Christian theology; and for that matter one's appreciation of Irish poets, novelists and playwrights writing in English is impoverished in the absence of some grasp of Catholic theology in particular. There's also the fact, already noted, that *Bunreacht na hÉireann*, the Republic's Constitution, continues to display traces of the influence of Catholic theological thinking.

One way of framing a debate in the academy that would probe important issues involving religion and public life is by way of exploring the concept of the common good. The term common good both has an ancient lineage and resonates in the contemporary mind, and not just in the West, even if it seems especially at home in western thinking; and it has now also passed into the rhetoric of western liberal democratic politics. It's hardly necessary to say that a term used by Plato and Aristotle, Augustine and Aquinas, the Irish bishops and the framers of New Labour's social policy in England, is unlikely to have meant the same thing to each of its users. Yet, as Patrick Riordan has recently shown, it remains useful as a way in which to talk about the purposes of politics and governance in contexts as diverse as all that's involved in globalisation and philosophy's disputations concerning the respective merits of liberalism and communitarianism (Riordan 2009).

It could, I think, play an especially useful role in an Irish debate just now, not only in the academy but also in the wider society. The "social teaching" of the Catholic tradition, of which the common good is a key concept, is acknowledged as valuable even by critics, and the fact that it is translatable into a secular idiom means that it can be a basis for the kind of discussion which can lead to a common mind and cooperative activity, whilst retaining its power to motivate and energise the believer. Few will doubt the importance of rigorous thought about the common good of a society which has been failed by all of the institutions to whose hands its good had been entrusted. And the distinguished work of Charles Taylor can enlighten the pursuit of a common good in a secular age.

References

Keogh, D, 1994. *Twentieth Century Ireland: Nation and State.* Dublin: Gill and Macmillan.

Lee, J, 1985. *Ireland 1912-1985: Politics and Society,* Cambridge University Press.

Rahner, K, 1973. Theological Reflections on the Problem of Secularization. *Theological Investigations* X. London: Darton, Longman and Todd, 318-48.

—. 1974. Theological Reflections on Secularization and Atheism. *Theological Investigations* XI, London: Darton, Longman and Todd.

Ratzinger, J., & J. Habermas, 2006. *The Dialectics of Secularization: on Reason and Religion,* trans. B McNeil, San Francisco: Ignatius Press.

Riordan P, 2008. *A Grammar of the Common Good: Speaking of Globalization*, London and New York: Continuum.

Steinfels P. Modernity and Belief, *Commonweal*, Volume CXXXV, Number 9, available at http://commonwealmagazine.org/modernity-belief-0. Last accessed 31/3/10.

Taylor, Charles, 1989. *Sources of the Self: The Making of the Modern Identity*, Cambridge: Harvard University Press.

—. 1992. *The Ethics of Authenticity*, Cambridge, Ma.: Harvard University Press.

—. 1995. *Philosophical Arguments*, Cambridge, Ma.: Harvard University Press.

—. *A Catholic Modernity? Charles Taylor's Marianist Award Lecture, with responses by William M. Shea, Rosemary Luling Haughton, George Marsden, and Jean Bethke Elshtain*, James L. Heft, ed. Oxford University Press, 1999.

De Vries H & L. Sullivan, 2006. *Political Theologies: Public Religions in a Post-secular World*. New York, Fordham University Press.

Whyte, J.H., 1984. *Church and State in Modern Ireland 1923-79*. Dublin, Gill and Macmillan.

Religious Inheritances of Learning and the "Unquiet Frontiers of Modernity"

Pádraig Hogan

Uniformity, Plurality and Parables

Where there is an established and widespread uniformity of religious belief in a society, as in the kind of society sketched by Charles Taylor in the early pages of *A Secular Age*, the handing-on of a religious tradition is a relatively unproblematic affair. That handing-on is accomplished through informal practices of upbringing in families and through more formal practices of learning in schools and colleges. The cultural world in which upbringing and education is carried on is itself suffused with familiar religious images and idioms, practices and rituals. This roughly describes the situation before the dawn of the Reformation, not just in individual countries, but more generally in those regions known as Western Christendom. Taylor captures the point well when he states, at the start of *A Secular Age*, that around the year 1500 it was "virtually impossible not to believe in God" (SA 26).[1]

The kind of secular age Taylor goes on to depict in his book presents a striking contrast to such uniformity. A distinctive feature of Taylor's case is the story he tells of secularisation coming about less through a successive falling away of belief occasioned by external factors, than through the consequences of reform efforts arising from within the church. This story has an abundance of insights—historical as well as philosophical. And whether or not one goes all the way with Taylor in his account of the reasons for the decline of the sacred, one can hardly contest the aspects of the decline that he highlights. These include:

> the yielding of the notion of cosmos (the Great Chain of Being with its inherent hierarchies) to that of a neutral universe;
> the demise of enchantment within the experience of religious belief, both socially and individually;

the decline of invocations and evocations of God in public society;
the decline of a capability to hold tensions in some equilibrium (e.g., between observance of religious authority, on the hand, and "festivals of unrule", such as Carnival, on the other);
the waning of a common understanding of time, especially sacred time.

For reasons like these, religious belief in the West no longer defines the identity of a culture or a society. Rather, as Taylor illustrates, in such cultures it presents an option, among others. Secondly, religious belief as an option is itself characterised by plurality rather than by uniformity—a plurality that is manifest not only between different traditions like Christianity, Islam, Judaism, but also within the traditions. And to this plurality can be added the further option of religious belief as a spirituality that disclaims an attachment to any established religious traditions; one that goes its own way – even a "privatized spirituality" to use Taylor's phrase. He points out that, within this radical pluralism, "our age is very far from settling into an age of comfortable unbelief", and that "unrest continues to surface" (SA 727).

When we consider these changes from an educational standpoint, we see that the unquiet frontiers of modernity have rendered the question of religious education newly problematic. Amid circumstances of "galloping pluralism on the spiritual plane" how is religious education to understand its own purposes? Would such purposes be different in schools under religious authorities and schools under public authorities? Can one speak coherently here, even within a particular denomination, of "handing on the faith" to new generations? Efforts to deal with the difficult issues raised by such questions have changed the face of denominational schools in many countries. For instance, many contemporary Catholic schools have a student body of up to 50% non-Catholic (Bryk et al. 1995), and the didactic emphasis long associated with programmes of faith-nurturing has all but disappeared.

It was widely assumed in the past that parents who sent their children to denominational schools within the Christian tradition did so to have their children's formal education characterised by a nurturing in the doctrines of the denomination in question. While that assumption can still be made today about many parents, there are also many, even multitudes, of whom it cannot be made, or can only be made in a weak sense. Even less so can it be made about the students in such schools today, especially in post-primary schools, where they spend half or more of their teenage schooldays.

I'd like to explore the problematic questions I've just mentioned by calling on an important distinction that the New Testament reveals about the teaching activities of Jesus Christ. The distinction is that between multitudes and disciples, and I believe it has much light to shed on these questions. In St. Matthew's Gospel, Chapter 13, verse 34 says: "All these things Jesus spoke in parables to the multitudes; and without parables he did not speak to them." In similar vein, St. Mark's Gospel, Chapter 4, verses 33-34 says:

> And with many such parables, he spoke to them the word, according as they were able to hear. And without parable he did not speak to them; but apart, he explained all things to his disciples.

Although the verses from St. Mark don't refer explicitly to "multitudes", it is clear that the "them" in question is the "great multitude" that had gathered by the sea, referred to in the opening verses of the chapter.

Many who know little enough about Christianity still know that parables were devices that Jesus sometimes used to capture the moral of a story (for instance, the prodigal son, the good Samaritan), or to avail of a good metaphor (for instance the mustard seed). And the verses I have just quoted are ones that most people brought up as Christians would have heard on many occasions during their upbringing and schooling. Yet, in my own case, it wasn't until the early nineties that something in these verses suddenly arrested my attention and made me rethink the whole question of parables and their significance. Some research I was doing at the time on practices of teaching sent me searching through the New Testament to study the recorded instances of teaching in the life of Jesus Christ. It was then that I noticed the abruptness of the verse from St Mark: "and without parables *he did not speak to them*". Did this mean a calculated decision? A quiet but determined refusal? "Yes" seems to be the inescapable answer. The more I thought about it, and the more I looked for evidence for a different kind of answer, the more it became clear that there was something decisive and determined in the dual approach to teaching adopted by Jesus: for the disciples, a language of direct explanation as well as of parable; for the multitudes, purely the more subtle language of parable. But why such a resolute difference?

Despite all that has been written on the Parables of Jesus, I've found little research that probes in depth the question I'm raising here: Why such a decisive difference of approach? And why decline to employ any approach but parables in engaging with the multitudes? The more common explanation that I have found (chiefly on the websites of Christian evangelical groups) is the following: "He employed parables to obscure the truth from unbelievers while making it clearer to His disciples."[2]

Plausible enough, perhaps. But such explanations emphasise what parables accomplish in a negative sense. Lines like "seeing, they do not see, hearing, they do not hear" (Matthew, 13:13) are drawn upon as support by those offering this kind of explanation, and sometimes to highlight a distinction between an elect minority and an excluded majority.

These arguments seem to me to be incomplete at best, and sometimes partisan. The partisanship seems to be tied into theological differences about the disciples as an elect group, and my concern here is not with theological controversies. Rather, I want to explore the positive, as distinct from the negative side of the issue: namely, the educational promise of parables, and of their modern day equivalents, where religious inheritances of learning are concerned. Whatever merits negative explanations for parables might have as strategies for confounding the enemy, such explanations seem to get it precisely the wrong way around where more constructive matters are concerned. Here, I have in mind particularly the revelatory power of parables. The direct answer Jesus gives to his disciples' questions about why he speaks in parables to the multitudes is: "Because it is given unto you to know the mysteries of the kingdom of heaven, but to them it is not given" (Matthew 13:11). But it was Christ himself who had already done this giving to the disciples. And it is clear that his continuing activity of teaching sought to bring such knowledge to those to whom it hadn't yet been given. The word "multitudes" describes just this group: a disparate assortment of the indifferent, the ardent seekers, the sceptical, the hangers-on, the mildly interested, the hostile, those on the make, and so on. In this kind of context the constructive possibilities of parables have everything to do with memorable disclosures, as distinct from keeping anyone in the dark. They might make available to the multitudes insights that they would reject, or fail to understand, if communicated more literally. Parables, in short, enable human communication to cut through a legalistic morality of outward observance and to summon thoughts to a quite different imaginative neighbourhood. They invite a disparate plurality of hearers to consider in their own hearts something that yet speaks individually to each and every one of them; something addressed to them as worthy of their deeper convictions, but which they might be embarrassed to acknowledge publicly, not least because of fears of losing face or social standing, or because of a variety of cultural pressures.

Unlike more direct forms of moral or religious teaching, parables make no substantive assumptions about the beliefs of hearers. The tales being told in the New Testament parables moreover are invariably about someone else (a traveller who comes across someone who has been mugged, a father enduring difficult relations with his two sons, a farmer sowing seeds and so on), so the spotlight is not on oneself—at least not explicitly. But the tale invites the hearer to consider anew some important point about which one might have some strong preconceived ideas, ideas that might be important to reconsider, but that one might resist doing in the public gaze. By granting one the dignity to consider quietly in one's own heart if the point of the tale applies to oneself – if the cap fits, so to speak—parables can be a potent way of enabling unhearing ears to hear. And taking a positive insight here from Christ's refusal to use a direct form of teaching with the multitudes, perhaps they may be the only successful way. This is an insight that I want to take up again in the final part of this presentation.

Buffered Self, Immanent Frame and Subtler Languages

Bringing our exploration of parables to bear on current educational concerns, I'd like to highlight now that the students in today's schools in Western societies can be described as "multitudes" in a strong pluralist sense of that word. This should surprise nobody, but I want to suggest that this is also basically true, though to a less radical degree, of students in schools run by religious denominations. While it would have been largely inaccurate to make this latter suggestion a generation ago, the last three decades have brought change on an unprecedented scale. The realities of a secular age and of postmodernity are now a familiar feature of experience even in rural parish schools. Although the inertia of inherited custom and practice in denominational education is sometimes disposed to overlook this, the conclusion increasingly presses itself as an inescapable one. The multitudes of students in today's denominational schools and colleges in the West are characteristically attuned to influences other than religious inheritances of learning.

An important distinction drawn by Charles Taylor is relevant to the change I have just mentioned. This is the contrast between what he calls the "buffered self" of the secular age and the more "porous self" of pre-modern times. The buffered self he describes as: "a new sense of the self and its place in the cosmos: not open and porous and vulnerable to a world of spirits and powers" (SA 27). Despite the cultural plurality of Western societies—in some ways because of it—the buffered self is an increasingly common feature of self-understanding and personal identity in such societies. The buffered self is unreceptive in particular to the claims of religious inheritances of learning, or to what Taylor calls "the great languages of transcendence" (SA 727).

At a number of points in *A Secular Age*, Taylor refers to "subtler languages", a term borrowed from the poet Shelley by Earl Wasserman for the title of his book *The Subtler Language* (1968). Acknowledging his debt to Shelley and Wasserman, Taylor had used the phrase "Subtler Languages" as the title for Part V of his book *Sources of the Self* (1989) and again for Chapter 8 of *The Ethics of Authenticity* (1991). In these two works he employed the term to capture the change from a mimetic to a creative conception of art which marked the rise of the Romantic movement in the late 18th century. Mimetic conceptions acknowledged resonances, or parallels, between human experience and an objective order of things in which the sacred was central: for instance, the Great Chain of Being. Mimetic art drew directly on these parallels and frequently featured well-known religious themes. The subtler languages of the Romantic period however—in literature, music and art—eschewed these parallels and turned inward, to draw strongly on the experienced quality of emotion, thus attempting to extend the powers of human originality to say something "for which there are as yet no established words" (SA 353).

The buffered self, Taylor points out, is susceptible to these subtler languages, not least because their creative achievements offer to modern unbelief, and to an undefined spiritual sensibility, a kind of substitute, or "a place to go", as he puts it (356). *A Secular Age* explores moreover how many of the subtler languages of modernity—in literature, painting, music—have become "absolute" in themselves. Where previously, the object of art included some kind of representation of a recognisable spiritual or cosmic order, more often now "the object is left unportrayed" (356). Subtler languages which take this "absolute" turn have greatly advanced the standing of the arts, not least by allowing aesthetic experience an unprecedented scope, but also an *undefined* scope—for instance, in the engrossed contemplation of a work of modern art by an individual connoisseur, or in the collective rapt attentiveness of a concert audience.

The buffered self, Taylor goes on to explain, is also a product of a range of disciplines: disciplines of self-control, of systematic devotion to work and progress, of well-used time, of individual achievement, and so on. Such disciplines, he points out, were historically cultivated by successive waves of reform. A distinctive part of his whole thesis is that these disciplines had their origins *within* Western Christianity rather than in external forces critical of Christianity. That is to say, over successive centuries many of the authorised practices of learning within Christian educational institutions contained unacknowledged tensions between their evangelising aspirations and their enduring practical consequences.

Later in the book, Taylor draws together some key features of the "buffered self" that have established themselves in place of earlier forms of self-understanding. Here I want to quote a relevant passage from *A Secular Age*:

> So the buffered identity of the disciplined individual moves in a constructed social space, where instrumental rationality is a key value, and time is pervasively secular. All of this makes up what I want to call 'the immanent frame'. There remains to add just one background idea: that this frame constitutes a 'natural' order, to be contrasted to a 'supernatural' one, an 'immanent' world over against a possible 'transcendent' one. (SA 542)

The immanent frame, Taylor argues, accommodates the buffered self with its own array of possibilities, and despite providing endless "places to go" for aesthetic sensibility, it remains for Taylor, who now draws specifically on Max Weber, something of an "iron cage". It rules out, or disregards, *other* places to go, especially those associated with impulses, influences and imaginings that are "transcendent", that's to say, religious in character. As Taylor himself concisely puts it: the buffered self cannot be easily "quickened from within" by God or the Holy Spirit. Taylor distinguishes, however, between open and closed readings of the immanent frame: the closed reading, or "closed spin", as he calls it, "sees immanence as admitting of no beyond" (SA 550). This spin, he suggests, has become "hegemonic" in intellectual and academic quarters in the West (SA 549-50). Notwithstanding this prevalence, Taylor argues that the closed reading assumes a stance of "anticipatory confidence" in its own naturalness, or logical unavoidability. In other words, it makes its own leap of faith in the non-existence of a "beyond". But it remains unaware of the element of credulity in this stance due to its own domestication in privative accounts of secularisation.

Religious Traditions, Educational Practice, and New Imaginative Neighbourhoods

What educational consequences follow from all of this? Do Taylor's searching historical analyses of the buffered self, the immanent frame and subtler languages mean the writing is on the wall for religious inheritances of learning? From most traditional educational perspectives the answer would have to be: "probably yes". But from another perspective, a distinctly educational one, a quite different answer suggests itself.

Taylor does not envisage as a realistic possibility any widespread return to the direct languages of a pre-secular age: either a public language of correlation between human experience and a natural-cum-supernatural order of things, or a more religious language of correspondence with a metaphysically ordered world view. Rather, what he is keen to bring to the fore is that the subtler languages of modernity themselves offer renewed possibilities for reaching beyond the immanent frame. How? Chiefly by seeking to do justice to the claims of human individuality, or authenticity, in the longing for and response to "a more-than-immanent transformation perspective". Taylor holds that such longing remains a "strong independent source of motivation in modernity" (SA 530), and underlines this with his explorations of "fragilization", "cross pressures", and the "unquiet frontiers of modernity", in the later pages of *A Secular Age*.

It is just here, amidst the turbulent cross-currents that underlie a conspicuous secularity, that Taylor's thoughts open a promising vista for educational encounters with religious inheritances of learning, especially in post-primary education. Most teachers today, and not only teachers of religion, will be familiar with how thoroughly "buffered" their teenage charges can be against such inheritances. Teachers are also aware of an unprecedented plurality among their students—cultural, ethnic, religious, familial, and so on. Yet there remains something central in conventional pedagogical approaches that is largely unheeding of the "massive unlearning" of "the great languages of transcendence" to which Taylor calls attention (SA 727). Take for instance the unacknowledged underside of the familiar point that a specific request from parents for the exclusion of a student from a religion class will invariably be granted by school authorities. The unacknowledged underside is the assumption that, in the case of students for whom such a request was *not* received (generally the majority of students), a direct language of faith formation can be employed as the norm.

If we make a full acknowledgement of factors like these, some striking consequences reveal themselves, particularly the following two: firstly, the use of a direct language of faith-formation with students who can fairly be regarded as "multitudes" in the New Testament sense, is problematic. Secondly, no less problematic are pedagogical practices that customarily link the work of religious education in schools with the work of preparation for sacraments in parishes. To put these points more succinctly: a clear distinction needs to be drawn between the assumptions on which religious inheritances of learning are introduced in schools and the assumptions on which such inheritances are introduced in a church. Now I'm not so naïve as to believe that practices of long ancestry can be wound up overnight, or indeed proscribed. And I'm more concerned in any case with what is pedagogically promising than with prohibitions and their justification.

Tracing a constructive pathway from the points just made, let us recall the remark of Matthew in chapter 13:34: "and without parables, *he did not speak to them*". This remark betokens an abundance of pedagogical insight. Parables, as used by Jesus, are subtler languages *par excellence*. As we have seen earlier, they respect the dignity and the privacy of a diversity of hearers. In doing so they summon the voice of conscience from its often-smothered depths. But they also acknowledge an individuality in each human being: of sensibility, of understanding and of aspiration. The examples provided in the writings of Matthew and Mark serve not so much as models to be emulated by today's teachers of religion (though they might sometimes be that). They serve more as illustrations of the fertility of a different pedagogical approach, suggesting the rich potential of modern-day counterparts of parables, or of a range of imaginative educational practices inspired by them.

Elucidating now this different pedagogical approach, if religious inheritances of learning are to speak seriously to the disparate sensibilities of learners in a secular age, the teachers who seek to bring about this engagement must forgo an urge to instruct or evangelise. Instead, their energies are called on to create new imaginative neighbourhoods in which the learners are invited to dwell awhile, in a wholehearted way. Exploring further the importance of subtler languages in this venture, I would like to draw here on some incisive observations by Michael Oakeshott— especially where he shows that the proper inspirations for educational efforts are those of conversation, rather than of any kind of planned socialisation, or pre-ordained destination. Where conversation is something genuine rather than forced or contrived, Oakeshott describes it as follows: "Thoughts of different species take wing and play around one another, responding to each other's movements and provoking one another to fresh exertions" (Oakeshott 1962, 198). And he goes on to add:

> Education, properly speaking, is an initiation into the skill and partnership of this conversation in which we learn to recognize the voices, to distinguish the proper occasions of utterance, and in which we acquire the intellectual and moral habits appropriate to conversation. (Ibid., 199)

Lest it be thought that this describes some kind of polite gentlemen's club with an elect membership, let me stress again the notion of multitudes, but now in connection with the pluralist learning environments of today's schools. It is in such contexts that teachers must attempt to get conversations underway, taking pains to cultivate among students the skill and partnership mentioned by Oakeshott. Efforts to do this, I need hardly add, are hindered by recurring pitfalls: by indifference, *ennui*, hostility, bravado, or fatalism on the part of students, or on the other hand by shortcomings in the teacher's capabilities and self-understanding.

Sufficient scope isn't available in a presentation of this kind to go into these difficulties in detail, but I'd like to provide, if I may, a summary illustration of what the fruits of such a venture might look like in practice. Let us take a teacher of Religious Education and group of pupils, aged between 16 and 17, in a co-educational secondary school. Over her first few weeks with this group, the teacher (let's call her Gráinne) has been putting a lot of energy into building healthy relationships of learning, working with the students towards a shared understanding of things like: purposes (enquiry rather than formation); mutual expectations; ground rules for the conduct of discussions and group work in class; strategies for follow-up work, including home-work, web-searching and so on. Though some of the students are still disposed to be disruptive of the community of learning that is gradually taking shape, Gráinne senses that a point has been reached where the critical mass of the group is now pulling with her and that the community learning idea is gathering an energy of its own. She has already profitably availed of a few parables, and now she is ready to introduce a new conversation with its own recurring notes of parable.

Gráinne reads to the class a news report that first appeared in newspapers internationally in April 2005, of a married woman in Afghanistan who was accused by her husband of adultery with an unmarried man. The report gives a few background details and reveals that the woman was stoned to death while the man was given 100 lashes and freed. Gráinne distributes a photocopy of the report to each of five groups of mixed gender, asks each group to examine and discuss it, and to prepare up to five key questions arising from it. The questions that are contributed by the students are then put together on a list. They include:

> Why was the woman treated differently from the man?
> Who condemned the woman to death?
> Is adultery considered a sin in all religions?
> Who did the stoning?
> Was the woman doing anything wrong if the unmarried man was her real love and if she was forced to marry this husband in the first place?
> Do different religions mean the same thing by adultery?
> Is this going to come up in an R.E exam?

In her initial review of the questions with the students, Gráinne refrains from giving answers of her own, but encourages students to refine some of the questions and place them in a fuller context. She monitors the quickening of interest in the questions, while now adroitly contributing to it herself—for instance by suggesting that the idea of adultery can't fully be understood without a good understanding of the notion of marriage. Towards the end of the lesson she suggests that these questions might become a shared research agenda for the class. She adds that the research might be more interesting and more fruitful if it could take the form of an investigation of what a marriage commitment actually involves in the case of the different religions. As examples, she poses questions such as: are the commitments entered into the same in the different religions? Are they the same for men and for women?

Both the students and Gráinne begin to anticipate that their enquiries could lead them to exciting places. Gráinne is keenly aware that thoughts of quite different species are likely to take wing in this venture, and that the agreed rules of engagement will be tested, but hopefully also strengthened and better appreciated, through the encounters that now lie ahead. She cannot say whether any of this material will come up on an exam, but she is happy in the knowledge that it is indeed central to the official programme for Religious Education.

Let me conclude by reviewing as succinctly as I can the emphasis that is being placed here on enquiry, as distinct from faith-formation. The teacher here understands that something of her own religious convictions is yet likely to be evident in her actions. She is quietly confident about this, but she also keeps an eye on it without letting her vigilance become a preoccupation, or stifle anything genuine in herself. She is aware, from her own fluent understanding of both educational experience and religious traditions, that there remains a crucial distinction between the teacher and the tradition. She understands that a teacher's evocations of the voices of a particular tradition may initiate enthusiasms and self-sustaining encounters between individual students and the tradition. But she also knows the teacher must seek to ensure that such enthusiasms remain conversational rather than adversarial, both in encounters *within* and *between* traditions. In this sense, she is aware that religious education in a secular age, far from being a combative voice on the unquiet frontiers of modernity, remains a fertile source for the renewed cultivation of humanity's ever-delayed maturity.

References

Bryk, A.S., V.E. Lee and P.B. Holland 1993. *Catholic Schools and the Common Good*. Cambridge MA: Harvard University Press.

Oakeshott, Michael, 1962. The Voice of Poetry in the Conversation of Mankind, in his *Rationalism in Politics and Other Essays*. London & New York: Methuen.

Williams, Kevin, 2007. *Education and the Voice of Michael Oakeshott*. Exeter: Imprint Academic.

CODES OF ETHICS IN A SECULAR AGE: LOSS OR EMPOWERMENT OF MORAL AGENCY?

ALAN J. KEARNS

Introduction

One of the defining features of any profession is its sense of having a moral dimension and a strong moral purpose; that they are there to provide a service to (sometimes vulnerable) people with their expertise and skills, in a professional and upstanding manner. A code of ethics can proffer a platform from which the values of the respective profession can be highlighted and promulgated among its members and the public at large. Professionals are often faced with difficult and ethically challenging situations in their work places. A code of ethics can provide useful guidance to professionals seeking ethical clarification on particular issues. Finally, the drafting of a code of professional ethics can be triggered by an event that throws up a shortfall in the present mechanisms that seek to guarantee professional behaviour. Codes often champion the rights of clients and seek to install measures to circumvent professional misconduct and attempt to guarantee high professional services.

With the introduction of more and more codes of ethics in professional activities, the question arises as to whether there is a dip in the balance of the scales from the individual professional's moral agency in the direction of the ethical codes themselves. Do codes empower the moral agency of professionals or can they sometimes lead to a loss of moral agency?

As someone working in the field of ethics education for student-teachers, health care practitioners and other professionals, I find Charles Taylor's latest insights on code-fixation in *A Secular Age* germane and provocative. His work poses some hard questions for the use of codes and indirectly raises questions about the impact of codes on moral agency in contemporary professional practices.

This paper presents an outline of Taylor's views regarding codes of ethics in his *A Secular Age*. It takes one contemporary example of a pan-

European code of ethics, namely *The Code of Ethics and Conduct for European Nursing*, and makes the argument that the intention of a code of ethics is not to diminish the moral agency of a professional, but to provide a scaffolding of support and guidance for professionals faced with work situations that pose increasingly complex ethical issues.

Setting the Context

My inquiry begins in the city of Tallinn, the capital of Estonia and the medieval pearl on the Baltic shore. Tallinn has many hidden attractions, one of which I fortunately stumbled upon while visiting the Church of St Nicholas. In this architectural jewel of Tallinn, the "Dance with Death" (*Dance Macabre*) by Bernt Notke is displayed. The painting is renowned for being one of the darkest works of art in history: Death is personified as someone who invites us to a dance (Notke 2004).[1] This particular masterpiece is one of the few surviving examples in the world that uses the "Dance with Death" motif. The original painting was thirty meters long and illustrated the personification of death dancing around twenty-four classes of people in society, from the very rich to the very poor, from the very powerful to the very weak, from the very young to the very old (Tähepõld 2004 p.7). This work of art suggests that all people are equal in the eyes of death, i.e. death comes to everyone and no-one is spared. Those who have power in society are reminded that their eminence is transient and will not guarantee immortality. Every person is called to this inescapable and inevitable dance with death no matter how he or she may wish to decline its invitation.

As I was observing this majestic masterpiece, I began to reflect on the fact that the advancements in technology and science and their employment in health care settings could be understood as ultimately a pursuit to avoid the invitation to the "dance with death". Technology and biomedicine are utilised in the world of health care to conquer illness and mortality. Yet, there often tends to be a confluence of excitement and uneasiness about the utilisation of technology and medicine in this area. This pursuit to do "all that can be done" for patients generates new challenges and ethical issues, especially when the use of technology only prolongs the life of a person who therefore experiences needless and unbearable suffering. Practitioners may, for example, be forced to do all that they can because of legal requirements and the threat of litigation from families left behind after the death of a loved one. This is a daily challenge in seeking to do what is in the best interest of the patient, while taking into account the law and the concerns of family members. In such situations, professionals may look to their code of ethics for guidance to help throw light on the moral quandary that they face.

In the world of business, there is another type of avid pursuit, not to avoid the "dance with death", but to generate as much profit as possible and to maximize shareholder value. The recent contraction of the world economies has unexpectedly led to an unintended cathartic experience where irregular and ethically questionable business practices, especially in the banking sectors, have come to light and have prompted the pressing need for really stringent regulation that protects consumers. In the race for the bottom line, principles of prudence, fairness, honesty and integrity seem to have taken second place. This phenomenon has led to a need for codes of ethics in business that are not cosmetic in nature but have real meaning, application and implication.

The complex world of health care and the cut-throat competitive nature of commercial activities demand codes of ethics to provide a moral compass in a world that is at sea in these morally turbulent times.

Charles Taylor on Codes of Ethics

In examining the moral sources[2] for the present day's standards of altruism, Taylor contends that much of the moral thinking of contemporary secular society has arisen from the modern understanding of moral order, which tends to focus primarily on moral codes (SA 703). He points to the fact that much effort in contemporary liberal society is given to defining and applying a code of conduct (SA 704). A lot of present-day moral theory takes it for granted that morality can be codified in terms of rules of conduct that are rooted in a single moral principle or source (SA 704). There is also a kind of "code-fixation" in the political world, which is "interwoven with legal entrenchment of certain fundamental principles of our society, whose most prominent and visible form is the constitutionalization of various charters of rights and non-discrimination, which is a central feature of our world" (SA 704). Taylor maintains that there is a belief that collective goods, including tolerance and respect, can be achieved through the establishment of a code of behaviour that outlines what is allowed and what is forbidden. Moral progress in any society—and perhaps by extension in any profession—is, according to this line of thinking, facilitated by the endorsement of a code.

For Taylor, the moral life of a person cannot be adequately captured in a code of ethics. Firstly, there are often unforeseen events in life that cannot be accommodated by a code. Therefore, any code will face the prospect of having to be constantly adapted to new situations. There is no one-size-fits-all approach to the moral life. In this context, Taylor points to the Aristotelian vision of the moral agent who uses practical judgement (*phronesis*) to discern the moral demand in each situation in light of the goods that are sought after (SA 704).

Secondly, codes of ethics often cannot cope with the fact that there is a plurality of goods which can clash with each other in various situations. For example, in health care the good of protecting and upholding the autonomy of the patient might demand that we respect the person's wishes to forego a particular treatment. This may mean in practice that the health care practitioner might have to go against the good of seeking what is in the "best interest" of the patient, especially when the benefit of utilising treatment would outweigh any potential harms or burdens to the respective patient. According to Taylor, a situation where there is a conflict of goods intensifies the need for practical judgment by the moral agent because the conflict of goods creates dilemmas that cannot be easily answered in a code of good practice. Taylor argues that the conflict of goods that engenders dilemmas may call for different responses and perhaps more than one possible resolution may present itself to the moral agent. This is due not only to the existence of a plurality of goods but also to the existence of a plurality of moral agents with various moral claims.

To illustrate his point, Taylor gives the example of strict commutative justice in cases of historical wrong-doings between nations. The residents of the offending country may have to live with the effects of full redress, which can frustrate the development of their home country. Taylor contends that if parties can be encouraged to enter into dialogue with one another—instead of having people insist on their rights as outlined in a respective code – a different kind of redress might be sought that does not perpetuate the suffering on any side.

According to Taylor, dilemmas that are caused by the clash of a plurality of goods sought by a number of moral agents with various moral claims, need to be understood in terms of a two-dimensional space, i.e. the horizontal and the vertical. The horizontal space is the point of resolution between two groups, which is often deemed to be the "fair award" in the case of commutative justice (SA 706). The vertical space allows the groups to rise above the point of resolution to a higher space where the fair award will be less damaging for all parties involved. This vertical space is one of reconciliation and trust (SA 706). It is one of the critical themes of the Christian approach to the resolution of conflict. To quote *in toto* from Taylor,

> ... Christian faith can never be decanted into a fixed code. Because it always places our actions in two dimensions, one of right action, and also an eschatological dimension. (SA 703)

Taylor refers to the biblical story of the parable of the vineyard workers that can be found in the gospel of Matthew (20:1-16). From the perspective of the horizontal space, the payment of one denarius does not seem acceptable in terms of a just wage in the strict sense. But from a vertical space perspective, it is an appropriate distribution of resources because of reconciliation and trust between the parties involved. Taylor concludes from this that the Christian moral life cannot be governed solely by a code of behaviour:

> ... there aren't any formulae for acting as Christians in the world. Take the best code possible in today's circumstances... The question always arises: could one, by transcending/amending/re-interpreting the code, move us vertically? Christ is constantly doing that in the Gospel. That's why there is something extremely troubling about the tendency of some Christian churches today to identify themselves so totally with certain codes (especially sexual norms), and institutions (liberal society). (SA 707)

As I read him, the horizontal space refers to the "right" action as specified by the code; it is the particular norm which governs conduct. The vertical space refers to the "values" underpinning the action, the *raison d'être* for the behaviour.[3]

For Taylor, the vertical dimension to the resolution of dilemmas returns us to the essential element that is missing in contemporary moral philosophy regarding its sources, i.e. moral motivation (SA 707). The experience of reconciliation and trust entails a "motivational conversion" that enables moral agents to respond to dilemmas, not in rigid ways of following rights and responsibilities as specified in a code of ethics (i.e., the horizontal space), but by engaging in dialogue and mutual trust with different moral agents (i.e., vertical space). Taylor contends that:

> ... the "code fetishism", or nomolatry, of modern liberal society is potentially very damaging. It tends to forget the background which makes sense of any code: the variety of goods which the rules and norms are meant to realize, and it tends to make us insensitive, even blind, to the vertical dimension. It also encourages a "one size fits all" approach: a rule is a rule. (SA 707)

Codes & Moral Agency

Taylor's insights on code-fixation in *A Secular Age* can be applied to questions relating to the impact of codes on the moral agency of the professional. Do codes empower moral agency or do they lead to an erosion of moral agency, where the code takes over and directs the moral agent to make an ethical choice in a certain way?

Firstly, the function of a code of ethics is not to replace the centres of ethical decision-making, i.e. the moral agent who can make ethical choices and who can be held morally accountable for his or her actions. The establishment of a code of ethics can be a hallmark of moral agency, i.e., codes are written *by* moral agents *for* moral agents.

Secondly, codes of ethics are not one of the distinguishing features of a secular age: they are not unique to this period of history. Codes seem to have always accompanied humanity in some shape or form. The Ten Commandments and the Torah are codes governing ethical living that are hugely important for the Jewish people as they are part of the covenental relationship between God and his chosen people as written in the Hebrew Scriptures.[4] The Beatitudes present normative instructions for Christians—in a kind of codal form—on how to live as a disciple of Jesus Christ.

Well before the emergence of Christianity, there are two historic codes that have significant implications for the governing of professional practices in medicine: The Babylonian Code of Hammurabi is accredited with being the first set of documented laws by a civilization and the Hippocratic Oath is considered to be a breakthrough in terms of physicians taking a pledge of not causing harm (*primum non nocere*) to all patients (Carrick 1985, 94).[5]

Such examples demonstrate that codes are the net result of moral agents articulating an experience of values, whether those values are grounded in divinely-revealed morality or solely in human rational reflection and evaluation of choices and actions.

Thirdly, although not unique to this period in history, the generation of codes has intensified in more recent times. Difficult episodes in the history of medicine, for instance, have prompted the establishment of codes of ethics to protect the public and to ensure high standards of medical research and care. In the twentieth century there was a significant surge in the number of codes such as Nuremberg (1948). Clearly in the pursuit of knowledge, humanity continues to learn that people can never be treated as mere objects in any experiment. The duty to care for the patient can be derailed in the pursuit to acquire knowledge that protects against the invitation to the "dance with death".

The Nuremberg Code establishes in clear and strong terms the absolute necessity for the attainment of voluntary, informed and valid consent when a person is being asked to participate in medical and scientific research.[6] This essential requirement has penetrated other areas of health care, especially in the area of invasive medical procedures. It has also penetrated other professional practices, including the world of education and the emergence of academic research ethics committees exemplifies this phenomenon.

Fourthly, codes of ethics are hugely important in defining professional practices. A code can provide a platform from which the values of the profession, and the institution in which professionals practice, can be embodied. Codes give professional organizations the opportunity to reflect on their value systems and to codify their normative insights in order to inspire as well as to inform their members. Mike Martin makes the following pertinent point about professionals in general and their respective codes:

> A code represents the formal and authoritative statement by a profession, through its representative professional society, of the standards for providing services. It constitutes the bedrock for a shared moral worldview within the profession.... Without codes, practitioners would have license to make up their own rules, and professions would lack moral coherence. (Martin 2000, 33)

Finally, codes also attempt to install measures to circumvent professional malpractice and misconduct. Codes attempt to champion the rights of clients, to detail the expectations of professional conduct and to install measures with disciplinary sanctions or penalties where professional behaviour does not meet the standards enumerated. The goal of any profession should be to contribute to the well-being of the person (Wogaman 1989, 71).[7] A professional generally offers a service or an expertise that the average person does not possess, which can place prospective clients in a somewhat vulnerable situation. The drafting of codes of professional behaviour can be triggered when an event or a situation throws up a flaw in the mechanism which had been designed to guarantee high professional service. According to Milton Jeganathan, "... ethical codes are the results of the attempt to direct the moral consciousness of the members of the profession to its particular problems. They crystallise moral opinion and define behaviour in these specialised fields" (1999, 4). It could be that the impulse to write a code may be reactionary rather than something proactive.

A Contemporary Example: *The Code of Ethics and Conduct for European Nursing*

Nursing is pioneering the development of a pan-European ethical code for professional practices with the introduction of *The Code of Ethics and Conduct for European Nursing* by the Federazione Europea delle Professioni Infermieristiche (FEPI).[8] The purpose of this code is to highlight the ethical values that ought to govern nursing professionals and to ensure that service-users receive the same quality of care whether they be in, for instance, Ireland, France or Croatia.

The Code of Ethics and Conduct for European Nursing is the net result of a consultative process between the FEPI and the various nursing regulatory bodies throughout Europe, together with patient representative groups and allied health care professionals. *The Code* "…arises from the new development of nursing knowledge, from the impact of technology and from the scientific advance regarding patient safety within the framework of a changing international context" (FEPI 2007, section 2). *The Code* has been influenced by certain European Directives, including human rights legislation and the European Council of the Liberal Professionals (FEPI 2007, section 2).[9]

The drafting of *The Code* is due to the recognition of the need for harmonious professional practices across Europe in the face of the ever-increasing mobility of practitioners. According to the President of the FEPI, Loredana Sasso, the project to create a trans-national code was:

> … aimed at harmonizing the ethical standards of nursing practice and the nursing profession in Europe by identifying, clarifying and analyzing the moral values underlying codes of ethics in nursing and to draw up a new code whose ethical principles could be shared at least by all FEPI members and in general throughout Europe (Sasso, Stievano, Jurado & Rocco 2008, 823).

Sasso points to the fact that the European Council of the Liberal Professions (CEPLIS) disseminated a questionnaire to various groups and organisations in an attempt to attain observations about the particular common values that should be demonstrated by various liberal professions.[10] They then went on to draw up a document, *Common Values for Liberal Professionals in Europe*, which was based on the feedback that they had received (Sasso, Stievano, Jurado & Rocco 2008, 824). FEPI responded to the invitation by CEPLIS for the liberal professionals to prepare European-wide codes of conduct for their respective professions that would be grounded in the following principles:

Confidentiality
Participation in Continuous Professional Development
Independence and Impartiality
Honesty and Integrity
Supervision of Support Staff
Compliance with Codes of Conduct and Practice
Professional Liability Insurance
Conflict with Moral or Religious Beliefs. (CEPLIS 2007, 2-4)

The bedrock of *The Code of Ethics and Conduct for European Nursing* is the protection of the public and the pursuit to ensure the safety of patients being given nursing care in all European countries (FEPI 2007, section 2). To this end, *The Code* provides direction to the various nursing regulatory bodies throughout Europe on the central common, professional and ethical principles that ought to be taken into account when they are drawing up their respective codes of ethics and professional conduct. In addition, the aim of *The Code* is to inform service-users/clients/patients of such common principles that penetrate all nursing practices in Europe and what they should expect from the delivery of health care (FEPI 2007, section 1).

The following are some of the key principles outlined in *The Code*:

Firstly, quality and excellence of the professional delivery of nursing care is paramount. *The Code* states that "nurses have professional competences linked to the good practice of the profession" (FEPI 2007, section 3.1). This principle governs the standard and quality of training and education of the profession.

The principle of human rights is the centrepiece of this code. It states that "patients have the right to human dignity..." (FEPI 2007, section 3.3).[11] *The Code* states quite clearly that it is formulated in such a way that the rights of patients are underscored and are given primacy (FEPI 2007, section 2).

Patients have a right to equitable access to quality health care. This reflects the traditional duty to care for the person irrespective of race, gender, age, religion, or culture (FEPI 2007, section 3.4).

The Code also states that patients have a right to expect honesty and integrity from nurses. Nurses are obliged to act in the best interests of the patient and to act as an advocate for them (FEPI 2007, section 3.6).

Other principles that are emphasized in *The Code* include the right to expect information that is communicated in an appropriate way and that can be comprehended (FEPI 2007, section 3.8).

The quintessential ethical principle of informed consent is also outlined in this code. It states that "patients have the right to decide whether or not to accept nursing care (informed consent) or to refuse to receive information, advice or care and that the nurse will respect this decision" (FEPI 2007, section 3.9). It should be added that *The Code* recognises the fact that valid consent should always be sought; that it must be free and non-coerced; and that the person must be legally competent.

The Code pinpoints the principle of confidentiality as the "cornerstone" of trust between professionals and clients (FEPI 2007, section 3.10). It also recognises that this is not an absolute principle as there may be legal limitations to confidentiality depending on the country in which the nurse practices.

Finally, in situations where the nurse has serious moral concerns about a requested nursing service, he or she is encouraged to find a solution through dialogue with the patient, the hospital and the regulatory board. *The Code* also allows for the nurse to voice conscientious objection. *The Code* is clear that it does not replace the conscience of the person.

The Code of Ethics and Conduct for European Nursing gives voice to the values of the profession of nursing across the European landscape. FEPI does not envisage *The Code* as something that is static and unchangeable but as something that is dynamic and adaptable to the changing context of health care in Europe. *The Code* is flexible enough to allow its central principles to be further specified by nursing regulatory bodies for their particular contexts and it is broad enough not to be seen to be replacing the role of the individual moral agent and inadvertently reducing the nurse to a moral robot.

In Response to Taylor

The following are some remarks in response to the criticisms raised by Taylor in relation to ethical codes. Firstly, Taylor is correct in his view that there are often unforeseen events in the moral life that cannot be accommodated by a code. I do not believe that all codes aspire to provide an answer to all ethical eventualities. This, of course, depends on the code and the profession. Some codes tend to give broad guidelines and aspirations whereas other codes are more detailed and are directive-focused. For example, Section 3 of the Association of Chartered Certified Accountants (ACCA) *Rulebook* (2009) contains a very detailed code of ethics and conduct governing the practice of accountancy in Ireland and Britain. Codes in health care tend not to be as detailed compared to codes in the accounting or aviation professions. But many codes do not present ready-made answers, aimed at resolving every possible type of ethical dilemma, nor do they claim to do so. They do not strive to replace the moral agent as the centre of moral decision-making.

Secondly, Taylor is correct when he states that there is a plurality of goods which can clash with each other in various situations. However, it may be unfair to state that codes often cannot cope with this fact. Once again, this would depend on the code. The pursuit of goods is generally weighed according to whether they are absolute or less stringent. For example, in some cases a professional may not be obliged to keep in confidence a possible harm to another person. In addition, the existence of a plurality of goods and moral agents would surely endorse the need to have a code when there is often a plurality of moral views on certain ethical dilemmatic situations.

Thirdly, Taylor is correct in his view that Christian faith can never be decanted into a fixed code in light of the fact that it places actions into two spaces: right action (i.e., horizontal) and eschatological dimension (i.e., the vertical). Indeed, Christ said, for example, that the Sabbath was made for the person and not the person for the Sabbath. In a similar vein, it could also be suggested that codes are made for the moral agent and not the moral agent for codes. Notwithstanding this, both the Ten Commandments and the Beatitudes demonstrate that codes are not necessarily foreign to the Christian faith. Religions have provided guidance and inspiration. Perhaps, today, for some people, codes of ethics may be replacing the role of religion in terms of ethical direction.

With the development of technology and with society becoming more and more complex, the importance of codes will only increase in the years to come become. Codes can give directives about "right" actions (i.e., horizontal space) grounded in some notion of the "good" (i.e., vertical space) of doing that action. The vertical space might provide the *raison d'être* of the horizontal code—but the following of the code will depend on the moral agents. Karen Lebacqz, correctly in my view, observes that a professional is a person who is called, not only to perform an action or provide a service, but to behave in a certain way. Therefore, she argues that "codes may be couched in actional language ('do this', 'avoid that'), but their meaning emerges only when we look behind these specifics to a sense of the overall picture of the type of person who is to *embody* those actions" (Lebacqz 1985, 71). Therefore, codes may not replace moral agency: they may empower agents by giving them direction and maybe even by offering inspiration.

A problem may arise in this age of ethical codes when there is a separation of the vertical from the horizontal space or when the code becomes the sole moral source of the moral life. There may also be a risk that codes of ethics are only generated for window-dressing purposes too. Perhaps a step towards preventing codes becoming static and helping moral agents to remain steadfast to the originating values of their profession, in the face of moral uncertainty and constantly changing world, is to ensure that the vertical values grounding the horizontal code are continually revisited and renewed.[12] In addition, with the introduction of a revised code for a given professional body, a new emphasis could also be placed on the importance of the individual professional as an agent of ethical decision-making. A code is there to assist rather than to replace moral agents who will need to face ethical challenges with strong character and conviction, rooted, for example, in the virtues of prudence and integrity. A renewed emphasis on the need for people to act as moral agents will not make codes redundant but will help to situate codes in their proper context as a horizontal guide for the day-to-day practices of professionals. Further education in the areas of ethics for professionals may help moral agents to refine their skills in making informed ethical decisions, in conjunction with their codes of ethics.

Conclusion

A code of ethics can provide a platform where a set of common values and aspirations, directions and sanctions, are articulated for moral agents working in their respective professions. As the world becomes more complex—with the pursuit of ingenious methods of forestalling the "dance with death" in health care, and the need for restraining the pursuit of unbridled profit-making and greed in business—codes will become increasingly important. I think that Taylor's view about code-fixation presents a significant word of caution to us, ensuring that codes do not replace the moral agent and become a substitute for ethical decision-making. However, innovative codes such as FEPI's *The Code of Ethics and Conduct for European Nursing* may not necessarily lead to a loss in moral agency but may assist the agent to make decisions in his or her professional capacity that is in keeping with the dignity of the person, which is central to ethical conduct.

References

American Pharmaceutical Association, 1994. *Code of Ethics*. Available from: http://ethics.iit.edu/codes/coe/amer.pharmaceutical.assoc.coe.html

Association of Chartered Certified Accountants, 2009. *Rulebook*. London: CPI William Clowes Beccles.

Bassford, H. A., 1990. Medical Ethics: The Basis of Medical Ethics, ed. Don MacNiven, *Moral Expertise: Studies in Practical and Professional Ethics*, London: Routledge, 128-143.

Carr, David, 2000. Professional Education and Professional Ethics, ed. Guillaume de Stexhe and Johan Verstraeten, *Matter of Breath: Foundations for Professional Ethics*, Leuven: Peeters, 15-34.

Carrick, Paul, 1985. *Medical Ethics in Antiquity: Philosophical Perspectives on Abortion and Euthanasia*, Dordrecht: Reidel.

European Council of the Liberal Professions, 2007. *Common Values for Liberal Professionals in Europe*. Available from: http://www.ceplis.org/indexengl.htm

FEPI, *The Code of Ethics and Conduct for European Nursing*, 2007. Available from: http://www.fepi.org/en/details_home.php?id=3

Hugman, Richard, 2003. Professional Ethics in Social Work: Living with the Legacy. *Australian Social Work*, 56.1, 2003, 5-13.

ICN Code of Ethics for Nurses, 2006. Available from: http://www.icn.ch/icncode.pdf

Kaptein, Muel, 2008. *The Living Code: Embedding Ethics into the Corporate DNA*, Sheffield: Greenleaf.

Kass, Leon R., 1985. *Toward a More Natural Science: Biology and Human Affairs*, New York: The Free Press.

Lebacqz, Karen, 1985. *Professional Ethics: Power and Paradox*, Nashville: Abingdon Press.

Martin, Mike, W., 2000. *Meaningful Work: Rethinking Professional Ethics*, New York: Oxford University Press.

Milton Jeganathan, W. S., 1999. *Professional Ethics among Teachers*, Delhi: ISPCK.

Sasso, Loredana, Alessandro Stievano, Máximo González Jurado and Gennaro Rocco, 2008. Code of Ethics and Conduct for European Nursing. *Nursing Ethics*, 15.6, 2008, 821-836.

Tähepõld, Kadri, 2004. *Nikolaikirche: Museum und Konzertsaal*, Tallinn: Ecce Revalia.

Taylor, Charles, 1989. *Sources of The Self: The Making of the Modern Identity*, New York: Cambridge University Press.

Telushkin, Joseph, 2006. *A Code of Jewish Ethics, Vol. I: You Shall be Holy*, New York: Bell Tower.

Tröhler, U. and S. Reiter-Theil, 1998. *Ethics Codes in Medicine: Foundations and Achievements of Codification Since 1947*, Aldershot: Ashgate.

Wogaman, J. Philip, 1989. 'Paternalism and Autonomy', *Studies in Christian Ethics: Professional Ethics*, 2.1, 1989, 66-78.

World Medical Association, 2006. *International Code of Medical Ethics*. Available from: http://www.wma.net/e/policy/c8.htm

Sources of the Sacred: Strong Pedagogy and the Making of a Secular Age

Andrew O'Shea

> From the very beginning of the human story religion, our link with the highest, has been recurrently associated with sacrifice, even mutilation, as though something of us has to be torn away or immolated if we are to please the gods. (Taylor 1989, 519)

At the end of *Sources of the Self*, having mapped the "conflicts of modernity", Taylor acknowledges, with an air of the almost inevitable, how all of what he had been writing about in the previous 520 pages was really just a warm-up for another book that he could scarcely then conceive. While so much of the groundwork was admittedly prepared, it seemed the really important work, the work that would yield the fruit of the labours thus far, lay in an exploration of a religious question concerning the true inspiration of secularization in Western culture over the past 450 or so years. Indicating the scale and nature of the problem, Taylor confesses his inability to demonstrate how the dilemma of mutilation is "our greatest spiritual challenge". With this confession he fires an arrow into the future along with a promise to return to the problem that had up until then eluded him. *A Secular Age* is his making good on that promise. One of its considerable achievements lies in the author's own perseverance as a philosopher with religion and its relationship to the sources of the modern identity. The issue of "mutilation" as the spiritual challenge he attempts to finally meet has to do precisely with the unravelling of the core of religious faith understood through the prism of the sacred from its earliest incarnations to the present day. What I wish to do is to draw out what I see as Taylor's "bi-focal" analysis of the sacred in the context of developments in secular culture: how is the self thus constituted in relation to the processes of "making sacred", or sacrifice?

What I attribute to Taylor, as a Catholic philosopher, is a way of reading "the signs of the times", or the meaning of Christianity today. It is a reading that earnestly confronts the historical reality of violence—its role in human communities and its intricacies and intransigencies in the human body and in human relationships—while also attempting a retrieval of the good. In this way Taylor's anthropology of the sacred is a strong hermeneutics: a "making" that is at once fully aware of the ontological dilemmas facing human beings in the 21st century and yet also, courageously, an attempt to define and clarify the conditions of hope for our world.

One of the central concerns of *A Secular Age* is how to recover some conception of sacrifice in a post-religious age, an age that places a premium on human flourishing and universal right. Arising from the historical disputes around religion and the nature of human flourishing, Taylor claims there is at least a three cornered battle raging in our culture.[1] "There are the secular humanists, there are the neo-Nietzscheans and there are those who acknowledge some good beyond life" (SA 636). Here we pick up the thread of the challenge mentioned above, since by pushing its own view independently of the others, each side of the debate today, in its own way, runs the risk of what Taylor calls "mutilation", or the process in which the human being—taken as a whole, with ordinary desires and fulfilments, including a longing for eternity (understood as either immanent or transcendent, or both)—is systematically reduced, cramped or denied its proper measure of life. This can occur in various ways in the "three cornered battle". For example, secular modernity has reacted strongly against transcendence, and in doing so it has drawn a fixed *cordon sanitaire* around its conception of the human. For those who have perhaps shaken off the "guilt" of a repressive religious upbringing, Taylor believes it is understandable that they might take the stance, "a pox on all transcendence" (SA 630). But he thinks this is wrong-headed, since this view of the human frequently holds "normative" assumptions that seek to explain our behaviour in terms of certain rational principles or modes of conduct that characterise deviance in ways that frequently undermine the integrity of individuals' own senses of their experience of why they can't quite hit the mark. In a civilized secular culture under the rule of law, the resistances to conformity and "the impulses toward violence, aggression, domination; and/or those to wild sexual licence" are characterised "as mere pathologies or underdevelopment" (SA 633). Describing the programme of reform concerning such "pathologies" Taylor says:

> These are simply to be extirpated, removed by therapy, re-education or the threat of force. They do not reflect any essential human fulfilments, even in a distorted form, from which people might indeed be induced to depart through moral transformation, but which cannot simply be repressed

without depriving them of what for them are important ends, constituent of their lives as human beings (SA 633).

Enlightenment culture tends toward mutilation by denying the pathways to *full* human flourishing. This "fullness" arguably requires a horizon of transcendence to help explain why things can and do frequently go so terribly wrong for individuals within our "civilized" culture.[2]

Those who follow Nietzsche take a different stance toward the irrepressible and constitutive nature of our most basic human impulses. They rejoice in them as an expression of the will to power: "their denigration by modern humanism in the name of equality, happiness and an end to suffering, was what was degrading the human being, reducing human life to something no longer worth living" (SA 635). Where, Taylor asks (polemically echoing this stance), is the "real sacrifice" in the "untroubled happiness" that attends this "normalcy"? Beyond the slavish impulse to cling to our chains, this side of the debate questions whether there really is anything worth dying for. Depending on the degree to which the Neitzscheans have imbibed their master's doctrine of the will to power, mutilation can come from either an undermining of human benevolence in the name of revolt (the mild form), or the expendable nature of human life in the name of great deeds and heroic values (the strong form). And Taylor speculates that along this "tragic axis" of anti-humanism we find an explicit embracing of the perennial human susceptibility to be fascinated by death and violence which he thinks is at bottom "a manifestation of our nature as homo religiosus" (SA 639).

Christianity clearly believes in human flourishing, but not as the last word in the drama of humanity. God's will does not equal "let human beings flourish".[3] Something may have to be given up, or our relationship to it reoriented, for the sake of transformation to a higher level in accordance with God's will. So Christians share with the Nietzscheans something that approximates the necessity of sacrifice—though unlike the latter, Christians clearly express this as self-sacrifice. But "believers", as Taylor calls them, also mutilate by renouncing sensuous pleasures, aggression and ordinary fulfilments in the name of a higher good; they frequently place the primacy of life elsewhere. Historically, he argues, the reaction to Catholic monasticism, during the Reformation, marks a move away from the higher spiritualities that were thought to cramp and stifle ordinary human fulfilments. However, he maintains that while there does appear to have been a slide into a negative obsession with the body during this period, the initial concern for renunciation, as a medium for passing on of titles, property and power, was not "in itself" a bad thing (SA 631). The problem is how it became a "disgust-cum-fascination with desire" which secular humanists, along with Taylor, want to reject (SA 631). This desire for transcendence can sacrifice ordinary fulfilments to some higher end, thereby stifling human flourishing. "Perhaps we should renounce this aspiration toward a fuller love on these grounds?" he asks, but then promptly answers: "I confess that this to me would be an even greater mutilation of the human than... cramped modern Catholicism" (SA 631). Thus the three corners of the battle in our culture today each risk mutilation, by: 1) reducing the limits of how it conceives of the human, and correspondingly reducing the bar governing our expectation of the highest good; 2) by radically undermining benevolence and equality, and perhaps even releasing some primordial violence (an outcome, Taylor suspects, that even the neo-Neitzscheans are not prepared to affirm); or 3) by undermining ordinary human desires and flourishing for the sake of some other-worldly good. Arising from these tensions Taylor puts the problem this way: "How to define our highest spiritual or moral aspirations for human beings, while showing a path to the transformation involved which doesn't crush, mutilate or deny what is essential to our humanity?" (SA 640). He calls this the "maximal demand". Achieving it in a secular age requires a new form of humanism. The issue of transformation turns out to be crucial here, and given that each of the above positions is in tension in terms of this very issue, the question becomes whether there are still resources within the Western tradition to help explain the problem and the possible solution better than the protagonists have so far themselves been able to do.

    Taylor argues that Christianity does offer the best account of how the transformation required might be achieved, but it is an interpretation that is perhaps as contentious among believers as non-believers. On one hand, he claims that Christian consciousness may not be comfortable with its own legacy of divine violence and God's gradualist approach to leading humankind away from *its own* punishing demands. On the other, he acknowledges that, in such a register as Christianity, change is always in the last analysis informed by faith and at least an implicit *eschaton*; it does not provide a purely historical solution. Some of the major distortions that create an obstacle to understanding the dilemmas we are in today have to do with: 1) Christianity's relationship to Platonism, 2) the issue of sacrifice, and 3) the need to integrate our lesser desires into a more improved way of life rather than trying to train ourselves away from them. All of this concerns a richer, deeper form of human transformation than is often proposed in today's climate, one that can get beyond the current malaises.

Taylor comes at the problem of transformation by comparing its Christian understanding with Plato's account of how we become lovers of wisdom. About Plato's account he says:

> [t]he transformation he foresees... means that some things which mattered very much to us before cease to do so... [They] will disappear, because we will come to see that they aren't really important, not part of what is required to realize the Idea of a human being. (SA 643)

Within this model, there is no point in protesting that our bodily desires and impulses matter to us—if we think so, then we are just not seeing things correctly. When we look at Christian sacrifice and renunciation (taken together), it is perhaps easy to elide one view with the other and see both Christians and Platonists as, more or less, preaching the same message. But when we do, Taylor thinks we make "nonsense of the sacrifice of Christ" (SA 644). Because what is implied in reading Platonic renunciation and Christian sacrifice as having the same meaning is that "nothing essential is given up". It is this issue that was part of the initial concern on behalf of the Reformers in their emphasising ordinary life: "It is precisely because human life is so valuable, part of the plan of God for us, that giving it up has the significance of a supreme act of love" (ibid.). This is of course a stumbling block for non-believers, who find it difficult to understand why one should give up the fullness of human flourishing unless there is something wrong with it. To do so implies that it is indeed how you see the fullness of human flourishing. Hence, "that's how unbelief reads Christian renunciation, as a negative judgement on human fulfilment" (SA 645). But secular humanism distorts the problem of transformation by "sanitizing" how profoundly deep-rooted the processes of human life and its aspirations are, and by thinking of the required change as perhaps suited to a therapeutic approach, or a programme of education. Once again nothing essential is at stake in the individual's own sense of her "underdevelopment" in this process of change.

From another angle modern Christian consciousness, by downplaying the violence and suffering that is unavoidably part of Christ's sacrifice, does not help get clear on the distortions. This move (to soften the message), Taylor thinks, is at one with the recent phenomenon referred to as the "decline of Hell"; which was an integral part of the traditional "juridical-penal framework": God pays the debt for humankind with his son; for those who repent and believe all is well, and for those who don't—damnation and eternal suffering (SA 651). Secular humanism balks at this talk of guilt and punishment. But if redemption is not simply about restoring God's "honour" as this framework suggests, then how are we to understand Christ's sacrifice? If suffering and destruction is not given such meaning, as in the older economy (i.e., "payback"), then the possibility opens up of seeing "the self-giving of Christ to suffering as a new initiative by God, whereby suffering repairs the breech between God and humans, and thus has not a retrospective or already established, but a transformative meaning" (SA 654). For modern Christian consciousness this possibility appears to break the grip of the juridical-penal model, but Taylor claims that, in doing so, it also tries to detach the central truths of the faith, regarding sin and atonement from "...the hermeneutics of divine violence, suffering as punishment or pedagogy" (ibid.). We see a complex picture emerging, but what concerns Taylor is that we do not play down the significance of the original breach—the sources of suffering and destruction—but rather he wants us to maintain some continuity with its Christian antecedents going right back "to the very beginning of the human story".

The whole account that Taylor brings forward is highly nuanced. It attempts to connect up the conflicts in our secular culture with the conflicts between the pre-Axial, the Axial, and the post-Axial religions (following Jaspers' terminology). So how does he do this? How does he recover a concept of sacrifice for a secular age—one that is charged with the earliest resonances of human violence, but can somehow respect (and even develop) both ordinary human flourishing and the religious aspiration to transcendence (or the maximal demand)? I suggest he makes an important move in this direction when he picks up on another theme, one that he explores extensively in *Sources of the Self*, regarding the aspiration to wholeness as it emerges in reaction to the disengaged self in the Romantic period. In chapter sixteen of *A Secular Age* he places this theme in the context of the move to rescue the body that has been such a feature of the modern reaction to religious renunciation:

> The [Romantic] protest here is that the rational disengaged agent is sacrificing something essential in realising his ideals. What is sacrificed is often described as spontaneity of creativity, but is even more frequently identified with our feelings and our bodily existence. (SA 609)[4]

This "sacrifice" forms the basis of the expressivist attack on Kantian autonomy, but Taylor singles out Schiller as a paradigm example of this protest with his concept of the union of opposites that achieve a higher form of life than either raw nature or reason can achieve on their own— hence overcoming division. As mentioned above, Taylor also suggests that we can read this understanding of wholeness which includes the body "as a legacy of our Christian civilization", though he acknowledges that this is clearly not an uncomplicated legacy (SA 610). What seems important here is the way this concern with wholeness and the body is connected up with the long history of religion.

Looking at it schematically we find that the pre-Axial religious life involved an enchanted world, which he describes as a "kind of acceptance of the two sides of things"; the way the gods and the world can be good and bad—beneficent and cruel (SA 611). Set against this, the Axial religions provided a source of empowerment, offering ways of "escaping/taming/overcoming this maelstrom of opposed forces" (ibid.), and thereby opening up pathways toward a higher good:

> In many cases, it was a good quite beyond ordinary human flourishing... But it promised a transformation in which we would find our deepest and fullest end in this higher good, and even one in which the struggle of forces would be transcended (the lion lying down with the lamb), or tamed into a coherent harmonious order (Confucian human-heartedness). (SA 611)

This transformation in and through something higher, Taylor claims, came at a price—one of denying and even crushing ordinary human desires. The price could be felt in two ways: first, in terms of an ethical demand that controls and restricts impulses toward unrestrained sexuality and violence; but, secondly, it could also be felt in its disenchanting effects, whereby these impulses were seen as obstacles to the good and thus "denied any depth resonance in the spiritual world" (SA 611). So, for example, certain forms of blood sacrifice are stamped out, denied any "numinous power"—the fascination that is bound up with the way ritual consecrates violence, harnessing it for social ends. This ethical pressure and disenchantment is felt all the more with the move beyond the Axial religions:

> With the coming of the 'higher', post-Axial religions, this kind of numinous endorsement is more and more withdrawn. We move toward a point where, in some religions, violence has no more place in the sanctified life, or its analogues. (SA 612)[5]

However, the two-fold price of the break with the Axial period continued to be felt, with repeated instances of regression into the more numinous and violent displays. Over the *longue durée* that Taylor traces these eruptions of the sacred can be witnessed in both higher religious cultures such as Christianity (the crusades), and secular cultures (the aftermath of the French Revolution).

While my account is even more "potted" than Taylor's is (on this issue), the point of introducing this history here is to show how he ties in the move away from violence and the excesses of desire to developments in the last few hundred years—when secular humanism comes into its own. In a post-Axial secular age—that rejects the higher transcendent dimension—there can be a number of responses to violence. Training people away from violence is one avenue open to us (he mentions Anthony Burgess's *A Clockwork Orange* as a critical exploration of this kind of disengaged social control). Another deeper response—this time on behalf of the Romantics—tries to rescue the body entirely, "to undo the disenchantment as well as the ethical suppression" (SA 613). Many of the expressivists of the eighteenth century looked to classical Greek culture to experience a purer form of religion—a development that is explored by Taylor in his *Hegel* and in *Sources of the Self*. In *A Secular Age* he picks up on this theme of modern paganism and the desire for a religion whose integral rituals connected human beings "through their desire and fulfilment with nature and the cosmos" (SA 613). And, he claims, the category of the "Dionysian", championed by Nietzsche and influencing many contemporary thinkers, is also a strong though later feature of these developments.

Now, what Taylor appears to be getting at here is that we can quite easily trace lines of connection and continuity between the Axial impulses and both contemporary higher religions and the Romantic reaction to the rational enlightenment. Yet the dominant strand of secular culture that values benevolence and universal right is, in a sense, also deeply implicated in this story:

> At its worst... Western modernity suppresses both poles of the religious. It inflicts the double wound on the pre-Axial; and it pours scorn on the post-Axial religions. But we might see it as another kind of post-Axial reform, seeking to establish a form of life that is unqualifiedly good, another mode of harmonious order. (SA 613)

The modern moral order is, after all, another order, one of mutual benefit. This too can be seen as part of the drive toward wholeness that Taylor believes is universal, and has come to include the recovery of the body, including all its numinous resonances.

What we begin to see opening up in the struggles toward fullness and wholeness today is a complicated story that must include some measure of human beings' unavoidable relationship to violence and excess. The trajectories stemming from our early connection to nature and the cosmos, and the "double wound" as the "price" of civilisation, in one way or another claims all sides of the debate. The conflicts of modernity not only run the risk of mutilation: they are also deeply sacrificial. Taylor gives this debate considerably more treatment than I can do justice to here, but if I am right to interpret him this way—of connecting up and showing continuity with a violent past—then what emerges is a set of rich and complex problems for secular culture whereby the following question appears apposite: Is it reasonable to believe that a divine power is gradually leading humankind away from forms of life that are destructive, and that something in the nature of the individual's relationship with this violence forms the basis of a progressive leap or transformation which brings about a radically new experience (not just for the subject involved), and thus is healing in a strong sense? This transformation of the world through human beings' participation and action is what he describes, at times alternatively, as a "meta-biological account" and "God's pedagogy".[6] However, he reminds us that "this is (at least) a three-cornered debate. There are accounts of the meaning of violence, which are inspired by Nietzsche... [and that] want to rehabilitate the impulsions to violence, destruction, and orgiastic sexuality" (SA 660).

Nonetheless, by assessing the dangers here in the context of the revolt from within humanism, Taylor also claims that this atheistic perspective opens paths for thinking about the place of violence and sacrifice in pre-Axial religions. His own narrative involves an attempt to explain how we have managed to move away from our being enthralled to violence. We can begin to imagine how sacrifice becomes internalised over time to involve a kind of self-sacrifice. A counter movement gradually emerges which tries to "break or at least purify" this link:

> Ancient Judaism starts a critique of this ancient levy on us... This critique applies to the unspiritualised, unmoralised forms of sacrifice where we just need to placate the Gods or spirits. But the Christian tradition retains various spiritualised forms, where the sacrifice is part of the road to perfection, or is our response to the kenosis (self emptying) of God. (SA 648)

An important development in this story of overcoming the ancient rupture occurs with the anthropocentric turn in modern Christianity—the Protestant affirmation of ordinary life—followed by a growth in unbelief and a fuller affirmation of the body in the here and now. According to Taylor this movement pushes the critique further and further:

> It portrays the older forms of Christian faith, and eventually religion as such, as a false spiritual perfectionism which sacrifices real, healthy,

breathing, loving human beings enjoying their normal fulfilment on the alters of false Gods. All religion is ultimately Moloch drinking blood from the skulls of the slain. The Old Testament critique of the Phoenician cults is now extended to faith in the transcendent as such. (SA 648)

It gradually but consistently debunks religion on the basis of it being incompatible with human flourishing. Until, finally, the critique is turned against the core human values of this movement through an affirmation of the "all too human" nature of religious violence, that can no longer be ignored at the expense of the will to power, but, on the contrary, must be unflinchingly faced and transcended, come what may. Hence, to take seriously this insight into the depth dimension of violence and still wish to respond from some kind of humanistic framework is to acknowledge that human beings are in something of a double bind when it comes to seeing a way through the apparently ineradicable nature of this violence. If Christianity is not a straightforward solution for Taylor, it does perhaps provide a way of holding the tensions in a space of transformative potential.

The strong pedagogy at work here ("God's pedagogy") is gradually leading human kind away from violence and destruction—healing the original breech—through revelation and the transformative power that comes through God's saving act. We make some concession to God's plan through what we give up, but in and through the violence we remain enthralled to its numinous power, which "concentrates into blood-lust" (SA 669). The sacred is both good and bad. Only slowly do we loosen its grip and reach a higher level. The revelation to Abraham is a leap forward. Something is brought within (the basis of a critique); violence begins to have a "double place" in human culture:

> It is there outside, in those pagan practices which have been declared abominable, like sacrificing children to Baal. But since these have to be combated, it is now also inside, in our mobilising as warriors to struggle against this paganism, defending the boundary against it. (SA 669)

And later, in Christ, there is a decisive leap and a new gift of power: "The victimhood of God, and the change it wrought, transforms the relation of violence and holiness" (SA 669). But even with the deeper critique wrought by Christianity there is still "blessed violence" and the sense of purity that can justify bloodshed, repression, and scapegoating.

Now to read Christianity in this way is to make sacrifice central to our experience as human beings—in a way that renunciation or "offering up our suffering" does not quite capture (though these forms of worship are clearly not unimportant). The transformation offered by Christianity involves acknowledging the numinous and violent legacy of "making sacred" and offering another spiritual direction. The wild dimensions of human life, articulated by Taylor in terms of Conrad's "Master Image",[7] and their rootedness in the body, are not easily overcome or indeed denied significance, since they have from the beginning been responses to God's pedagogy: in different ways,

> [they] express resistance to God, an attempt to capture and inflect the path of agape he calls us on, and bend it into something we find easier to live with. But that doesn't mean that these forms are simply all bad. They are bad qua inflections, but good qua responses to God's call. (SA 673)

On the whole, modern Christian consciousness is continually reminded that it is involved in a steep learning curve. When considering the small gains of earlier ages it should recognise them as such and not be parochial about the present by comparing our most recent achievements to them with unreflective pride.

The double place of violence owing to its historical roots, i.e., that it is still both "outside" and "inside", means that we respond to its deep resonances in at least two ways: "In the immediate context, we have to defend the innocent against attack" (SA 673). Taylor sees this as "damage control", by which he presumably means that it prevents the violence taking over. And then there is the transformative way where we "think of how we can collaborate with God's pedagogy, help along the turning into the directions of God's plan" (SA 674). This second way is closed to us, however, if we deny the resonances at work their numinous meaning: something that perhaps both secular humanists and neo-Nietzscheans do respectively (the first by "reducing them to pathology", the second by "celebrating them as intrinsically human, regardless of the form they take" (SA 674)). Yet all sides of the debate today share similar concerns regarding the human being and fullness as such. Seeing this involves a kind of "reality check" that can help each side get clear on its own deeply held values and commitments.

But why does Taylor believe that this revolt from within humanism has such a powerful hold on us? The discussion above addressed this question in terms of the constitutive nature of sacrifice for human experience and its resonances from a violent pre-Axial age. The explanation of the power of the post-humanist stance, according to Taylor, can be found in the unravelling of the problem of *homo religiosus* within the context of our modern imaginary. It is here that the issue of his "bi-focal" analysis takes on heightened significance since we are now dealing with a qualified form of transcendence (i.e., not strictly speaking "good"), *and* the conception of a personally derived identity as a hallmark of modern selfhood. In chapter nine of *A Secular Age*, entitled "The Dark Abyss of Time", we find an example of the struggle to find a new, reliable horizon of meaning. Taylor gives an account of the transition to modernity that attempts to take stock of the impact of a disenchanted cosmos on those who experienced this upheaval. He makes the case that our whole sense of things changes with the advances in science—especially with developments in astronomy, biology and evolutionary theory. We shift from an experience of a cosmos of fixed variety to a vast alienating, immeasurable universe of infinite variety, whereby the sacramental modes of the older "higher time" are relegated. We go from porous, permeable selves where signs and spirits in nature were part of our every day meanings connecting us to a larger whole, to buffered, disciplined disengaged selves disconnecting us from the world of mystery and strong value/meaning. Compared to our new cosmic imaginary and its image of "deep time", Taylor suggests that the biblical imagination in the narrative that preceded it was that of a "shaft of light right to the bottom of a rather shallow well" (SA 326-7). The new imaginary must contend with the fact that "...the extension in space not only flees outward into the immense, it also opens an inner frontier of the microscopic... Reality in all directions plunges its roots into the unknown and as yet unmappable" (SA 326). The new sense of the universe is deep in a way that the earlier understanding of cosmic order was not. The dark abyss comes to represent the vast expanse of time behind us that "hides the process of our genesis, of our coming to be" (ibid.).

The significance of our sense of awe in face of the expanse of time and untamed nature breaks us out of our rigid "buffered selves", accustomed as they are to order, purpose, and what could be seen as a narrow range of internally generated goods (tolerance, mutual benefit, etc.). The dark abyss experienced as the sublime in nature can create an agreeable frisson by shaking up our too rosy picture of the human condition. Thus, for Taylor, the dark side of creation, deep time, the very terror of the wilderness, has a moral purpose. It awakens something of the primal in us that can enable us to live proper lives even though we are long since civilized. It is here, in this experience of being open to our deep nature, that we recognise what will become the Romantic reaction to modern mechanistic science and its objectifying stance. For Rousseau nature has a voice within that awakens our moral sentiments, and for Herder, after him, language gives us access to an expressive power from the beginning. Taylor sees this as a significant development from the pre-modern cosmic imaginary of "fixed variety" where personally derived identity was never a question. For the modern imagination, meanings have to be refracted (or inflected) through the self—as the very condition of identity.

In *Sources of the Self*, Taylor explores this shift to a more subjective stance in poetry from the eighteenth century onwards. A public language of reference, employed frequently, for example, by Shakespeare, is no longer available. As a result of the disenchanting consequences of modernity "the great chain of being" is undermined. The significances in nature that were essential to this older ontic order are no longer seen as a valid basis for science. Our contact with its gamut of meanings is gradually broken, and the result is a radical disconnect from a profoundly reliable source of meaning, a loss expressed clearly in the first of Rilke's *Duino Elegies*: "Who if I cried out would hear me among the order of angels?"[8] One of the characteristics of modern selfhood is that the significance of things must be now brought out through the poets own engagement. We can recognise this change, Taylor argues, in the difference between Pope and Wordsworth— between a providential order and a personal vision.[9] But the latter "modern view" is not content to imagine a unity from the present experience of the world; it also seeks to "recapture the great moments and achievements of other times" (Taylor 1989, 465). The modern epiphany in literature seeks a unity over time, a "retrieval of experience that involves a profound breech in the received sense of identity and time, and a series of re-orderings of a strange and unfamiliar kind" (ibid.). More and more the poet's imagination must enter the dark abyss.

What is coming through here? Well, Taylor believes that the modern epiphany "doesn't come to us in the object or image or words presented"; for Taylor, "it would be better to say it happens between them. It's as though the words or images set up between them a field of force which can capture a more intense energy" (Taylor 1989, 475). Words and images from the past—from the archive of traditional symbols—are given a new power and a new meaning. Taylor sees the constitutive role of language as a crucial mode of access to the moral sources that can motivate us beyond the atrophy of dead formula or "code fixation". Over and against the poststructuralist view of language that downplays the strongly expressive aspects of subjectivity, he is attempting to recover something of the poetical power of ordinary speech, and its ability to capture and release the good. Thus the act of meeting the spiritual challenge of our age requires a space for personal vision.

However, in *A Secular Age* the problem of re-ordering and indexing a personally derived identity as a defining feature of secular culture is addressed alongside of and balanced with the *foci* of the transitions from pre-Axial to post-Axial age. We learn that, to one degree or another, the individual is confronting a foundational element of culture in the struggles to define and give meaning to his or her life. The roots of our dilemmas resonate across time. The uncertainty and urgency today of the act of bringing forward and clarifying one's identity is evident here in the deep time from which human beings emerge. The Nietzschean affirmation of the Dionysian reminds us that the post-humanist stance in its "yea saying" to death and destruction also attempts to meet our spiritual challenges without disconnecting from a pre-Axial understanding of the sacred. Hence the work of retrieval, the very articulation of sources can bring us out of our cramped postures of suppression that shrink our moral and spiritual horizons *or* fuel the darker forces of the modern story.[10]

The double focus, or *bi*-focal hermeneutics, of sacrifice and selfhood, come together at the end of *A Secular Age* in an acute way in the figure of Gerard Manley Hopkins, whose struggles and conversions in many ways personify the tensions of the three-sided battle discussed above, though for Taylor he undoubtedly is a model of a certain kind of Christian consciousness that ought to be affirmed. Hopkins is operating within a modern, disenchanted paradigm, and while tragedy appears always near he manages not to lose faith and even to maintain an orthodox view of Christianity and a sacramental view of nature. In other words, despite if not because of the wholly different context of the nineteenth century he manages to affirm the central Christian focus on communion as the goal of God's action in Creation, hence bringing "to the fore once again the deep connection between this telos of communion and a recognition of the particular in all its specificity" (SA 764). His achievement is accomplished through language, exemplified in his poetry when it captures the extremes of human experience and at times achieves a breakthrough in the otherwise cramped and deadening tendencies of the spirit. And, Taylor argues, especially in the so-called "terrible sonnets" we can find an opening up to the Other, a communion, that allows us to truly be ourselves, something that "requires an abandonment, a letting go, a sacrifice" (SA, 763).

If the conflicts of modernity are to be placed in the context of a transcendent pedagogy, a divinely inspired journey from pre-Axial to post-Axial times, then the narratives of reorientation must also be placed in the context of a *longue durée* from cosmos to universe; a narrative that reaches into the dark abyss of time and, in the very act of participation in the creative action of the divine pedagogue, goes beyond the temporal and purely subjective skein of things. The problematics of sacrifice are a central feature of the transformation involved here, but the Romantic notion of the symbol and its translation into the language of epiphany also do a lot of work for Taylor in helping him to marry the numinous resonances of the sacred and the modern turn to the subject *with* a sacramental view of nature that we find, for example, in Hopkins, and of course in Genesis, where the goodness of Creation is guaranteed. The deeper meanings that are brought about today by being refracted through the self and its struggles can be understood as part of a hard-won human development that can still acknowledge the good through some personal indexing of its significance. This personal agency in the world can never be purely instrumental or disconnected from its own ontological investment in the processes of differentiation, but is rather always grappling with the body in its bid for authenticity and wholeness. Of course, this is one story, which may or may not be convincing. As we have seen, Taylor suggests there are other accounts, ones that may well concede he is half-right, but nonetheless place their hope elsewhere, eschewing entirely what Hopkins in the poem "God's Grandeur" calls "the dearest freshest deep down things".

References

Taylor, Charles, 1989. *Sources of the Self: The Making of the Modern Identity*. Cambridge: Cambridge University Press.
—. 1992. *The Ethics of Authenticity*. Cambridge, MA: Harvard University Press.
O'Shea, Andrew, 2010. *Sacrifice and Selfhood: Rene Girard and Charles Taylor on the Crisis of Modernity*. New York and London: Continuum Books.

"CODE FIXATION", DILEMMAS AND THE MISSING VIRTUE: PRACTICAL WISDOM IN A SECULAR AGE

FÁINCHE RYAN

In the 1960s Alisdair MacIntyre gave a course at the University of Oxford entitled "What was Morality?" He suggested that the 1960s, which he considered an age of irrational emotivism and existentialism, where liberty was conceived of as an absence of constraint, might best be described as a time "After Virtue". This evaluation came to mind while reading Charles Taylor's *The Secular Age*. The absence of the concept of virtue is striking. Virtue is mentioned on page 589, where Taylor writes of the virtue of imaginative courage, and perhaps in some other places; but the term does not feature in the Index. However, on page 501 we find a sentence which indicates that Taylor accords with MacIntyre's labelling of this era as "after virtue". He notes: "We are in a different universe from that of, say, Aristotelian ethics, where a concept of *phronesis* doesn't allow us to separate a knowledge component from the practice of virtue" (SA 501).

Objectively this may be true, but one is led to ask "Why?" Why should we wish to separate a knowledge component from the practice of virtue? Why should knowledge be separated from practice? As Taylor perceives it, in modern culture "objectified knowledge" is taking over ethics (SA 501). "It goes without saying", Taylor suggests, "that this emphasis on objectified expertise over moral insight is the charter for new and more powerful forms of paternalism in our world" (SA 501). If Taylor's observations are correct, and there is ample evidence to support his claims, it seems that what is being spoken of is a changed conception of what it is to be human, a different understanding of human flourishing, if indeed flourishing remains the correct term, in this world wherein what Taylor so adroitly terms the "code-fixation" of the twenty-first century dominates. This is a world in which everything can, and indeed should, be legislated for, or so it seems in contemporary western society. The moral issue of the abuse of alcohol, and its attendant problems, are deemed to be controllable by tighter laws, or more flexible ones, depending on your stance, regarding the sale of drink. Legislation regarding food and obesity is not far away. The Church is not immune from this vision: currently in Ireland, in 2010, Church and State are co-operating in a bid to legislate to save future generations from the abuse of paedophilia. While all these movements are necessary, the focus on "code-fixation" and legislation may be deemed to indicate a certain satisfaction with a minimalist version of human order. Harmony, stability and social order seem to be the goal, and not great deeds motivated by a belief in the Transcendent, or the great dignity of human kind. Rule-keeping, and not flourishing, seem to be the goals of the secular world. Taylor writes:

> A great deal of effort in modern liberal society is invested in defining and applying codes of conduct. First, at the highest theoretical level, much contemporary moral theory assumes that morality can be defined in terms of a code of obligatory and forbidden actions, a code moreover which can be generated from a single source or principle. Hence the major importance in our philosophy departments of the battle between Utilitarians and (post)-Kantians; they agree that there must be a single principle from which one can generate all and only obligatory actions, but they wage a vigorous polemic over the nature of this principle. (SA 704)

Moving from the academy to society at large the picture is no different. Charters of rights and laws of non-discrimination are being presented in increasingly more elaborate legally binding codes; tolerance and mutual respect are seen to be achievable through legislation, or codes of behaviour. Thus we have arrived at a situation where "the contours of disrespect are codified, so that they can be forbidden, and if necessary sanctioned. Thus will our society march forward" (SA 704).

This cannot work and indeed is not working. Human moral life can never be adequately captured in a code. Situations and events are various, and change; that which is good is manifold; and goods can sometimes be in conflict. Hence dilemmas abound and admit of more than one solution. And so, Taylor concludes, "we need *phronesis* even more" (SA 705). At this point, bearing in mind the particular focus of this essay, it is appropriate to shift the focus toward moral theology, a stance not overly distant from that of moral philosophy, but distinct nonetheless. Good moral theology is rooted in a belief in the human as image of God as a necessary foundation for wholesome moral empowerment. Taylor ponders the influence this starting point might have on human action in the opening pages of the chapter entitled "Dilemmas 2". Here he presents Luc Ferry's exploration of the meaning of life, as articulated in his work *L'Homme-*

Dieu ou Le sens de la vie (Ferry 1996). In seeking to address the question of the meaning of meaning, "le sens du sens", Ferry opts to remain within the natural-human domain, to propose an answer which remains immanent. The work of *Médecins Sans Frontières* (an independent humanitarian medical aid agency) is presented as a setting wherein people can experience a kind of transcendence which is horizontal. Ferry postulates that transcendence of our ordinary existence by extra-worldly acts, by living according to extra-worldly values, can be experienced while still remaining within the human domain (SA 677). Taylor sees Ferry's theory as very much part of the modern "discovery" or "invention" of intra-human sources of motivation for universal benevolence, and admits:

> It is a powerful answer. Whether it is enough for us will depend partly on whether we sense that it captures the full force of the call we feel to succour human beings as human; whether there is something still left out which is articulated, for instance, in the language of the human as image of God. (SA 678)

It is possible for humans to act well in a secular world, to do good, even in a rule-bound world, through agencies such as *Médecins Sans Frontières*. At the same time, Taylor wonders if there is not more to human flourishing, whether the Christian story has anything unique to contribute? Yet, as he admits, the good news of Christ has become distorted. The movements of the Reformation era, while not the sole cause of this distortion, were instrumental in contributing to the growth of a secular Europe. The Reformation, and many Catholic responses to it, grew from an understanding of reason and will as separate functioning parts of the human, hence religious practice focused more on self-discipline than on grace, and the "natural" and the "supernatural" worlds became separated. Incarnational theology came to be replaced by an "excarnation" of religious practice.[1] Decision making, deliberation and conscience came to the forefront. Catechisms and manuals were used to seek the right thing to do, and Thomism was born, and flourished. This age, what Taylor labels the Secular Age, is the fruit of these changes in world view.

Prudentia

For those who stand at the crossroads, in the midst of the dilemmas of secular living, perhaps what is called for is a recovery of the virtue of *prudentia*, or at the very least the Greek virtue of *phronesis*. In order to explore this suggestion a return to the theology of St Thomas Aquinas will prove helpful—but not to the legalist and essentially voluntarist interpretations of Thomas oft times termed "Thomism", or perhaps more accurately "neo-Thomism" (Pesch 2003). In an authentic re-reading of Aquinas, what is central is not rules, or natural law, "but the virtue of *prudentia*—and not just the human virtue of *prudentia*, but a sharing in divine *providentia* by which we are guided in the life of *caritas* (sharing in divine love)" (McCabe 2008, 103). Rules do not define human goodness, and virtues as understood in the theology of Aquinas do not lend themselves to an easy concept of rule keeping. The rehabilitation of virtue, begun in the 1950s in Oxford by people such as Phillippa Foot and Elizabeth Anscombe, and put on the international stage by Alisdair MacIntyre, does not seem to have succeeded in putting *prudentia* at the centre of moral thinking. A different concept of what it is to be human, and of human action, both in the secular world and the Christian world, contribute to this difficulty.

For this reason, any contemporary consideration of the virtue of *prudentia*, and its place in the secular world, needs to first consider its concept of the agent of this virtue. For Aquinas this is the human animal, the only animal created after the image and likeness of God (ST I q.93). Like all animals, the human is an "auto-mobile", a self mover (McCabe 2008, 7). Yet the human is a very distinct type of "auto-mobile", for each human being is simultaneously a human becoming, an actor in one's own life story, with a part to play in the many life stories encountered in this world. This is what ethics studies, or at least this is how Aristotle and Aquinas would have understood things. In their world, the concept of Applied Ethics would have been incongruous. Acting and thinking about how one would act are inseparable. Each human story has a similar purpose in life, to learn how it is we might live well together on this earth. For Christians this story is part of a larger story which sees the point of human living as lying beyond itself, "in God, who is beyond but not outside ourselves" (McCabe 2008, 53). This *telos* of a life beyond death still leaves people with the task of learning how to live well here on earth, to learn, as it were, the game of life, together. It is as we live together that we create our various human cultures, and indeed our traditions. This ability that humans have is firmly rooted in that which differentiates us from other animals, language. We are symbol-using animals. Language is used to communicate with others and to talk to ourselves, in other words, in our thinking. Talking, thinking, understanding, are all distinctively human actions. Humans are not born able to speak, but are born with the capacity to learn how to speak, and thus to acquire the skills of thinking. These are learnt within the community one grows into. This is an important point, for this is what makes the human animal unique amongst all other animals. Humans create, act and respond—in other words the human animal operates in structures that are of its own making. The age Taylor describes as secular is so because of human action, and decision.

Inasmuch as human action is intentional, rather than instinctual, it is, for Aquinas, a unity of thought and will (ST I q.16 a.4, ad.1, *voluntas et intellectus mutuo se includunt*). At the same time he is aware that thought and will represent two different faculties of the soul, a distinction based on the difference between their objects (ST I q.77). The intellect is a person's ability to recognise reality and truth (*verum*), while the will is the ability to be attracted toward the good (*bonum*) as specified by the intellect. The will loves only what the mind conceives for "some knowledge of a thing is necessary before it can be loved" (ST q.27, a.2, c). For practical reasoning "both intellect and will need to be active *at the same time*. Apprehension and inclination are simultaneously necessary for action," (Westburg 1994a, 53). It is understood good, *bonum apprehensum,* which moves the will, as for "an object to move the will it must be given its character as good by the intellect" (ST I q.82, a.4). Both the will and reason act in choice, activating and guiding each other, the reason apprehending the good, the will desiring it.

Having established that rational creatures always act on the basis of a perceived good, and simultaneously recognising the ambiguity of all good apart from God, Aquinas is sure that choice is free—because unless "confronted by sheer goodness itself (God) the will may have a rich variety of reasons for being attracted and so choice/decision, *electio,* is free," (McCabe 1996, 164).[2] Here lies the distinguishing mark of all intelligent beings: we are free because we act for reasons, we choose. This is what Aquinas sees as the essence of *liberum arbitrium*, free choice.[3] In sensitivity to Aquinas' use of the term, *liberum arbitrium* is better interpreted as free choice, or "freedom to choose", and not as free will. This linguistic interpretation implies that it is always possible to have acted differently. In Aquinas' thought we are free not because we act randomly or unpredictably, but because we act for reasons, and there are many possible available reasons. Who we are, who we have become, with our virtues and vices, will affect our choices. The proper act of free will, for Aquinas, is choice (ST I q.83, a.3). However, choice, human action, takes place within a story, and human thoughts have meaning within a language system. The world of human experience, which humans seek to conceptualise, can be spoken of in an indefinite number of ways. This is key:

> It is this capacity to conceptualise the world in an indefinite number of ways, and to construct an indefinite number of sentences that lies at the

heart of human freedom. It is because, and to the extent that, we act not simply in terms of how we have to sensually *experience* the world, but of how we symbolise it, that our activity is free. (McCabe 2008, 50)

But how do we exercise this freedom? Freedom, free-will, human rights, are very much concepts of the current age, an era which Taylor sees as one of "exclusive humanism" (Taylor 1999, 19).[4] Freedom, in this world-view, is often viewed as freedom from all constraints, freedom to do what I wish, when I wish to do it.[5] This type of freedom is inevitably doomed. Perhaps it is no surprise that a therapeutic culture is flourishing in a world which fosters this vision of being human, as it seeks to try and pick up the broken pieces of those who fail to be "successful" humans, at least according to what much contemporary culture proclaims. Aquinas' understanding of life, and of being human, is different. Humans are here on earth with the central task, not of pursuing personal happiness, but in order to learn the game of life, to learn how to live together with other human beings, and in doing so, to create cultures. Central to living well, to playing the game properly, is the acquisition of the skills of living. Aquinas sees these skills as dispositions, *habitus*. The Latin *habitus* (from *habere*) is not to be translated as "habit". Translation is key for, as Servais Pinckaers notes in an article entitled "Virtue is not a Habit", the "question of words bespeaks different conceptions of virtue and morality" (Pinckaers, 1960).[6] Anthony Kenny explains the difference well: "a disposition or skill or *habitus* makes it easier for you to do what you want to do; a habit makes it harder for you not to do what you do not want to do" (Kenny 1989, 85). A *habitus* is a "disposition", a faculty which lies "half-way between a capacity and an action, between pure potentiality and full actualisation" (ST I-II q.50, a.4 ad. 2).[7] The development of a *habitus* is somewhat akin to learning to drive a car, or to write. Initially it is difficult, complex, and everything must be thought of before it is done. With practice, it becomes second nature, but driving, or writing, never become habits. It is similar with dispositions, *habiti*, which, when fully realised, when they have become second nature, are most properly termed virtues. These are what humans need on their journey toward becoming what humans were created to become. Unlike with other animals this does not happen "naturally", so to speak. The human animal has to be educated into the skills of humanity, and a good education is essential. Before we explore where and how this education might happen, we must as it were lay the ground rules, and explore how it is that Aquinas perceives the human person, negotiating a way of living life well in a complex world.

Hence we come to the question of decision making. If one is given a choice, how does one choose between two, or more apparent goods? In what may be deemed an unusual step, Aquinas treats of decision (ST I-II q.13) before discussing deliberation (ST I-II q.14, 15). This accords with the principal that a person who is skilled with the virtues will often decide without deliberation. The question on decision (*electio*) is preceded by one on intention, and this is how human action occurs. Humans pay attention to what they want to attend to. They think of it and are attracted to it. Intending and deciding are acts of will and intellect, they are rational activities. As Aquinas sees it, human action is always rational, but not necessarily reasonable, not always moral. In the exercise of practical intelligence, intellect and will work together. "By nature we tend to will whatever can present itself to our reason as good to pursue" (McDermott 2007, 46). Yet, while it is true that humans have a willing for the good in general,

> we do not choose the good in general, but only in particularised form, and it is the reason that performs the function of specification. ... The difference in the nature of the apprehended good as intellect translates it from general to particular is the essence of the psychological process of action. (Westburg 1994, 89)

In other words the difficulty in living well lies not only in the doing of the truth but also in identifying it (McNamara 1998, 159). As the work of Simone Weil and Iris Murdoch indicates, "to see things as they are is a morally difficult task" (MacIntyre 1983, 12).

Aquinas sees human behaviour as best understood in terms of virtues and vices rather than in terms of episodic individual good or bad acts. Deliberation does not necessarily precede decision making. This is where the significance of the virtue of *prudentia* becomes apparent. People who have developed the virtue of *prudentia* are skilled at decision making, at making choices. They can deliberate where necessary, delay a decision if required, and they have the courage to make difficult decisions, at the correct time. While the theological virtue of *caritas*, the virtue by which we share in the divine life, may be the queen of the virtues, in order to live well here on earth *prudentia* is identified as the linchpin of the virtues. For Aquinas, *prudentia* is an intellectual virtue, and human beings are called upon to be intelligent: as he puts it, "the intellect is the subject of virtue" (ST I-II q.56 a.3). Its chief concern is with selecting and deciding the best means to achieve an end. As practical wisdom about human action, *prudentia* is intimately related to the moral virtues. Knowing what to do, and wanting to do it, exist in a symbiotic relationship.

Prudentia is dealt with in two places in the *Summa*, briefly in ST I-II, and in more detail (10 questions) in ST II-II. As a virtue, prudence is deemed to render a person good in an unqualified sense.[8] It is a disposition of the mind which operates in view of the ends judged to be good ends. A difficulty with seeing *prudentia* as an intellectual virtue is that the human intellect deals not with concrete individuals but with meanings, with universal ideas. Human action, on the other hand, deals in specifics, with individual actions at particular times, and so the virtue of prudence, if it is to carry out its proper operation, has to involve the senses in its operation. Hence *prudentia*, (Aristotle's *phronesis*) so central to Aquinas' understanding of human action, is a disposition not only of the intellect but also of human sensibility.

The role of the senses in decision making is not something readily associated with Aquinas; indeed, it is a part of the human that does not tend to be considered as involved in intellectual decision making. Aquinas recognises its importance. A sense, he understands, as a "bodily activity by which we interpret the world" (McCabe 2008, 111).[9] There are five exterior senses, and we are familiar with these. They are concerned with receiving information, data, and experience. The four interior ones he refers to are less familiar, but are deemed to function in the very important role of perceiving a meaning in things. These senses are identified as the *sensus communis* (co-ordinating sense), the *imaginatio* (retaining the experience), the *sensus aestimativus* (evaluating significance), and the sense memory, or memorative power. Aquinas understands the *sensus communis* as an interior co-ordinating sense (ST I q.78 a.4). This co-ordinating sense is an operation of the brain which interprets and "co-ordinates" in order that what we perceive sensually are not isolated colours, sounds etc., but organised patterns of sensation. It is the "common sense" insofar as it receives information from all the other senses and interprets, or channels the information as it deems appropriate. It is this *sensus communis* which enables a human to sensually perceive objects over against themselves. It discerns and integrates. That humans have a sensual self-awareness apart from intellect is significant, and contributes to a wholesome vision of what it is to be human.

To retain and preserve experience, *imaginatio* (the storehouse of the forms an animal has sensibly received) or *phantasmata* are needed. *Phantasmata* are similitudes of particular things, and for Aquinas it is not possible to have any cognition of a material thing without a phantasm.[10] Our *imaginatio* is a storehouse of *phantasmata*, making our experiences available to us when we can no longer perceive them. This is where we move into what distinguishes human animals from other animals, the sense memory. We reminisce. Aquinas distinguishes between two types of memory, intellectual (e.g., learning a language, a telephone number) and sense memory (e.g., about one's first time arriving in Dublin). The memorative power "is the storehouse for sensory impressions and is distinct from intellective memory" (Stump 2003, 248). It gives us a sense of pastness, "a power of reminiscence, a quasi-reasoning search into the memory of past individual sense-meanings" (See ST I q.78 a.4) (Stump 2003, 248), but it can deceive, it can be wrong. The *sensus aestimativus*, the estimative sense, is a power of sensual evaluation which helps us to grasp meanings. It is similar to those animal instincts by which non-human animals sense what to seek out and what to flee, what is useful to them and what is hurtful (ST I q.78 a.4). In human beings, the estimative power also compares "individual intentions", as intellect compares universal intentions; it apprehends individual things insofar as they are "the terminus or the source of some action or passion" (Stump 2003, 248).

In exercising the virtue of *prudentia*, right practical reasoning, sense knowledge is of central importance. Each person's storehouse of experience influences decision making. Practical wisdom about human action, since human actions are always concrete and individual (unlike rules), is not an intellectual disposition like mathematics, or any other science; it must involve human sense knowledge and sense experience. As McCabe writes:

> the way we have stocked and ordered the storehouses of our *imaginatio* and our sense-memory, and the extent to which we are willing honestly to look into them, will be of great importance to the exercise of *prudentia* in our deliberation and equally important to our decision, our choice of what to do, bearing in mind who and what kind of a character we really are. (ST I q.79 a.6) (McCabe 2008, 139)

Before continuing, a word is needed on the emotions—are not the emotions that which drives us astray? Aquinas did not hold a dualist view of human nature (ST I-II q.22 a.1). *Anima mea not est ego*: the soul is containing, not contained, in the whole person. He spoke of *passione animae*, the passions of the soul. These are bodily responses of the soul, responses to our world of sensual experience. The world of sensual experience is experienced in two ways: in an undemanding way, when the world simply affects us; and as presenting us with things which need to be dealt with, the world as demanding, *ardus*. The ability to deal with the latter, to lead a good life, is the fruit of human emotions being guided by virtues.

The Game of Human Life

This leads to the final part of this exploration of the dilemma of decision making in a complex world. How can a human be formed, educated, into a person of *prudentia*? How can we learn how to act wisely in today's secular world? Or to put it differently, how can one learn to play well the game of human life? A particularly, but not exclusively, Catholic response to the secular age described by Taylor will be attempted here. While Taylor seems to emphasise the idea of conversion, the focus here will be on virtuous living—on process and not on moment. The centrality of the sacraments in the communal formation of the baptised member of the human race, baptised so that they might more easily learn the game of life, will receive particular consideration.

In the opening stages of this paper the code fixation of the world of the 21st century was identified as central to human life in the "western world", and yet it was suggested that it was stultifying to human flourishing, encouraging a minimalist standard of behaviour. The Aristotelian tradition, within which Aquinas worked, put the idea of rights and law in a secondary place: "[t]hey have their validity and necessity within, and only within, the quest for human excellence or satisfaction" (McCabe 2005, 6). Community, the *polis*, is primary, and as a community develops it discovers the need for law to help maintain the community. Insightfully, and challengingly, Herbert McCabe, in his work *On Aquinas*, writes: "Of course, being thoroughly familiar with laws does not help you to play well—indeed it is quite compatible with never playing the game at all. It is an exercise of theoretical intelligence rather than practical intelligence" (McCabe 2008, 69). One almost feels like adding a caveat: let theologians and Church leaders beware. It is by practice that the skills of human living are learnt, by practicing in accordance with Christian teachings.[11] The skills of human living, more properly termed virtues, are transformative of the practitioner. While they are totally "my" work, they are completely God's work in me, a personal response to God's presence in my life. They are a beginning of the sharing of God's life, the beginning of the road toward deification, begun here on this earth.

The game of human life is that of friendship, of learning how to live well in society. While friendship is deemed central to human flourishing in both moral philosophy and moral theology, in theology friendship is understood differently. Aristotle's *philia*, understood as right social relationships among the members of the *polis*, is concerned with their flourishing, a concept which concerns much more than justice. For an Aristotelian happiness is an activity, and essential to the activity of happiness is the fostering of friendship. This ability to foster friendship, while a central activity towards becoming human, is a skill that humans have to learn, to acquire. Firstly, we have to learn to identify what it is that makes a person "good", so that we attempt to learn the skills of goodness as we learn the skills of friendship. Aquinas, following Aristotle, identified virtue as fundamental to living well in community. The practice and acquisition of the virtue of *prudentia,* the linchpin of the virtues, consists of what might be termed a training in moral understanding. It is the process by which we learn "to want some things rather than others, to enjoy some things rather than others, and it is learning to behave reasonably in view of these wants" (McCabe 2005, 8). In asserting this, Aquinas was following not only in the footsteps of Aristotle but also of Plato, who too saw ethics as being about *paideia,* education. This understanding of the good life is based, not on law, but on tradition, and hence the question becomes how this tradition can be passed on, how people in a diverse and contradictory world can be "schooled" in an ancient philosophical tradition, and even more radically, how one can educate Christians to become Christians. This tradition is passed down in our families, our institutions, our Churches. Our critical reception of the tradition is not, according to Herbert McCabe's interpretation of Aquinas, "simply a matter of changing words and ideas but of changing fundamental structures of human living. It is a political matter" (McCabe 2005, 11).

One can be good at the project of becoming a human being, or less good, or indeed some of us may be poor specimens of what it is to be a human being, if the criteria rests in creation after the image and likeness of God. Thus becoming a good human being, flourishing, fulfilling God's dream for this particular human, necessitates learning about God and the Christian tradition, the way in which linguistic animals have, over generations, made real God's message among us. Here Sacred Scripture, and in particular the Decalogue, the ten commandments, must be of central importance in the process of learning about human flourishing in a multifaceted, complicated and secular world, where the justice which ensures an agreed peace amongst individuals is often deemed sufficient for human existence. But is not sufficient for the human flourishing which Christianity calls for. The Decalogue seeks to establish human friendship as the fundamental relationship by which people might live well together and flourish. This friendship, the *philia* in question, from the point of view of moral theology, is *agape* or *caritas,* the "friendship God shares with us and enables us to share with each other" (McCabe 2005, 88). That is the goal, the motivation, and the Decalogue gives us the guidelines as to how we might play the game of friendship, of life, well. Yet, as has been said, knowing the rules is insufficient, for the game of life is an exercise of practical and not theoretical wisdom. Living well does not consist in exercising one's will power to follow the laws of a country or an institution, but is better understood as a process by which one is educated into the practices of a virtuous life. Of course, Christianity has often been perceived as an exercise in learning to obey laws and regulations. The Decalogue can be read in this way: do not kill means, for some people, simply that I should not kill another human being. Read through a different lens, however, a wider interpretation can be made: this commandment does not simply prohibit the taking of life, but it also teaches us that we should value and respect life, all life, and other human beings in particular. We should not kill, hurt, or damage by words or actions. This is where we learn to respect others quite simply because they too have been made after the image and likeness of God, not because we are following laws regulating rights and discrimination. We are growing to see them as friends. In a similar way, the other commandments can be interpreted much more richly: thou shalt not steal means, not simply that one should not take the material possessions of another, but that one should not steal their good name through, for example, gossip. In short, the Decalogue was a gift from God to the People of God to help them to learn to live well together, to form a community in which *caritas* and God's justice would be the overriding goal. The Hebrew concept of *Sedaqah* encapsulates what the Decalogue was trying to teach.[12] It suggests a way of living which Christians believe comes to a certain climax in the life and teaching of Jesus the Christ. The term *Sedaqah* refers to a way of living which is rooted in God's holiness and calls for moral rightness, right relationship amongst people, and between people and God.

The road toward this ideal is not an easy one, and more than the guidelines of the Decalogue are needed for, as McCabe reminds his readers: "If you ask the question: what is the most dangerous wild animal, the answer is, as everyone agrees, the human one" (McCabe 2008, 158). Human beings do not seem to be well suited for life on earth—since the linguistic animal arrived on earth, acid rain, the destruction of rain forests, the atomic bomb, have followed relatively swiftly. We kill one another in a reasoned way. This is what those within the Christian story refer to as "original" sin, the disorder in our life due to our rejection of God's plan, and divine grace is needed to facilitate correct response to it (Nolan 1996). Disorder is at the root of the social and personal disorders manifest in Aquinas' world and in our Secular Age. Due to this alienation, humanity needed religion, *religare*, rules, guidelines, to learn how to live well. Living well in this life is essentially a preparation for life eternal with God. For a Catholic, the pilgrim's progress back to God takes place in and through the sacraments. There are seven of them, and while not everyone can receive them all, all share in the initiating, the "engulfing" sacrament of baptism (Moriarty 2007, 12). To be baptized into Christ is to be baptized into newness of life,

> to be baptized into Christ is to be baptized into Chrysalis Christ, it is to be baptized into a principle of transformation, into a principle of metamorphosis, it is to be baptized into life disposed to further faring, into life disposed to further Christian faring. To be baptized into Christ is to be baptized into a new genetics. The genetics of Parable and Passion. The genetics of our continuing Genesis. ... And so it is that a Christian can say, whatever my postal address might be at any one time, my real address, my genetic address, is my baptism. (Moriarty 2007, 14, 15)

Baptism begins the journey, it facilitates the journey into order, it confirms human origin in God and points toward human destiny, in God.

As we seek to walk the path pioneered by Christ our baptism grows with us. Baptism is an initiation into a life of virtue. It is a making visible of God's gift to humankind, for those within and outside the Christian community. A powerful symbol, it requires nourishment if it is to grow. Liturgy and the other sacraments enable Christ to grow in us. The Christian sacramental road for Catholics has potentially seven significant moments—baptism, eucharist, reconciliation, confirmation, marriage, ordination, sacrament of the sick. All these are of importance in the journey in a world of dilemmas and decision-making, but the most important is that which is celebrated and ritualised regularly—the Eucharist. The "drip drip drip drop drop drop of water being poured into wine" and the "sound of the dry, wafer-thin bread being broken" are what Moriarty calls the "most serious sounds in Christendom... sounds of the universe being redeemed" (Moriarty 2007, 25). This regular ritual reminds Catholics that we live toward God. Slowly but surely, if we are willing, the words and ritual form and transform our imagination so that we slowly learn to recognise the good, and only then can we freely choose it. Sacramental assimilation into Christ is a process fully human and fully divine. It is a schooling in the virtues, a process of conversion in which Christian sacraments are, as Moriarty describes it, like "seals' breathing-holes in which we breathe transcendentally. Without such breathing something essential to our humanity dies, or rather, something essential to our humanity doesn't come to life" (Moriarty 2007, 61). *Prudentia* is needed simply to recognise this fact. *Prudentia* is needed to know and to do that which is good for us, so that we might flourish as community, and individually. The difficulty in today's world is that *prudentia* has all but disappeared, and slowly rules have become the guidelines for human action in both the secular and religious world. The formation of people along the Christian road has become more complex—many still celebrate the moments but few are willing, or encouraged, to follow a path that inevitably and with regularity leads into Passiontide, into suffering as well as resurrection.

The thoughts of David Thompson, erstwhile professor of Modern Church History at Cambridge University, provide some interesting material with which to end this paper. Thompson began his valedictory lecture with a quote from another Taylor, A.J.P. Taylor who, in a review of Kitson Clark's *The Making of Victorian England*, noted that "while Kitson Clark was not the first to point out that Victorian England was intensely religious, he did so in greater detail, and with the sharp reminder that, even at the height of religious devotion, hardly more than half the population attended any place of worship."[13] In this paper Thompson goes on to ask if there ever was an "age of faith," if it is "in the nature of Christianity ever to be popular, or whether we should always look in suspicion upon any Christian movement which is gaining in popularity". Gabriel le Bras, in a posthumously published article makes the same point. His research led him to wonder if there ever had been an age of faith, and therefore if the notion of "dechristianization as applied to eighteenth-century France was misconceived."[14]

Taking all this into account perhaps we can say that Taylor's *Secular Age* is nothing unusual: maybe it is normal for religious practice to be a minority activity? This was conceivably no less true in the time of Aquinas than it was in the time of Jesus. Yes, external obedience to religious laws, which were often laws of state, may have been much stronger, but actual Christian faith may have been no stronger than it is today. And perhaps it is better this way, perhaps this better respects the gift of *liberium arbitrium*, the freedom to choose, given to humans by their Creator God. Christianity is not best conceived as the obedience of laws, or as practices followed for fear of teachings such as "outside the Church no salvation", but as a radical following of the living Christ.[15] The life of virtues is a call both to resurrection and passion, it is a call to sacrament, to become sacrament, to be living signs of God's love for the world. In order to live this life well, to learn the skills of human friendship, to be empowered to live a life of indiscriminate welcome, a community is needed. This community is called Church and it exists to form its members into living sacraments. The wisdom to do this requires the virtue of *prudentia*.

References

Aquinas, Thomas. *Summa theologiae*, textum Leoninum 1888 editum. English translation used is the Leonine edition by the Dominican Fathers of the English Province. Cincinnati, Chicago: Benziger Brothers, 1947.

—. *Quaestiones disputatae de veritate*, textum Leoninum 1970 editum. English translation: *St. Thomas on Truth*. Vol. 3. trans. R.W. Schmidt. Chicago, Henry Regnery Company, 1952-54.

Achtemeier, Elisabeth R., 1976. Righteousness in the Old Testament, eds. George Buttrick et al. in *The Interpreter's Dictionary of the Bible*. Vol. 4, 80-85.

Epszter, Leon, 1986. *Social Justice in the Ancient Near East and the People of the Bible*. London: SCM Press.

Gilley, Sheridan and Brian Stanley eds. 2006. *The Cambridge History of Christianity: World Christianities c.1815-c.1914*. Volume 8. Cambridge: Cambridge University Press.

Ferry, Luc, 1996. *L'Homme-Dieu ou Le sens de la vie*. Paris: Grasset.

Kenny, Anthony, 1989. *The Metaphysics of Mind*. Oxford: Clarendon Press.

—. ed., 1964. *Summa Theologiae*, vol.22. London: Eyre & Spottiswoode; New York: McGraw-Hill.

Kerr, Fergus ed. 2003. *Contemplating Aquinas. On the Varieties of Interpretation*. London: SCM Press.

MacIntyre, Alasdair, 1981. *After Virtue*. Duckworth: London.

—. 1983. Moral Philosophy: What Next?, in *Revisions: Changing Perspectives in Moral Philosophy*, eds. Stanley Hauerwas and Alasdair MacIntyre, Notre Dame: University of Notre Dame Press, 1-15.

McCabe, Herbert, 1996.Virtue and Truth. *Irish Theological Quarterly* 62: 161-169.

—. 2005, *The Good Life. Ethics and the Pursuit of Happiness*, Edited by Brian Davies. London: Continuum.

—. 2008, *On Aquinas*. Edited by Brian Davies. London: Continuum.

McDermott, Timothy, 2007. *How to read Aquinas*. London: Granta Books.

McNamara, Vincent, 1998. The Distinctiveness of Christian Morality, in *Christian Ethics: An Introduction*, ed. Bernard Hoose, London:

Cassell, 149-160.
Moriarty, John, 2007. *Serious Sounds*, Dublin: The Lilliput Press.
Nolan, Michael, 1996. Aquinas and the Act of Love, *New Blackfriars* 77: 115-130.
Pesch, Otto-Herman, 2003. Thomas Aquinas and Contemporary Theology, in *Contemplating Aquinas. On the Varieties of Interpretation,* ed. Fergus Kerr, London: SCM Press, 184-216.
Pinckaers, Servais, 1962. Virtue is Not a Habit. *Cross Currents* 71: 65-81.
Sullivan, Francis A., 1992. *Salvation outside the church: tracing the history of the Catholic response.* London: Geoffrey Chapman.
Stump, Eleanore, 2003. *Aquinas*, New York: Routledge.
Taylor, Charles 1999. A Catholic Modernity?, in *A Catholic Modernity? Charles Taylor's Marianist Award Lecture with responses*, ed. James L. Heft. New York/Oxford: Oxford University Press, 13-38.
Thompson, David, 2009. Is Popular Christianity a contradiction in terms? Some historical reflections for the twenty-first century. A valedictory lecture (unpublished) given in Cambridge University on the 13 May, 2009.
Westburg, Daniel, 1994a. Did Aquinas Change His Mind About the Will?. *The Thomist* 58: 41-60.
Westburg, Daniel, 1994b. *Right Practical Reason. Aristotle, Action and Prudence in Aquinas.* Oxford: Oxford University Press.

CONTRIBUTORS

Ruth Abbey is Professor of Political Science at the University of Notre Dame. She is the author of *Nietzsche's Middle Period* and *Charles Taylor*.

Eoin Cassidy is a Lecturer in Philosophy at the Mater Dei Institute, Dublin. His publications include *The Common Good in an Unequal World*, *Who Is My Neighbour?* and *Community, Constitution and Ethos*.

Michael Conway is Professor of Faith and Culture at St Patrick's College, Maynooth. He is editor of the *Irish Theological Quarterly*, and Director of the Irish Centre for Faith and Culture.

Stephen J. Costello is a Lecturer in Philosophy at the Dublin Business School. His books include *Basil Hume: Builder of Community*, *The Irish Soul: In Dialogue* and *What Are Friends For? Insights from the Great Philosophers*.

Joseph Dunne is Cregan Professor of Philosophy of Education at Dublin City University and Head of Human Development at St Patrick's College, Drumcondra, Dublin. He is author of *Back to the Rough Ground: Practical Judgement and the Lure of Technique*.

Michael Paul Gallagher is Professor of Fundamental Theology at the Pontifical Gregorian University, Rome. His books include *Clashing Symbols: an Introduction to Faith and Culture* and *Faith Maps: Ten Religious Thinkers from Newman to Joseph Ratzinger*.

Patrick Hannon is Emeritus Professor of Moral Theology at St Patrick's College, Maynooth. His books include *Church, State, Morality and Law* and *Moral Decision Making*.

Pádraig Hogan is a Lecturer in Education at NUI Maynooth. He is the author of *The Custody and Courtship of Experience: Western Education in Philosophical Perspective*.

Alan Kearns is a Lecturer in Ethics and Moral Theology at the Mater Dei Institute, Dublin. He is the author of *The Concept of Person in a World Mediated by Meaning and Constituted by Significance*.

Ian Leask is a Lecturer in Philosophy at the Mater Dei Institute, Dublin.

Andrew O'Shea is a Senior Tutor and Associate Lecturer in Philosophy and Human Development at St Patrick's College, Drumcondra, Dublin. He is the author of *Sacrifice and Selfhood: René Girard and Charles Taylor on the Crisis of Modernity*.

Fainche Ryan is a Lecturer in Systematic Theology at the Mater Dei Institute, Dublin. She is the author of *Formation in Holiness: Thomas Aquinas on Sacra Doctrina*.

Mary Shanahan is completing a PhD in philosophy at University College Dublin.

NOTES

Chapter One
A Secular Age: The Missing Question Mark

[1] For some indication of Taylor's life-long commitment to Catholicism, see Redhead 2002, 13-16.

[2] Cf. James Miller's claim that Taylor "is committed to denying any assumption that the evolution of modern societies or the spread of enlightenment will render obsolete religious belief" (Miller 2008, 6).

[3] My analysis dovetails in two important ways with Miller's. Firstly, as the title of his article indicates, Miller maintains that "the title of Charles Taylor's book *A Secular Age* is misleading": see Miller 2008, 5; cf. 9, 10. Secondly, Miller invokes empirical evidence to cast doubt upon "the sorts of sweeping generalizations about secularity that Taylor invites us to take for granted" (ibid., 6), and in this context appeals to opinion poll data from the US. However, in contrast to the analysis offered here, Miller does not hinge his argument on any discussion of Taylor's definition of religion. Instead, he asserts that "around the world religious communities of belief are still quite robust" (ibid., 5). Given Taylor's focus in *A Secular Age*, evidence from non-Western countries is not relevant to the argument. When it comes to Westernized societies, most of Miller's evidence refers to the US alone (ibid., 7).

[4] The Introduction runs from pp 1-22, while Chapter 13 to the end occupies pp 473-776.

[5] Cf. Miller 2008, 6-7, on these three forms of secularity.

[6] For a fuller discussion of Taylor's views on these issues, see Abbey 2000, 58-62, and Smith 2002, 120-128. For a much more systematic approach to the study of self-interpretations, inspired by some of Taylor's insights, see Rosa 2004.

[7] See Gordon 2008 and Jay 2009.

[8] For a different interpretation, see Gordon 2008, 670-671, who reads Taylor as holding that "the sacred is … always and only God. Other experiences (for example, a Romantic's experience of the natural sublime, or a concertgoer's experience of a Beethoven symphony) do not count in his view as actual transcendence since they are ultimately reducible to an exclusive humanism." Gordon refers to Taylor's "a priori conviction that the title of the sacred belongs to monotheistic transcendence alone" and infers that "Taylor wants his transcendence in traditionally religious form." Cf. 673.

[9] Part III is entitled "The Nova Effect". See *passim.*, esp. 423, 599, 727.

[10] For earlier discussions of religious authenticity and of cross pressures and fragilization, see Taylor 2002, while the Three Cornered Contest is discussed in Taylor 1999.

[11] On the following page he repeats this point again, stating: "The crucial change which brought us into this new condition was the coming of exclusive humanism as a widely available option" (SA 21; see also 322, 423).

[12] I wonder if it is appropriate to characterize Epicureanism as "a self-sufficing humanism". By Taylor's own admission, this doctrine "admitted Gods, but denied them relevance to human life" (SA 19). While I suggested above that the relevant denying clause precludes Epicureanism from qualifying as a religion in Taylor's sense, it nonetheless seems strange to call a doctrine which recognizes the existence of gods a form of self-sufficing humanism—especially when, as just noted, atheist humanism serves as a synonym for this. Modern versions of self-sufficing humanism do not, after all, even admit gods. Taylor might be better off saying, as he sometimes suggests, that the denial of the transcendent altogether, rather than just of its relevance to human life, is a uniquely modern phenomenon— and thus avoiding classifying ancient Epicureanism as a form of self-sufficing humanism.

[13] Gordon 2008, 654, suggests, however, that Taylor does not see such ideals of fullness as being as full as religious ones: "An operative assumption throughout the book is that those who deny religion are missing something, and that, even if they do not recognize it themselves, their lives are lacking in a certain fullness, an awareness of higher meaning or dimensionality."

[14] For a fuller depiction of this view, see Taylor 1995.

[15] It is possible that Taylor intends rock concerts to also fit this category—"they are plainly "non-religious"; and yet they also sit uneasily in the secular, disenchanted world. Fusions in common action/feeling, which take us out of the everyday, they often generate the powerful phenomenological sense that we are in contact with something greater, however we ultimately want to explain or understand this" (SA 517-518). However, the fact that he soon goes on to discuss views he typically associates with the immanent counter-enlightenment makes me wonder if rock concerts fit that rubric instead.

[16] Gordon rules out this aspect of Taylor's position, holding instead that "[o]ther experiences (for example, a Romantic's experience of the natural sublime)... do not count in his view as actual transcendence since they are ultimately reducible to an exclusive humanism" (Gordon 2008, 654).

[17] On strong evaluation, see Taylor 1985a, 16ff; for "Self-Interpreting Animals", see ibid., 65-68. See also Taylor 1989, 4, 20, 47. For a fuller discussion of Taylor's conception of strong evaluation, see Abbey 2000, 17-26, and Smith 2002, 89-97.

[18] Taylor mentions strong evaluation at SA 544.

[19] See Gourgouris 2008, who, in "A Case of Heteronomous Thinking", concludes that "the "immanent frame" is, in the last instance, a frame of closure, of self-enclosure, whose greatest failure is that it inhibits humanity's openness to the transcendental [sic]."

[20] Taylor claims that living within the immanent frame "is something we all share, regardless of our differences in outlook" (SA 594). Yet he also wants to underscore the difference between living the immanent frame in an open or closed way. The latter claim complicates the former and leads Arto Laitinen to ask what it means to

say that all Westerners live within this frame. Surely the differences within the frame rival its commonalities? Is there really any sense in which the supposedly immanent aspects of the frame remain the same in the open and closed versions? Does not openness to transcendence fundamentally turn the frame into a "non-immanent" one? Personal Conversation with the author, June 2009.

[21] Cf. Jay 2009, 81: for Taylor, religion is "sometimes understood in generic terms, sometimes in specific ones".

[22] Once again we see the wider notion of religion being substituted for belief in God.

[23] I quote from the "Summary Report", *American Religious Identification Survey*, Trinity College, Hartford Connecticut by Barry A. Kosmin and Ariela Keysar. This was published in March 2009:
http://livinginliminality.files.wordpress.com/2009/03/aris_report_2008.pdf

[24] See SA 522 and 526 for remarks on differences between the US and Europe.

[25] Pew 2008a, 3, distinguishes, in the American context, between the secular unaffiliated and the religious unaffiliated. While the former "say that religion is not important in their lives (6.3% of the adult population)", the latter report "that religion is either somewhat important or very important in their lives (5.8% of the overall adult population)." For an interesting discussion of how to interpret the meanings of "no religion", albeit one again confined to the American data, see Polebaum & Gelman 2009; as they point out, "The 'None' category would… appear to be capable of housing diverse configurations of belief no less than unbelief."

[26] Greeley 2002, 23, even contends that there has been an increase in religious faith in Europe: "belief in a transcendental order has increased among many Europeans born since 1950… in twelve of twenty two European countries there has been a statistically significant increase in belief in life after death since 1955." Seven of these are former communist countries; three are Scandanavian.

[27] See: http://ec.europa.eu/public_opinion/archives/ebs/ebs_225_report_en.pdf

[28] Poland joins Ireland in being closer to the US in its levels of religiosity than to most of its European neighbors. Cf. Casanova 2003, 18.

[29] The study was conducted by Michael MacGreil from a national sample of just over 1,000 adults. See John Cooney, "Keeping the Faith: 95pc of us still believe there is a God", *Irish Independent*, June 10, 2009, 1.

[30] I am not suggesting, of course, that all sociologists employ quantitative methods.

[31] Martha Nussbaum draws attention to the "top-down" bias in *Sources*, with the cultural creations Taylor discusses being those of the middle and upper classes in her Our Pasts, Ourselves, Review of *Sources of the Self*, by Charles Taylor, *New Republic*, April 9, 1990, 32.

[32] For Kant, see SA 8-9, 589; for Nietzsche, 589; for Romanticism, 9.

[33] On Hardy, see SA 564, 592-3; on Arnold 570; on Camus 583, 589.

[34] Further information about Taizé is available at http://www.taize.fr/en

[35] By "vicarious religion" Davie means "religion performed by an active minority but on behalf of a much larger number, who (implicitly at least) not only understand, but, quite clearly, approve of what the minority is doing." See Davie

2006, 24. But vicarious religion is a European, rather than American, phenomenon. According to Davie (ibid., 27), "[t]here are exceptions, but to act vicariously is not part of American self-understanding."

[36] Although it is beyond this chapter's scope to elaborate on this, it warrants mention that the Pew findings are also in keeping with Taylor's depiction of the quest for religious authenticity, especially among younger people.

[37] Cf. Berger 2005, 114, on the pluralism that marks religious life in both the US and Europe. Woodhead, Heelas & Davie 2003, 1-2, 6, 7, point to the diversification, rather than disappearance, of religion in their "Introduction". Hervieu-Léger (whose work Taylor cites) 2008, 246, likewise observes that, in modernity, religion "resurfaces, is reborn, circulates, and displaces itself ..." She speaks of its "transformations" "displacements" and "revivals" in the western world; cf. 247-248. So Taylor is here reiterating a point agreed upon by many contemporary students of religion. Cf. the claim in Miller 2008, 6, that the "well-known sociological hypothesis... that, in industrial or industrializing countries, religion loses much of its former authority over men and social institutions—a hypothesis advanced in perhaps its purest form by Karl Marx" was "more widely credited a generation ago than it is today".

[38] Some of these arguments were made in a paper I presented at the American Political Science Association Annual Conference in Boston, 2008. I thank Michael Gibbons for convening the panel and Jean Bethke Elshtain for her comments as respondent. Bill Dodge, Joe Nawrocki and Paul Weithman also provided helpful comments on that version of my paper. I am also grateful for the opportunity to have aired some of these ideas at the conference "A Secular Age: Tracing the Contours of Religion and Belief" convened by the Mater Dei Institute in Dublin, Ireland in June 2009. Clifford Ando provided helpful comments on a draft of this version of the paper.

Chapter Two
"Transcending Human Flourishing"

[1] The importance of this issue should not be underestimated. One could in fact make a convincing case that the book has emerged precisely out of a need to explore the cultural effects on religious and societal beliefs and values of the growth of an increasingly immanent horizon of meaning. See, for example, the following: "But if we are prudent (or perhaps cowardly), and reflect that we are trying to understand a set of forms and changes that have arisen in one particular civilization, Latin Christendom—we see to our relief that we don't need to construct a definition of religion that covers everything 'religious' in all human societies in all ages" (SA 15). See also the following: "[w]e are trying to understand changes in a culture for which the transcendent/immanent distinction has become foundational" (SA 16).

[2]The cumulative evidence of internationally reputable statistical analysis suggests that Ireland, in company with many other newly "developed" nations, has begun to embrace many of the features classically associated with a secular age. See Eoin

Cassidy, "Modernity and Religion in Ireland: 1980-2000", in E. Cassidy (ed.), *Measuring Ireland: Discerning Values and Beliefs*, (Dublin: Veritas, 2002), 17-46.

[3] For an exploration of themes associated with secularisation in dialogue with the work of Taylor, see Eoin Cassidy "The Right Notes in the Right Order: Faith and the Challenge of a Therapeutic Culture", *Milltown Studies*, No. 48, 2001, pp. 1-20

[4] Two other eminent commentators on modernity who come to mind, both currently working out of a North American cultural context, and both of whom share with Taylor the same desire and indeed ability to undertake this challenging endeavour, are the sociologist Robert Bellah and the philosopher Alasdair MacIntyre. Bellah's book was first published in 1985 and remains a benchmark for all that is best in the discipline of sociology. MacIntyre 1981 is rightly regarded as a classic of its genre.

[5] The most detailed and sustained expose of this thesis is to be found in a book written in the 1960's by the Italian philosopher Cornelio Fabro, *God in Exile: A Study of the Internal Dynamic of Modern Atheism, from its Roots in the Cartesian Cogito to the Present Day*, trans, A Gibson, (New York: Newman Press, 1964)

[6] This is the theme which in many respects is the focus of Taylor's earlier, 1991 publication. Although it is quite a short book, it offers a remarkably penetrating and fair analysis of the issues.

[7] It is in the introduction to *A Secular Age*, where Taylor outlines the rationale for the book, that we find the most extensive treatment of this theme. See, esp., SA 5, 6, 8 and 10.

[8] A fuller rendition of the passage reads as follows: "[D]oes the highest, the best life involve our seeking, or acknowledging, or serving a good which is beyond, in the sense of independent of human flourishing? In which case, the highest, most real, authentic or adequate human flourishing could include our aiming (also) in our range of final goals at something other than human flourishing. I say "final goals", because even the most self-sufficing humanism has to be concerned with the condition of some non-human things instrumentally, e.g., the condition of the natural environment... It's clear that in the Judaeo-Christian religious tradition the answer to this question is affirmative. Loving, worshipping God is the ultimate end. Of course, in this tradition God is seen as willing human flourishing, but devotion to God is not seen as contingent on this. The injunction "Thy will be done" isn't equivalent to "Let humans flourish", even though we know that God wills human flourishing." (SA 16-17)

[9] See, e.g., SA 18: "[F]lourishing and renunciation cannot simply be collapsed into each other to make a single goal... There remains a fundamental tension in Christianity. Flourishing is good, nevertheless seeking it is not our ultimate goal. But even where we renounce it, we re-affirm it, because we follow God's will in being a channel for it to others, and ultimately to all."

[10] See Eoin Cassidy, "Augustine's Homilies on John's Gospel", in T. Finan & V. Twomey (eds.), *Studies in Patristic Christology* (Dublin: Four Courts Press, 1998), 122-143; idem., "Pathways to God: Beauty, the Road Less Travelled", in A. M. Murphy & E. Cassidy (eds.), *Neglected Wells: Spirituality and the Arts* (Dublin: Four Courts Press, 1997), 11-27; and idem., 'Le rôle de L'Amitié dans la

quête du Bonheur Chez Augustin', in J. Follon & J. McEvoy (eds.), *Actualité de la Pensée Mediévale*, (Louvain: Peeters, 1994), 171-201.
[11] This emphasis is particularly pronounced where Taylor, in the final chapter of SA, discusses the experiences that gave rise to religious conversion. See also his references to Bede Griffiths in the introduction, esp. SA 5.
[12] See Taylor 2003, 12 – 22
[13] In this analysis, Taylor would seem to be adopting a position that is close to the cultural pessimism that is characteristic of both Bellah's description of radical individualism (Bellah 2007) and indeed Alaisdair McIntyre's harrowing description in the first three chapters of *After Virtue* of the loss of moral discourse in the emotivist culture of today (MacIntyre 1981).

**Chapter Four
"Our Ethical Predicament"**

[1] Famously, "incredulity towards meta-narratives" is taken to be the most defining characteristic of the "post-modern" in Lyotard, 1984.
[2] See especially, Taylor 1992, Part 1, "Identity and the Good".
[3] The titles of chapters 12 and 13 of *A Secular Age* are, respectively, "The Age of Mobilisation" and "The Age of Authenticity".
[4] Taylor 2004 and Taylor 1991.
[5] Earlier, I said that Taylor has provided me with terms in which to articulate a benign formative experience with church figures in my childhood. Perhaps I might also claim, as a measure of the range of his work, that it *also* offers some resources for understanding, if not coming to terms with, the sexual abuses of children by clerics that have increasingly come to light in recent years.
[6] Although references to Hegel or Heidegger are not very frequent in the writings in which Taylor sets out his own views, one might say that their influences have been so deeply absorbed that he *does* Heidegger and Hegel rather than simply writing *about* them. But for such writing, too, see Taylor, 1993; "Heidegger, Language and Ecology", in Taylor 1995, 100-26; Taylor, 1975c; and Taylor, 1979.
[7] The experienced relationship that Taylor invokes here, while saying tantalisingly little about it, is the one established with God through prayer. For a fuller and more explicit elaboration of prayer and religious devotion as an insider experience within a social practice that is no less legitimate than, for example, the tasting and discernment developed within wine connoisseurship—and that similarly affords an otherwise unavailable mode of access to the real, governed by its own proper norms of validity—see Archer, 2004a and Archer 2004b. While I'm unsure whether Archer's elaboration would receive Taylor's endorsement, it comes out of a philosophical perspectives that seems very close to his—a "critical realist" one, positioned between positivism and post-modernism, that rejects the 'epistemic fallacy' of allowing 'epistemology completely to swallow up ontology' (cf. his essay, "Overcoming Epistemology", Taylor, 1995, 100-26, and his forthcoming book, co-authored with Hubert Dreyfus, *Rescuing Realism*, flagged in a footnote in SA); and he might well identify with the statement in the book's preface that its

editors/contributors 'had all until recently written purely secular... books, but had arrived at religious positions about which we wanted to go public.'

[8] Given some of its connotations in current usage, I use the word "spirituality" here with some hesitation; see Dunne 2003.

[9] Critique of what might be called "reductive naturalism" was the driving force in Taylor's first book (Taylor, 1964) and has remained integral to his whole philosophical project over the ensuing half century.

[10] Taylor 1996.

[11] See Csikszentmihalyi 1991.

[12] See Taylor 1992, chapter 13, "God Loveth Adverbs".

[13] It is this affirmation of the ordinary that Declan Kiberd attempts to rescue from pedants and Joycean specialists and to restore to lay readers in his recent book arguing that *Ulysses* 'set out to restore the dignity of the middle range of human experience [and]... to celebrate the common man and woman' (Kiberd, 2009, pp. 6-7).

[14] Taylor here draws on and repeats the analysis of a three-cornered fight, in which any two of the protagonists can gang up on the third, which he had offered in his Marionist award lecture (Taylor, 1999).

[15] This is the text of an opening keynote lecture given at the conference on *A Secular Age* at the Mater Dei Institute Dublin in June 2009; I've made little attempt here to alter the style of its oral delivery. For stimulation in reading the book, and thus more remotely in preparing the paper, I'm indebted to richly enjoyable discussion with fellow-members of the "Taylor group", which met monthly in a Dublin city-centre bar from January 2008 until April 2010.

Chapter Five
Deism, Spinozism, Anti-Humanism

[1] Cf. Taylor 1989, ch.14, 234-247.

[2] Of course, the Spinozistic character of Deism is manifest well beyond the work of Tindal and Toland: significantly, what might be regarded as the first "official" Deist text, Charles Blount's *Miracles, no Violations of the Laws of Nature* (1683) was, in effect, the rendition of ch.6 of Spinoza's *Theological-Political Treatise*. For a general survey, see Rosalie Colie, "Spinoza and the Early English Deists", *Journal of the History of Ideas*, 20, 1959, 23-46.

[3] Taylor does note, in *Sources of the Self*, that "Deism developed its own forms in France, evolving much more clandestinely, passionately anti-clerical and anti-Catholic, and often inspired by the work of Spinoza" (Taylor 1989, 334). However, the point remains under-developed (or even under-determined) and never applied to anglophone formations—a significant lacuna, given the influence that Toland, in particular, had on thinkers such as La Mettrie, Diderot and d'Holbach.

[4] In *Sources of the Self*, Taylor had already described Deism as rewriting Christian faith "around the picture of a natural order designed inter alia for a self-contained human good" (Taylor 1989, 271).

[5] Taylor depicts a general Lockean influence—radical enlightenment thinkers "were all very much followers of Locke", he asserts (Taylor 1989, 320)—but leaves any Spinozistic source unexplored.

[6] Cf. Gilles Deleuze, *Expressionism in Philosophy: Spinoza*, trans. Martin Joughin, New York: Zone Books, 1990, 256: "Parallelism... excludes any eminence of the soul, any spiritual and moral finality, any transcendence of a God who might base one series on the other."

[7] *Ethics* Book 3, Preface.

[8] *Ethics* Book 2, Prop.10.

[9] Cf. Edwin Curley, *Behind the Geometrical Method. A Reading of Spinoza's Ethics*, Princeton University Press, 1986, 74-78: he suggests that the *consequence* of Spinoza's thinking here is, inevitably, a kind of materialism.

[10] See, for example, Spinoza 2002, 250 ff. (*Ethics* Book 2, Prop.11 ff.).

[11] *Ethics* Book 3, Prop.2. As the original has it: "Nec Corpus Mentem ad cogitandum, nec Mens Corpus ad motum, neque ad quietem, nec ad aliquid (si quid est) aliud determinare potest."

[12] *Ethics* Book 3, Prop.2, Proof.

[13] Deleuze, *Expressionism*, op.cit., 255, describes Spinoza's position, in this regard, as "practically a war cry". Warren Montag, *Louis Althusser*, Basingstoke: Palgrave, 2003, 56, describes it as "perhaps the most heretical moment in this very heretical text".

[14] *Ethics*, Book 3, Prop.2, Schol.

[15] In general, Taylor's treatment of Spinoza's thought tends to highlight its Romantic and "expressivist" appropriation (e.g., Taylor, 1975, 27, 34, 40-41); at one point (Taylor 1989, 316), he will even posit Spinoza's "intellectual love of God" as a kind of spiritual opposite to natural reality (and not, as Spinoza himself understood it, as the full understanding of natural laws and processes).

[16] *Ethics* Book 3, Preface.

[17] Officially, of course, mental "decision" and physical "determination" are "one and the same thing" seen under different attributes—see, for example, *Ethics* Book 2, Prop.7, Schol.

[18] Cf. Peter Winch, 'Mind, Body & Ethics in Spinoza', *Philosophical Investigations*, 18 (3), July 1995, 216-234. For a detailed discussion of how the body might be fundamental—given that, for Spinoza, the modes of one attribute cannot be explained in terms of another—see Michael Della Rocca, *Representation and the Mind-Body Problem in Spinoza*, Oxford University Press, 1996, esp. ch.8, 141-156.

[19] Cf. Wallace Matson, 'Spinoza's Theory of Mind', *The Monist*, 55, 1971, 568-578.

[20] Cf. Warren Montag, *Bodies, Masses, Power. Spinoza and his Contemporaries*, London & New York: Verso, 1999, xvii: "[Spinoza's] refusal to set the human apart from nature, mind from body, thought from action... makes him perhaps the most thoroughgoing anti-humanist in the history of philosophy".

[21] See, for example, the famous Appendix to Book 1 of the *Ethics* (Spinoza 2002, 238-243).

[22] See Letter 73, to Oldenburg (Spinoza 2002, 942-943)
[23] Cf. Letter 56 (Spinoza 2002, 904): "... I believe that, a triangle, could it speak, would... say that God is eminently triangular, and a circle that God's nature is eminently circular".
[24] Again, see Ethics Book 1, Appendix (Spinoza 2002, 238-243).
[25] For an excellent survey, which concentrates on Tindal and on Toland's *Letters to Serena*, see Justin Champion, '"The Men of Matter": Spirits, Matter and the Politics of Priestcraft, 1701-1709', in Gianni Paganini et al (eds.), *Scepticisme, Clandestinité et Libre Pensée*, Paris: Honoré Champion, 2002, 115-150.
[26] See: Jonathan Israel, *Radical Enlightenment: Philosophy and the Making of Modernity 1650-1750*, Oxford University Press, 2002; idem., *Enlightenment Contested: Philosophy, Modernity and the Emancipation of Man 1670-1752*, Oxford University Press, 2008.
[27] See, for example, Margaret Jacob's review of Israel's *Radical Enlightenment*, in *The Journal of Modern History*, 75 (2), June 2003, 387-389.
[28] See, as well: Paul Vernière, *Spinoza et la pensée française avant la Révolution*, Paris: PUF, 1954, 355-360; Rosalie Colie, 'Spinoza and the Early English Deists', op.cit., esp.43-46; Erwin Pracht, 'Einleitung' to G.Wichmann's translation of the *Letters to Serena, Briefe an Serena. Über den Aberglauben, über Materie und Bewegung*, Berlin: Akademie-Verlag, 1959, vii-lxvi; Günter Gawlick, 'Einleitung' to facsimile (English) edition of Toland's *Letters to Serena*, Stuttgart-Bad Cannstatt: Friedrich Fromann, 1964, 5-23; Robert E. Sullivan, *John Toland and the Deist Controversy. A Study in Adaptations*, Cambridge, Ma.: Harvard University Press, 1982 (esp. ch.6); Giuseppe Tognon, 'Leibniz, Toland et Spinoza: une lettre inédite à propos des *Lettres à Serena*', in *Bulletin de l'Association des Amis de Spinoza*, 12, 1984, 2-11; Stephen H. Daniel, *John Toland. His Methods, Manners and Mind*, Kingston & Montreal: McGill-Queen's University Press, 1984, esp. ch.7; Pierre Lurbe, 'Le Spinozism de John Toland', in *Spinoza Au XVIIIe Siècle*, ed. Olivier Bloch, Paris: Méridiens-Klincksieck, 1990, 33-47; Stuart Brown, 'Theological Politics and the Reception of Spinoza in the Early English Enlightenment', *Studia Spinozana*, 9, 1993, 181-200; Rienk Vermij, 'Matter and Motion: Toland and Spinoza', in Wiep van Bunge and Wim Klever (eds.), *Disguised and Overt Spinozism Around 1700*, Leiden: Brill, 1996, 275-288; Justin Champion, *Republican Learning. John Toland and the Crisis of Christian Culture, 1696-1722*, Manchester University Press, 2003, 173-177, 252-253; Tristan Dagron, 'Introduction' to Toland's *Lettres à Serena et autres textes* (ed. & trans. Dagron), Paris: Honoré Champion, 2004, 9-60; idem., *Toland et Leibniz. L'invention du néo-spinozisme*, Paris: Vrin, 2009; Daniel C.Fouke, *Philosophy and Theology in a Burlesque Mode. John Toland and 'The Way of Paradox'*, New York: Humanity Books, 2007, esp. 273-275.
[29] See, especially, Chapter 12 of *Christianity as Old as Creation*. Compare Spinoza, *Theological-Political Treatise* ch.7 (Spinoza, 2007,100).
[30] See, as well, Tindal 1995, 116: "there is nothing so indifferent, but may, if believ'd to have Divinity stamp'd upon it, be perverted by designing men to the vilest Purposes";

[31] Compare Spinoza, *Theological-Political Treatise* ch.6 (Spinoza 2007, 86-7), where—in opposition to so-called supernatural rationalists—Spinoza refuses to accept both what is contrary to nature *and* above nature.

[32] Compare Spinoza (in Letter 73, for example; Spinoza 2002, 942-3) on the need to rid ourselves of the various (and ridiculous) anthropomorphisms that cloud our thinking—for example, the notion of 'final cause', or the notion that we have a special place in the universe, or that God has a kind of personal interest in humanity (and even took human form).

[33] *The Religious, Rational and Moral Conduct of Matthew Tindal* [etc.] (Oxford, 1735), 25.

[34] See *Spinoza Reviv'd*, 7-11. See, as well, Stuart Brown, "Theological Politics and the Reception of Spinoza in Early Enlightenment England", *Studia Spinoziana* 9, 1994, 181-200.

[35] Other noted voices of opposition to Tindal include: John Turner's *A Vindication of the Rights and Privileges of the Christian Church* (1707); Samuel Hill's *A Thorough Examination* (1708); and William Oldisworth's *A Dialogue between Timothy and Philalethes* (1709).

[36] See *Theological-Political Treatise*, ch.6, par. 9 (Spinoza 2002, 448). For more extensive treatment, see I. Leask, 'Personation and Immanent Undermining: On Toland's Appearing Lockean', *British Journal for the History of Philosophy*, 18 (2), 2010, 231-256.

[37] *Ethics* Book 2, Prop.13, Second Corollary.

[38] For context, see Fichant, 'Leibniz et Toland', op.cit.; and Dagron, *Toland et Leibniz*, op.cit.,15-58.

[39] For a famous example of Leibniz apparently drawing a metaphysical conclusion from empirical premises, see his *Discourse*, pars. 17 & 18 (Leibniz 1969, 314-315). Leibniz states, at par.18 (315), that "the general principles of corporeal nature [*la nature corporelle*] and of mechanics themselves are nevertheless metaphysical rather than geometrical and pertain to certain forms [*formes*] or indivisible natures as the causes of what appears..." For general commentary, see the classic study of Martial Gueroult, *Leibniz: Dynamique et Métaphysique*, Paris: Aubier-Montaigne, 1967.

[40] The subtitle to the 1698 essay *De ipsa natura* is particularly illuminating, in this respect: *sive de vi insita actionibusque Creaturarum, pro dynamicis suis confirmandis illustrandisque* ('Or, the Inherent Force and Activity of Created Things—Confirming and Illustrating the Author's Dynamics'). See Leibniz 1969, 498-508.

[41] Individual substances can be seen, ultimately, as *fulgurations* of God; meanwhile, God is the sufficient reason required to explain an infinity of substances, or monads. See, for example, *Monadology*, pars.36-38, Leibniz 1969, 646.

[42] *Monadology*, par 87.

[43] Tristan Dagron refers to Toland as advancing "a more scandalous naturalism (*un naturalisme plus scandaleux*)" than that of the *Ethics* itself; see *Toland et Leibniz*, op.cit., 193.

[44] See, as well, E.5. Prop.23, Schol. Spinoza's claim that 'something' of the mind continues to exist after the destruction of the body (E.5, Prop.23) is not, strictly speaking, a *theological* point; rather, it is supposed to follow from his conception of the human mind as a mode of the infinite idea of God.
[45] See Richard Mason, *The God of Spinoza. A Philosophical Study*, Cambridge University Press, 1997, 77.
[46] See *Die philosophischen Schriften von Gottfried Wilhelm Leibniz*, ed. C. I. Gerhardt, 7 vols., Berlin: Weidmannsche Buchhandlung, 1875-1890, vol.5, 509-512.
[47] Ibid.
[48] Cf. Lurbe, 'Le Spinozism de John Toland', op.cit., 42: he regards the points made in the *Pantheisticon* as the culmination (*l'aboutissement*) of Toland's explicit reduction of thought to matter.
[49] As Frederick Lange would comment, in his *History of Materialism*, vol.1, London: Routledge, 2000 (reprint of 1925 Second Edition), 329: "Toland obviously regards thought as a phenomenon which is an inherent accompaniment of the material movements in the nervous system, much as the light which results from a galvanic current."
[50] Sullivan, op.cit., 18.
[51] Lurbe, 'Le Spinozism de John Toland', op.cit., 45-4.

Chapter Six
Establishing an Ethical Community

[1] Plato's consideration of friendship is largely confined to the *Lysis*, *Symposium* and *Phaedrus*; in each of these dialogues, friendship is considered within the parameters of the erotic relationship. Granted, Plato recasts such friendships in largely "desexualised" terms; however, the erotic framework persists nonetheless.
[2] For consideration of the wider context, see Kenneth Dover's impressive work *Greek Homosexuality* (Dover 1978).
[3] Scholars remain divided (no pun intended) regarding whether or not the *Phaedrus* should be treated as a unified dialogue. Certainly, the theme of speech-making runs throughout the dialogue, the first part being concerned with the making of speeches (both false and true) and the second part being concerned with a critique of speech making and writing. In *Listening to the Cicadas: A Study of Plato's Phaedrus*, G. R. F. Ferrari argues that the first and second parts of the dialogue are not neatly linked but that this is a necessary 'rough edge' to the dialogue (see Ferrari 1987, especially Chapter Seven, "Writing the Conversation", 204-232). Similarly, James L. Kastely argues that the dialogue is not unified and neither should we attempt to force unity where there is none (see Kastely 2002). Josef Pieper, on the other hand, whilst noting that the latter section of the dialogue certainly appears to be at odds with the first in its manner of "jumping" from one matter to the next, is of the view that the dialogue is, in fact, unified. See Pieper 2000, especially 97-103.

[4] I.M. Crombie has remarked of Plato's concern with "soul-harmony", correctly I think, that: "Virtue is the kind of conduct which we are obliged to approve of and enjoin, the kind of conduct, that is to say, which in others, makes them useful and not harmful to us, and which, in ourselves, makes us tolerable to ourselves; and the knowledge which makes a man love virtue is the knowledge that a human being is, in the end, a rational soul, and that happiness is not to be identified with the gratification of impulse but with the rational organization of the whole of life, and with the pursuit, so far as each man is capable of it, of the proper interests of the mind" (Crombie 1964, 145).

[5] To emphasise this point, I will limit my analysis of the *Phaedrus* solely to an exploration of Socrates' Palinode. The speech of Lysias and Socrates' first speech are, of course, interesting but their investigation would necessitate following up a line of argumentation which does not entirely fit with my concerns in this chapter.

[6] The term "metaphysicality" is sometimes used in scholarly discussions of poetry (see, for example, Hannoosh 1987). In popular culture, the term is also used on occasion to refer to the paranormal and the supernatural (there are, for example, numerous websites dedicated to such matters). However, my use of the term is quite distinct from the aforementioned interpretations of the term. When I use the term "metaphysicality" I refer to that aspect of our being (the soul) which responds to the metaphysical whilst retaining its status as physical. So, for example, one might contend that when, in the *Symposium*, Socrates-Diotima describes how the philosopher "turns towards the great sea of beauty [*kalou*]" (210d) and gazes upon it, he is immersed in the "metaphysicality" of his being.

[7] Consider Book VII of the *Republic* where, when considering the nature of the Good and its importance for the philosopher, Socrates remarks that: "the power and capacity of learning exists in the soul already; and that just as the eye was unable to turn from darkness to light without the whole body, so too the instrument of knowledge can only by the movement of the whole soul be turned from the world of becoming into that of being, and learn by degrees to endure the sight of being, and of the brightest and best of being, or in other words, of the good."

[8] Of course, a discussion of friendship is also carried out in the *Lysis*; however, for clarity's sake, I have omitted a detailed study of this dialogue here. That is not to say that the *Lysis* is not an important dialogue: far from it. An important aspect of this dialogue, in terms of the Taylorian-Platonic concern with ethical community, is the notion that reciprocity is key in friendship and that such reciprocity must occur between good (that is, ethical) persons who are friends (this is something that Aristotle also makes much of, cf. *Nichomachean Ethics*, 1156b6-35, and *Rhetoric* 1381a1). At 212d Socrates puts this quite succinctly: "So nothing is a friend of the lover unless it loves him in return." This is a step removed from the traditional Greek understanding of the relationship, whereby the beloved was expected to feel, and to show, his gratitude (such was the understanding expressed in the first two speeches of the *Phaedrus*). However, the more "authentic" line of Plato's thought, that is, what is implicitly expressed in the *Lysis*, but more explicitly expressed in the second speech of the *Phaedrus* and also in the *Symposium*, exhibits an awareness that the boy has feelings too and, more to the

point, that these feelings are *valuable*. Furthermore, the notion that the friendship relationship can be of real (that is, ethical) benefit to both parties continues to lend weight to my contention that the Platonic account of friendship is an account of ethical co-development.

[9] At 254d, noting the incorrigible will of the dark horse, Socrates comments: "Then, when the promised time arrives, and they are pretending to have forgotten, it reminds them; it struggles, it neighs, it pulls them forward and forces them to approach... again with the same proposition; and as soon as they are near, it drops its head, straightens its tail, bites the bit, and pulls without any shame at all." Later, at 256b, Socrates comments on the benefits afforded to the lovers when the dark horse does not win out: "...their life below here is one of bliss and shared understanding [*homonoetikon*]".

[10] Although Alcibiades essentially fits the model of Greek perfection, he does not reflect the Platonic conception of the morally beautiful. Dover notes that: "It must be emphasised that the Greeks did not call a person 'beautiful' by virtue of that person's morals, intelligence, ability or temperament, but solely by virtue of shape, colour, texture and movement" (*Greek Homosexuality*, 16). In general terms, we might say that Alcibiades, being notably attractive, fits the traditional Greek definition of beauty because he is beautiful "by virtue of shape, colour, texture and movement". However, he is not, like Socrates, as Vlastos puts it: "[a] masterwork of excellence" (Vlastos 1981, 3-34).

[11] Consider, for example, John Donne's comments in Meditation XVII ('Nunc Lento Sonitu Dicunt, Morieris'), that: "No man is an island, entire of itself; every man is a piece of the continent, a part of the main... Any man's death diminishes me, because I am involved in mankind..." (Donne 2004, 61).

[12] Ruth Abbey notes that, for Taylor, the notion of a shared good is of intrinsic importance in an ethical community. In *Charles Taylor* she comments on this in relation to Taylor's *A Catholic Modernity?*: "What the phrase 'irreducibly social goods' captures is a category of that cannot be disaggregated or decomposed into individual goods but that they must be shared by two or more individuals—hence their description as irreducibly social. These shared goods are, at one level, goods for individuals, things that they experience and enjoy. However, Taylor argues that it is a category error to think of them as only individual goods. They are both goods for individuals and goods that can only be generated in common with others. He uses the example of friendship to illustrate this rather abstract claim. When two people are friends, their friendship becomes a good that is shared between them... some things [such as friendship] can only be appreciated when they are understood as shared; some goods can only be realized in concert with others" (Abbey 2000, 118-119). Interestingly, Plato's philosophy of friendship, as I have shown, also operates at the level of being understood as a shared good.

[13] Alasdair MacIntyre has also written of the need for a return to shared projects. MacIntyre, correctly I think, argues that: "For if the conception of the good has to be expounded in terms of such notions as those of a practice, of the narrative unity of a human life and of a moral tradition, then goods, and with them the only grounds for the authority of laws and virtues, can only be discovered by entering

into those relationships which constitute communities whose central bond is a shared vision of and understanding of goods. To cut oneself off from shared activity in which one has initially to learn obediently as an apprentice learns, to isolate oneself from the communities which find their point and purpose in such activities, will be to debar oneself from finding any good outside of oneself" (MacIntyre 1981, 258). See also MacIntyre 1999, especially Chapter 9 ("Social Relationships, Practical Reasoning, Common Goods, and Individual Good") and Chapter 12 ("Proxies, Friends, Truthfulness"), 99-118 and 147-154 respectively.

[14] This is especially clear in *A Secular Age*, in addition to his comments in Taylor 1999.

[15] See, for example, Taylor 1989.

[16] Such a non-religious horizon has what Taylor terms an "immanent frame of reference" (SA 539). Michael Paul Gallagher has also written perceptively on this movement towards what he terms "religious anaemia". See Gallagher 2003, especially Chapter 10 ("Cultural Discernment"), 129-144.

[17] Taylor argues that when the community does not operate in a cohesively ethical manner, each member of that community is damaged in some way. In "The Politics of Recognition", he puts this in the following way: "...our identity is partly shaped by recognition or its absence, often by the *mis*recognition of others, and so a person or group of people can suffer real damage, real distortion, if the people or society around them mirror back to them a confining or demeaning or contemptible picture of themselves" (Gutman 1994, 25-74). Interestingly, Emmanuel Levinas also makes much of the problematic of recognition. However, unlike Taylor, such a problematic cannot be surmounted by a reconstruction or reconfiguration of the "politics of recognition", for it is the very possibility of recognition, and not merely that of misrecognition, which itself poses the ethical problem for both the individual and the community. In *Ethics and Infinity*, Levinas explains his position in the following terms: "So, too, I wonder if one can speak of a look turned toward the face [*un regard tourney vers le visage*], for the look is knowledge [*connaissance*], perception [*perception*]. I think rather that access to the face is straightaway ethical [*d'emblée éthique*]. You turn yourself toward the Other as toward an object when you see a nose, eyes, a forehead, a chin, and you can describe them. The best way of encountering the Other is not even to notice the colour of his eyes! [*La meilleure manière de rencontrer autrui, c'est de ne pas meme remarquer la couleur de ses yeux!*] When one observes the colour of the eyes one is not in social relationship with the Other [*on n'est pas en relation sociale avec autrui*]. The relation with the face can surely be dominated by perception, but what is specifically the face is what cannot be reduced [*réduit*] to that" (Levinas 1985, 85-86).

[18] Again, the reference to the political society as a community is reminiscent of the Platonic philosophical project (consider the *Republic* for example).

[19] A similar line of thinking is also espoused in paragraph 4 the 1965 Vatican II document *Gaudium et Spes (Pastoral Constitution on the Church in the Modern World)*: "Never has the human race enjoyed such an abundance of wealth, resources and economic power, and yet a huge proportion of the worlds citizens

are still tormented by hunger and poverty, while countless numbers suffer from total illiteracy. Never before has man had so keen an understanding of freedom, yet at the same time new forms of social and psychological slavery make their appearance. Although the world of today has a very vivid awareness of its unity and of how one man depends on another in needful solidarity, it is most grievously torn into opposing camps by conflicting forces. For political, social, economic, racial and ideological disputes still continue bitterly, and with them the peril of a war which would reduce everything to ashes. True, there is a growing exchange of ideas, but the very words by which key concepts are expressed take on quite different meanings in diverse ideological systems. Finally, man painstakingly searches for a better world, without a corresponding spiritual advancement. Influenced by such a variety of complexities, many of our contemporaries are kept from accurately identifying permanent values and adjusting them properly to fresh discoveries. As a result, buffeted between hope and anxiety and pressing one another with questions about the present course of events, they are burdened down with uneasiness. This same course of events leads men to look for answers; indeed, it forces them to do so" (Abbott 1966).

[20] Taylor argues that: "So the buffered identity of the disciplined individual moves in a constructed social space, where instrumental rationality is a key value, and time is pervasively secular. All of this makes up what I want to call "the immanent frame". There remains to add just one background idea: that this frame constitutes a "natural" order, to be contrasted to a "supernatural" one, an "immanent" world, over against a possible "transcendent" one... This finally yielded our familiar picture of the natural, "physical" universe as governed by exceptionless laws, which may reflect the wisdom and benevolence of the creator, but don't require in order to be understood—or (at least on a first level) explained—any reference to a good aimed at, whether in the form of the Platonic Idea, or of the Ideas in the mind of God." (SA 542). Of course, for Taylor (and one might quite justifiably speculate that this would also be the case for Plato) a world that is not perforated by the possibility of the transcendent is not a world that is open to the power of objective ethical norms and values; without the transcendent, there can be no transformation.

[21] This is also reminiscent of Plato, who views the failure to enter into an ethical life with a philosophical partner to be not only morally but also mortally dangerous (consider the life of Alcibiades, for example).

[22] The notion of responsibility is a feature of many contemporary ethical philosophies. In particular, the work of Emmanuel Levinas is a case in point. Levinas argues that: "The positivity of the infinite is the conversion of the response to the infinite into responsibility [*c'est la conversion en responsibilité*], into approach of the other. The Infinite is non-thematizable, gloriously exceeds every capacity, and manifests, as it were in reverse, its exorbitance in the approach of a neighbour, obedient to its measure....the glow of a trace is enigmatic, equivocal....The trace left by the infinite is not the residue of a presence; its very glow is ambiguous [*la trace laissée par l'Infini n'est pas le résidu d'une présence; sa luisance même est ambiguë*]" (Levinas 1998, 12).

[23] Consider paragraph 361 of the *Catechism of the Catholic Church* which states that: "This law of human solidarity and charity", without excluding the rich variety of persons, cultures and peoples, assures us that all men are truly brethren."

[24] Despite his differences from Taylor, Levinas is also committed to espousing a philosophy which holds, at its heart, a fundamental respect for difference. In *Time and the Other*, for example, Levinas makes the following claim: "To be sure, the other [*l'Autre*] that is announced does not possess this existing as the subject possesses it; its hold over my existing is mysterious. It is not unknown but unknowable, refractory to all light. But this precisely indicates that the other is in no way another myself, participating with me in a common existence" (Levinas 1987, 75). See also note 52, inserted by the translator Richard A. Cohen.

[25] Consider Mark 12:31, where the evangelist renders Jesus' words as follows: "You shall love your neighbour as yourself." Christians are called to view all persons as their neighbour and thus love of one's neighbour is transformed into love of humanity. Consider, for example, the words of Pope Benedict XVI: "Human nature, in its deepest essence, consists in loving. Ultimately, a single task is entrusted to every human being: to learn to like and to love, sincerely, authentically and freely" (Benedict 2009).

[26] Paragraph 2819 of the *Catechism* states that: ""The kingdom of God [is] righteousness and peace and joy in the Holy Spirit." The end-time in which we live is the age of the outpouring of the Spirit" (Chapman 2002). Also, at paragraph 1042 the *Catechism* states that: "At the end of time, the Kingdom of God will come in its fullness. After the universal judgment, the righteous will reign for ever with Christ, glorified in body and soul" (Chapman 2002). In addition, the 1965 Vatican II decree *Apostolicam Actuositatem* (*Decree on the Apostolate of the Laity*) emphasises the importance of the establishment of the Kingdom in the following way at paragraph 4: "They who have this faith live in the hope of the revelation of the sons of God and keep in mind the cross and resurrection of the Lord. In the pilgrimage of this life, hidden with Christ in God and free from enslavement to wealth, they aspire to those riches which remain forever and generously dedicate themselves wholly to the advancement of the kingdom of God and to the reform and improvement of the temporal order in a Christian spirit. Among the trials of this life they find strength in hope, convinced that "the sufferings of the present time are not worthy to be compared with the glory to come that will be revealed in us" (Rom. 8:18)" (Abbott 1966).

[27] Consider also Plato's advice in the *Republic* that we should orient our concerns towards the "good beyond being". This elusive Platonic idea is also explicitly and implicitly drawn upon by Levinas, see Levinas 1998. In *Emmanuel Levinas: Basic Philosophical Writings*, the editors, Adriaan T. Peperzak, Simon Critchley and Robert Bernasconi, note: "The title [of *Otherwise Than Being or Beyond Essence*]... is a double translation of Plato's characterization of the Good as "beyond the *ousia*"; it declares Levinas's intention to overcome ontology" (Pererzak, Critchley & Bernasconi 1996, xi).

[28] In the *Phaedrus*, the friend-lovers who fail to always uphold the non-sexual bonds of their friendship are not entirely lost—if they guide one another, they can find their way back along the right path together. See 256 c-e.

Chapter Seven
Chaste Morning of the Infinite

[1] The entry continues: "As such it is an aspect of a general trend toward structural differentiation in a society, a trend that is manifested in an increasing emergence of specific institutions to solve the functional problems of maintenance or survival" (s.v. Secularization, R.H. Potvin, 867, vol. 12). I should add that there is second entry dedicated to "Secularization of Church Property," 869-874.

[2] Although it is true that Comte was the first to so designate the discipline, one must clarify that his conception was not what we understand today under this term, but was much more a "physics of society." Indeed, he divided this new science into two branches: a "social statics" as the theory of the natural order in society and a "social dynamics," which studied the development and progress of society. This conception has only a remote connection with the contemporary understanding of the discipline. See Störig 1965, 587.

[3] It should be said that the term "ontological" is a term that is often used carelessly in these discussions to designate what are no more (or less) than phenomena in a technical sense.

[4] "My point is that the assumption that we live in a secularised world is false. The world today, with some exceptions to which I will come presently, is as furiously religious as it ever was, and in some places more so than ever. This means that a whole body of literature by historians and social scientists loosely labelled 'secularisation theory' is essentially mistaken. In my early work I contributed to this literature" (Berger 1999, 2).

[5] Encyclical Letter *Fides et Ratio*, 53. This, in fact, is a quotation from *Dei Filius*, IV (DS 3017).

[6] See Weber 1917, 611. It is of note that the English translation of this remark is modified with respect to the usual one (which is somewhat inaccurate).

[7] Like Hegel before him, Taylor does attempt to break out of an exclusively theoretical stance, particularly with the notion of a "social imaginary," which reflects the phenomenological idea of a background. The social imaginary is far more, for example, than a socio-cultural theory of the social world. It is articulated in a myriad of ways beyond the strictly discursive (e.g., in stories, myths, social dynamics, assumptions, etc).

[8] Social scientists, it seems to me, must, to some degree, take responsibility for misleading generations of students in some of their statements on religion, making uncritical claims that went well beyond the parameters of competency of the discipline, such as those that undermined the credibility of religious statement, and, in doing so, contributing to blinding several generations to the possibility of the dawn of the transcendent in human consciousness.

[9] The same point is made by Hegel in his well known observation on the "Owl of Minerva": "Um noch über das *Belehren*, wie die Welt sein soll, ein Wort zu sagen, so kommt dazu ohnehin die Philosophie immer zu spät. Als der *Gedanke* der Welt erscheint sie erst in der Zeit, nachdem die Wirklichkeit ihren Bildungsprozess vollendet und sich fertig gemacht hat. Dies, was der Begriff lehrt, zeigt notwendig ebenso die Geschichte, dass erst in der Reife der Wirklichkeit das Ideale dem Realen gegenüber erscheint und jenes sich dieselbe Welt, in ihrer Substanz erfasst, in Gestalt eines intellektuellen Reichs erbaut. Wenn die Philosophie ihr Grau in Grau malt, dann ist eine Gestalt des Lebens alt geworden, und mit Grau in Grau lässt sie sich nicht verjüngen, sondern nur erkennen; die Eule der Minerva beginnt erst mit der einbrechenden Dämmerung ihren Flug" (Hegel 1821, Vorrede).

[10] "[E]s gibt einen Grad von Schlaflosigkeit, von Wiederkäuen, von historischem Sinne, bei dem das Lebendige zu Schaden kommt und zuletzt zugrunde geht, sei es nun ein Mensch oder ein Volk oder eine Cultur [sic]" (Nietzsche 1874, 246, highlighted in the original).

[11] "Das Unhistorische ist einer umhüllenden Atmosphäre ähnlich, in der sich Leben allein erzeugt, um mit der Vernichtung dieser Atmosphäre wieder zu verschwinden" (Nietzsche 1874, 248).

[12] "Die historische Bildung ist vielmehr nur im Gefolge einer mächtigen neuen Lebensströmung, einer werdenden Cultur [sic] zum Beispiel, etwas Heilsames und Zukunft-Verheissendes, also nur dann, wenn sie von einer höheren Kraft beherrscht und geführt wird und nicht selber herrscht und führt" (Nietzsche 1874, 253).

[13] And this in two senses: firstly, more philosophically, it is determined immanently by freedom and as such cannot be subsumed into any monistic discourse that would amount to a reductive determinism; secondly, more theologically, it is directed to the future, to the coming of the Kingdom of God, and as such is inherently eschatological. See, for example,Valadier 2007.

[14] For a discussion of the positive tradition and Blondel's philosophy, see Conway 2000, 2006.

[15] Note that, although De Lubac is mentioned on page 752, this is not acknowledged in the index!

[16] Thomas Kuhn's discussion of changing paradigms is simply a reflection of this fact. It is clear that in such a setting one needs to be particularly critical around ascriptions such as "objective", "neutral", "scientific", "real", etc.

[17] There can be many competing versions to explain the same set of facts.

[18] The mistake that Peter Berger and company made in the 1960s was in their understanding of the nature of the very research that was being carried out and in its legitimate interpretation with respect to the wider framework of human life and action. In more technical terminology, they presumed an ontological bearing for what was in fact simply a stage in a phenomenological analysis, ascribing substantial reality to what was only a constituent aspect (and this not in any additive sense).

Chapter Eight
Translating Taylor

[1] A different version of this paper appears in Michael Paul Gallaher, *Faith Maps: Ten Religious Thinkers from Newman to Joseph Ratzinger*, London: Darton, Longman and Todd, 2010.

Chapter Ten
Religious Inheritances of Learning

[1] Of course, outside of this centuries-long uniformity in European Christendom stood the traditions of Judaism and Islam, the first comprising significant minorities mainly in the regions of eastern Europe, and the second being influential in southern Spain from the early 8th Century to the 15th.
[2] See: http://www.gotquestions.org/Jesus-parables.html.

Chapter Eleven
Codes of Ethics in a Secular Age

[1] See commentary on the *Dance Macabre* by Bernt Notke in K. Tähepõld, *Nikolaikirche: Museum und Konzertsaa*.
[2] One definition offered by Taylor regarding moral sources is that they are the "... considerations which (for us) inspire us to embrace this morality, and evoking of which strengthens our commitment to it" (SA 693).
[3] In the *Sources of the Self*, Taylor argues that "... moral philosophy has tended to focus on what it is right to do rather than on what it is good to be, on defining the content of obligation rather than the nature of the good life" (Taylor 1989, 3).
[4] Joseph Telushkin presents a comprehensive presentation of Jewish ethics in *A Code of Jewish Ethics*.
[5] In *Medical Ethics in Antiquity*, Paul Carrick provides a detailed and informative analysis of the Hippocratic Oath. Leon R. Kass also provides an extensive analysis of the Oath in *Toward a More Natural Science*.
[6] Other codes that have emerged include the 1949 World Medical Association, *International Code of Medical Ethics* (amended 2006), the 1953 ICN *Code of Ethics for Nurses* (revised 2006), the American Pharmaceutical Association, *Code of Ethics* (1994). In the Irish context, there are national codes of professional conduct such as the Irish Medical Council and An Bord Altranais (Irish Nursing Board). In addition, individual hospitals have codes of conduct together with mission statements.
[7] And see Bassford 1990, 129.
[8] I would like to express my appreciation to FEPI for allowing me to send this paper to them for review.
[9] The FEPI Working Group included Croatia, Greece, Ireland, Italy, Portugal, Romania, Spain, UK together with other non-FEPI members, such as France and Cyprus (Sasso, Stievano, Jurado & Rocco 2008, 823).

[10] According to Directive 2005/36/EC of the European Parliament and of the Council of 7 September 2005 on the Recognition of Professional Qualifications, "Liberal professions, [...] are, according to this Directive, those practised on the basis of relevant professional qualifications in a personal, responsible and professionally independent capacity by those providing intellectual and conceptual services in the interest of the client and the public."

[11] I would argue that people have a dignity that is a given and that it is from their inherent dignity that various rights ensue.

[12] As Kaptein maintains, in *The Living Code*, "... life has to be breathed into a code" (2008, 1-2).

Chapter Twelve
Modernity, Sacrifice...

[1] See SA 604-5:"I want to stress again that the crucial debate in modern culture turns not just on rival notions of fullness, but on conceptions of our ethical predicament... [which include]: (a) Some idea of what the motivations are which can carry us towards it; these may sometimes be implicit in the very notion of fullness—as in the Christian case where agape is both path and destination—but this is not always so. (b) The motivations which bar our way to it... (c) There will also be some notion of how integrally fullness can be achieved; is it merely a utopian ideal which no human will reach in its entirety, but which can be approximated? Or is an integral transformation possible which will realize it totally?... (d) Closely related to (c) is another cluster of issues: to what extent can negative emotions under (b) be vanquished? Will they always remain, although they can be diminished? Or can they really be transformed, or gone beyond?... (e) Closely linked to (d) is another issue: if the negative motivations (b) cannot be utterly set aside, what are the costs of denying or over-riding them? Does this require serious sacrifice, even mutilation of human life?"

[2] See SA 634: "In modern terms, ethical transformation involves engaging both the will and the vision of the agent. It is beyond the reach of a therapy designed to cure an agent who doesn't endorse his deviancy, beyond the reach of an education which inculcates knowledge and capacities; it can be resisted to force and error."

[3] See Taylor 1989, 218-227.

[4] What is being called "sacrifice" here is obviously not part of the self-understanding of the rational enlightenment. Those who take the objectifying stance do not see nature (and hence the kind of higher experience that Schiller had in mind) as "essential".

[5] Taylor expands on this point, at SA 612: "This is true of Christianity, of Buddhism; and we might find in Hinduism a steady spread of the demands of *ahisma*, so that even *jatis* who were previously allow and expected to kill animals, now try to rise through abandoning these practices."

[6] About the "meta-biological" account Taylor writes: "We enter the realm of the meta-biological when we come to needs like that for meaning. Here we can no longer spell out what is involved in biological terms, those with animal analogues,

nor state in these terms what kind of things will answer this need, like a sense of purpose, or of the importance or value of a certain kind of life..." (SA 658).
[7] Conrad's Master Image is provided by Marlow's description of the African "natives" when he first encounters them on the shores of the river, in *The Heart of Darkness*. For Taylor, this image, of "truth stripped of its cloak of time" is emblematic of what he calls the Schopenhauerian turn in modern thought. See Taylor 1989, 407.
[8] Quoted in Taylor 1992, 84.
[9] See Taylor 1989, 465:"Where Pope could call on the established gamut of references with the great chain of being afforded, Wordsworth or Hölderlin are finding new words by which something can become manifest to us through nature."
[10] See Taylor 1989, 107.

Chapter Thirteen
"Code Fixation"

[1] By "excarnation" Taylor understands the movement which official Christianity has gone through, "a transfer out of embodied, "enfleshed" forms of religious life, to those which are more "in the head". *A Secular Age*, 554. See also 288.
[2] Decision making will remain difficult until "the certitude enjoyed through seeing God proves the necessity of this link (between particular choices and our final good) the will clings by necessity neither to God nor to the things of God" (ST I q.82, a.2 c).
[3] See *De Veritate* q.24, a.1.
[4] A notion of human flourishing which recognises no valid aim beyond this world. Charles Taylor, "A Catholic Modernity?" 1999, in *A Catholic Modernity? Charles Taylor's Marianist Award Lecture with responses*, ed. James L. Heft (New York/Oxford: Oxford University Press), 13-38: 19.
[5] This privileged view of human freedom is a "western" one. Indeed in reading Taylor one must be aware that one is reading the work of a "western" scholar, and a Canadian. His work is written from this perspective and addresses this "world".
[6] The title of this article, "*La vertu est tout autre chose qu'une habitude*," was translated into English as "Virtue is Not a Habit," thus loosing something of the meaning in the process of translation. The common dictionary definition of *habeo, habitus* is as a state of being, a condition, a manner, a character.
[7] For a defence of this translation see *Summa Theologiae* Vol.22 ed. Anthony Kenny (London: Eyre & Spottiswoode; New York: McGraw-Hill, 1964), "Introduction," xx, xxi.
[8] A virtue is that which renders a person good *simpliciter*, without qualification.
[9] See also Eleonore Stump, *Aquinas* (New York: Routledge, 2003), 247 ff.
[10] "The experience (*passio*) of *phantasia* is in us whenever we wish, because it is in our power to form something, as it were, "appearing" before our eyes, such as gold mountains, or whatever we wish." *In De Anima* III.4.633.

[11] See Alasdair MacIntyre, *After Virtue* (Duckworth: London, 1981) 175, for a description of how practice is being understood.

[12] "Righteousness is in the Old Testament the fulfilment of the demands of a relationship, whether that relationship be with people or with God." Elisabeth R. Achtemeier 1976, "Righteousness in the Old Testament" in *The Interpreter's Dictionary of the Bible*, ed. George Buttrick et al. Vol. 4, 80-85: 80. See also Leon Epszter 1986, *Social Justice in the Ancient Near East and the People of the Bible* (London: SCM Press).

[13] A.J.P. Taylor, "The Victorians: Revised Version", *The Observer*, 17 June 1962. The reference is to G. Kitson Clark, *The Making of Victorian England* (London: Methuen, 1962). Cited in Prof. David Thompson, "Is Popular Christianity a contradiction in terms? Some historical reflections for the twenty-first century." A valedictory lecture (unpublished) given in Cambridge University on the 13 May, 2009.

[14] G. Le Bras, *L'église et la village* (Paris: Flammarion, 1976) cited in *The Cambridge History of Christianity: World Christianities c.1815-c.1914*. Volume 8. Edited by Sheridan Gilley and Brian Stanley (Cambridge: Cambridge University Press, 2006), 210.

[15] For an informative account of the history and theology of this teaching see Francis A. Sullivan, *Salvation outside the church: tracing the history of the Catholic response* (London: Geoffrey Chapman, 1992).

INDEX

Alcibiades 86-7
Athusser, L 72
Aristotle 39, 61, 132, 182, 184, 185
Arnold, Mathew 20
Aquinas 41, 124, 177-8, 179-80, 181-3, 185, 186
Augustine 31-2, 107, 124

Bakhtin, M 60
von Balthassar, H.U 107
Barth, K 107
Bataille, G 4, 57
Bayle, P 76
Bentham, J 61
Berger, P 100, 108
Blondel, M 105-6
le Bras, G 188
Bultmann, R 107
Burgess, A 167

Camus, A 20, 46
Carroll, W 76
Casanova, J 19
Chenu, M-D 107, 113
Clark, G Kitson 188
Claudel, P 20
Comte, A 99
Congar, Y 107, 113
Conrad, J 170
Cudworth, R 76

Davie, G 21
Daniélou, J 107
Deleuze, G 57
Derrida, J 42
Descartes, R 72
Durkheim, E 105

Einstein, A 107
Evans, A 76

Ferry, L 13, 176-7
Foot, P 178
Foucault, M 57

Gauchet, M 118
Geertz, C 101
Giancotti, E 78
Girard, R 4
Griffiths, B 20, 40, 43, 46, 47, 48, 62, 119
Gordon, P 105

Habermas, J 99, 130, 131
Hardy, T 20
Havel, V 21, 47, 48, 62
Hegel, G.W.F 50, 57, 124
Heidegger, M 57, 70, 124
Herder, J.G 171
Hopkins, G.M 56, 119, 173, 174
Hudson, W 71

Ignatius 48
Illich, I 56
Israel, J 74

Jacob, M 74
Jaspers, K 165
Jeganathan, M 152
John Paul II 101
Joyce, James 63

Kant, I 20, 61, 124
Kenny, A 180

Lacan, J 41, 57
Locke, J 76
Lebacqz, K 156

Lecky, W.E.H 97
Levinas, E 33-4, 42, 206
Lonergan, B 2, 39, 40 42, 44, 48-51, 107, 118
de Lubac, H 107, 113
Lyotard, J-F 57

Macherey, P 82
Marx, K 35, 57
Mc Cabe, H 178, 179, 180, 184, 185, 186
Mac Gréil, M 128
MacIntrye, A 61, 174, 178, 197
Mallarmé, S 46
Maslow, A 41
Merleau-Ponty, M 57
Metz, J.B 107
Mill, J.S 61
Moriarty, J 187
Murdoch, I 40, 54, 61
Murray, L 110
Musil, R 20

Newman, J.H 107, 116
Nietzsche, F 20, 27, 45, 46, 57, 64, 103, 104, 162, 167, 168
Norman, E 124
Notke, B 147
Nussbaum, M 65, 195

Oakeshott, M 142

Peguy, C 56, 119
Pelagius 107
Plato 1, 2, 84-8, 89, 91, 92, 132, 164, 185, 203-8
Pope, S 172
Purcell, B 91

Rahner, K 50, 107, 119, 130, 131
Ratzinger, J 130
Ricoeur, P 46, 116

Rilke, R.M 48, 172
Riordan, P 132
Rousseau, J-J 57, 171

Sartre, J-P 44, 57
Sasso, L 153
Schillebeeckx, E 107
Schiller, F 44, 56, 165, 212
Shakespeare, W 172
Shelley, P.B 139
Shklar, J 57
Spanheim, F 77
Socrates 85-7
Spinoza, B 2, 69, 72-4, 75, 76-8, 79-81, 82, 199, 203
Steenbakkers, P 74
Steinfels, P vii, 128
Stephen, L 71, 74

Taylor, A.J.P 188
Teresa of Avila 47
Thompson, D 188
Tillich, P 107
Tindal, M 69, 74-77
Toland, J 69, 72, 74, 75, 76, 77-81, 201-3
Turner, V 60

Valadier, P 109
Vanier, J 119
Van Dale, A 77
Verbeek, T 74
Voegelin, E 40, 43, 44, 45, 51

Walsh, D 39
Wasserman, E 139
Weber, M 99, 101, 140, 209
Weil, S 40, 181
Whyte, J 126
Williams, B 61
Wittgenstein, L 59
Wordsworth, W 44, 172, 213